To Wayne,
for your winter garden
enjoyment —
love,
Julie & Barry

TOUCH—ME—NOT

MY
BEST
WEEDS

PICK—A—BACK—
PLANT

The 3,000 Mile Garden

An Exchange of Letters on Gardening, Food, and the Good Life

&

Leslie Land and Roger Phillips

VIKING

VIKING
Published by the Penguin Group
Penguin Books USA Inc., 375 Hudson Street,
New York, New York 10014, U.S.A.
Penguin Books Ltd, 27 Wrights Lane, London W8 5TZ, England
Penguin Books Australia Ltd, Ringwood, Victoria, Australia
Penguin Books Canada Ltd, 10 Alcorn Avenue,
Toronto, Ontario, Canada M4V 3B2
Penguin Books (N.Z.) Ltd, 182-190 Wairau Road,
Auckland 10, New Zealand

Penguin Books Ltd, Registered Offices:
Harmondsworth, Middlesex, England

This edition first published in 1996 by Viking Penguin,
a division of Penguin Books USA Inc.

1 3 5 7 9 10 8 6 4 2

Grateful acknowledgment is made for permission to reprint an excerpt from "Big Yellow Taxi," words and music by Joni Mitchell. © 1970 Siquomb Publishing Corp. All rights reserved. Reprinted by permission of Warner Bros. Publications.

LIBRARY OF CONGRESS CATALOGING IN PUBLICATION DATA
Leslie, Land
    The 3,000 mile garden: an exchange of letters on gardening,
food, and the good life / Leslie Land and Roger Phillips.
    p. cm.
    Includes index.
    ISBN 0-670-86714-4
    1. Gardening—England—London. 2. Gardening—Maine.
3. Phillips, Roger, 1932—Correspondence. 4. Land, Leslie—
Correspondence. 5. Photographers—England—Correspondence.
6. Authors, American—20th century—Correspondence. 7.
Phillips, Roger, 1932—Homes and haunts—England—London. 8. Land, Leslie—Homes and haunts—Maine. I. Land,
Leslie. II. Title.
SB455.P48   1996
635´.09´2—dc20   95-24621

This book is printed on acid-free paper.

Printed in the United States of America

Set in Granjon
Designed by Katy Riegel

The 3,000 Mile Garden

Eccleston Square,
London

6 September 1989

Dear Leslie,

I loved your articles in the *New York Times*. You aren't a garden writer, you're a poet! I have been thinking about you and your garden and then my mind jumps to what must be done in my own garden: planting, pruning, trimming, manuring or just the plain digging up and chucking out.

It was terrific chatting to you up in New Hampshire at the mushroom bash. Our conversation just got started and then suddenly it was so late at night that it just got ended, there are lots of other things I wanted to say but never got round to. I would like to hear what you are up to and thought you might like to hear what I am doing in the Eccleston Square garden. So here are a few more things I wanted to say to you but now I am going to have to paper speak.

This year the weather in England has been like Egypt: dry, dry, dry and hot, hot, hot. Watering has been the top priority. I got back from New England to find that the very day I had left for a month in the States, 31 July, the water authority had imposed a hose-pipe ban which has now lasted over a month and, as we have had no rain at all for the last three weeks, it looks as if it will be November before we get the hoses out again.

Let me give you some idea of our garden. It is about three acres, a typical London square, fenced and locked with what Thomas Cubitt, the architect, referred to as 'Good iron railings' in a letter to the then landowner, the Duke of Westminster, when asking to take a lease on the land to build the square 'as from Lady Day 1828'.

We have no records of the date the first trees were planted but I have always supposed that the laying out of the garden would have been concurrent with building the first houses which means 1832 or so. In those days there was only one tree that would grow in the thick, polluted London air: the trees that we call London plane and you call sycamore – *Platanus* × *hispanicus*. (Now the Latin name has changed to *Platanus acerifolia* – these things are sent to try us.) The first plan I can find of the square shows thirty-six trees and the beds, lawns and paths laid out just as they are now. Being an historic area the basic layout of the garden is protected by statute and cannot be interfered with. I don't find this a limitation but an inspiration: it concentrates my mind on the plants and structures, and forces me to find cunning ways to enhance what is already there. To me a garden should be full of surprises and secrets, areas where you can wander, wonder and generally lose yourself; there should be scents and colours to excite, shapes and textures to stimulate you.

The garden is run by the residents of the square and we each pay a garden rate. At the moment it is £65 per year. The residents elect a committee of twelve to do all the work. I was elected to the committee eight years ago and at the first meeting I attended someone mentioned that I had written books on plants, so they immediately asked me to take over the planting and care of the garden. What they didn't realize was that all my books were on wild flowers and wild plants. I loved the thought of doing it and so did not enlighten them. The garden at that time had just staggered on for years not totally neglected but lacking any loving care. The soil on examination turned out to be dry dust that could not even be watered; water ran off in globules as it does from a duck's back. We were living in a London desert. Large areas had been used for dumping – old leaves, bricks, rubble, cans, bottles, wood, glass, wire – in fact the detritus of the whole period since the beginning of the Second World War.

Two gigantic problems needed to be dealt with before planting could be considered: clearing up the rubbish and improving the soil.

I have a theory that bankers, insurance men, stockbrokers and the like are underneath it all frustrated athletes or weightlifters. I put this to the test by planning a series of Sunday digs. What was really needed was a bulldozer and earth-moving equipment but what I had to hand was city gents. I was right. They all wanted to sweat and ruin their clothes and get generally filthy, moving the fifty or so tons of accumulated rubbish. Under one heap we found all the Tarmac that had been lifted from an ancient tennis court!

In the first area cleared with their sweat I planted a fern garden with a tiny path through the middle. The main ferns are *Matteuccia struthiopteris,* the Shuttlecock Fern, which spreads like mad and *Osmundia regalis,* the Royal Fern. I found a clump of Royal Fern in the New Forest in southern England that was about thirty feet across and seven feet high. My clump is only about six feet across and no more than three feet high at present, despite the fact that we dug out a pit and lined it with plastic to hold the water around it − it thrives in bogs. The ferns do not come into their own until about June so I lined the path with snowdrops and all the surrounds with *Dicentra eximia* supported by a few specimens of *Dicentra spectabilis,* the real Bleeding Heart, to arch over them. On another corner of this bed I have planted a massive clump of blue comfrey, *Symphytum caucasicum,* overshadowed by an ivy-covered holly. It flowers very early in March when it is only about ten inches high and keeps on flowering until it is about three feet high two months later.

On my travels looking for mushrooms in Washington State, two of the wild plants I saw there stuck in my mind. One was the little Pick-a-Back plant *Tolmiea menziesii,* that grows its new plants from the middle of its leaves − hence its name; and the other was *Aralia spinosa*, the Devil's Walking Stick. The first was easy to get: it is commonly grown as a house plant in England. Anyway I got one and in a few weeks I had propagated about fifty more by just putting mature leaves in pots with a tiny pinch of soil to hold them down. As far as the *Aralia* went, I decided in the end to go for *Aralia elata* 'Variegata', a lovely form of the Japanese angelica tree. Now its gigantic leaves with their multiple leaflets arch gently above the ferns, adding to the already rather dense shade.

At one end of the path I have two camellias, 'Apollo' and 'Yours Truly', both of which do well. The 'Apollo' is very free flowering, the 'Yours Truly' has fewer flowers but is well worth having as they are a lovely veined pink with a narrow pure white edge. At the other end of the bed, cutting the whole thing off from the rest of the garden, is a gigantic clump of *Rosa* 'Canary Bird', so charming with its rows of tiny, single yellow flowers. There are also some delicate polygonum fighting their way up through the ferns. We have two species, *P. bistorta* 'Superbum' for spring and the tall, red *P. amplexicaule* for autumn. My other surprise plant for autumn is a disaster this year because of the lack of water. It is *Ligularia hodgsonii*. It has super great big leaves with purple backs and stems and then spires of orange-yellow daisy flowers in August. That is, in the past it had, this year it is a sad, lonely, drooping creature.

I nearly forgot. In the early spring there are two other things. A bank of Greek anemones, *Anemone blanda,* both white and blue. They carry on from the snowdrops, seeming to leap from the earth and then flower overnight the way an Amanita mushroom expands almost before your eyes in the summer woods. The second thing is a small clump of *Uvularia grandiflora,* the delicate relative of Solomon's Seal. To me, on this side of the Atlantic, it is rather rare and special, but as it's an American plant, you probably think of it as a weed.

Back to today. I have bulbs to order from my wholesaler. I am planting a little, round bed in the middle of the garden for next spring – at present it is full of cosmos and sunflowers, surrounded by the common pink sedum. I am ordering: 1000 *Narcissi* 'Thalia', the orchid-flower narcissi, which will produce two or four flowers per head in early to mid April; 250 Greenland tulips; and 250 spring green tulips – these two from the 'Viridiflora' group, their green flowers edged with cream or old rose, will, I hope, make a subtle but fascinating combination. They should flower right after the narcissi, or so I hope. I am also ordering 1000 *Scilla bifolia* which are going to be planted in the grass amongst a little grove of the Himalayan birch, *Betula jacquemontii*. The scillas were at the request of an Old Etonian on the committee with a rather overbearing manner. He's called Oliver Baxter, a ball organizer by profession (balls as in dances), and when he isn't organizing he plagues me with some new plan or theory for the garden. Not that I mind, it keeps me on my toes. There is a super planting of scillas in Windsor Great Park near the Savill Garden. The Savill is one of the great gardens of southern England, with the most exciting collection of woodland plants I have ever seen. I have been making regular visits there to study the collection of rhododendrons – it includes many of the original plants collected by Forrest and other great plant collectors. Anyway, I digress. The reason I give the quantities of the bulbs is that the total cost amounts to only £187.50. At today's exchange rate that is $288. Although it's a lot of money it doesn't seem too bad for 2500 bulbs!

My arm is aching so I'm going to stop now. I hope you can read my scrawl.

Love,

Roger

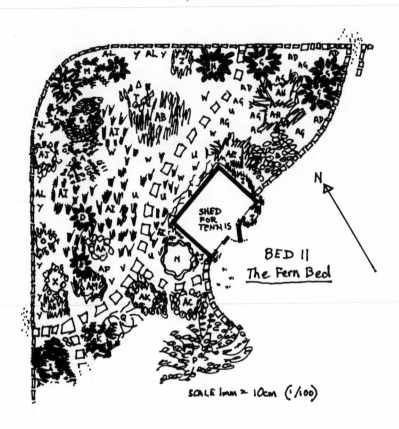

SCALE 1mm ≈ 10cm (¹/₁₀₀)

Bed 11: The Fern Bed

Shrubs

A = *Aralia elata* 'Variegata'
B = *Azalea* 'Hino-mayo'
C = *Rhododendron* 'Alice'
D = *Camellia* 'Edwin H. Falk'
E = *Camellia* 'Adolphe Audusson'
F = *Camellia* 'Innovation'

G = *Camellia* 'Apollo' × 3

H = *Camellia* 'Yours Truly'

I = *Euonymus japonicus*

J = *Hedera helix*, common ivy

K = *Ilex aquifolium*, common holly

L = *Mahonia confusa*

M = *Mahonia japonicus*

N = *Platanus acerifolia*, the common London plane

O = *Prunus subhirtella* 'Autumnalis'

P = Rose 'Canary Bird'

Q = Rose 'Fragrant Cloud'

R = Rose 'Zephirine Drouhin'

S = *Viburnum tinus*

Perennials

T = *Arum italicum*

U = *Athyrium filix-femina*, the Lady Fern

V = *Dicentra eximia* and *Dicentra spectabilis*

W = *Dryopteris filix-mas*, the Male Fern

X = *Epimedium alpinum*

Y = *Geranium endressii*

Z = *Hemerocallis flava*

AA = *Hosta sieboldiana*

AB = *Iris pseudocorus*, the wild yellow flag iris

AC = *Ligularia hodgsonii*

AD = *Petasites fragrans*, the winter heliotrope

AE = *Polygonum bistorta* 'Superbum'

AF = *Polygonum amplexicaule*

AG = *Onoclea sensibilis*, the American Oak Fern

AH = *Osmundia regalis*

AI = *Matteuccia struthiopteris*, the Shuttlecock Fern

AJ = *Scrophularia nodosa* 'Variegata', the variegated figwort

AK = *Symphytum caucasicum*, blue comfrey

AL = *Tolmiea menziesii*, the Pick-a-Back plant

AM = *Uvularia grandiflora*

Cushing,
Maine

Dear Roger,

I was delighted by your letter. Reply in kind shall be forthcoming whenever I can find the time. Shortly off to New York for a week to see editors, etc., and before I go much work to do, not least of which is dealing with frost-probably-before-I-return. Plastic on the tomatoes, peppers, eggplants and shell beans. My shell beans this year are something called "Bert Goodwin," reputedly a hundred-year-old family (not mine) heirloom from New Hampshire, and a nameless, big, white-seeded mystery bought last year at a grocery store in Hungary by my foody friend Nancy Jenkins.

Of course the *Acidanthera* are just starting—these things are sent to try us—but by and large it has been a good summer in spite of a ferocious drought. It's tempting to say conditions are not so different on our two sides of the Atlantic after all, but the truth is they really are. My garden is raw and new and carved out of something that could almost be called wilderness—at least it's wilderness compared to your venerable and unchangeable square in the heart (*is* it the heart?) of London.

I call the garden mine because I planned it and plant it, maintain and harvest it, but it actually belongs to Lois Dodd, a dear friend who has been kind enough to let me perch a little house (about which more some other time) on her property. There are five acres here, in a roughly triangular piece with one edge on the road. A deep gully with a stream at the bottom forms the other two sides, which meet at Lo's "shore frontage," a ten-foot toehold on the bank of the Saint George River. I can see a sliver of silver and the neighbor's lobster boat from my upstairs workroom, but that's about it for water views.

The old (well, roughly 1850s) farmhouse where Lois spends her summers has been my winter home since 1973, but until I came to live here year round I never did much work in the gardens because I had gardens of my own—ten miles down the road—that took all my time and attention. When I set up my summer studio here, at the other end of the land from the main house, I had to start again from scratch.

The place Lois bought in 1960 was a former sort-of-farm, potatoes the principal product, gone idle already for several decades. The entire hillside where my gardens are was badly overgrown with burdocks, roses, blackberries, and seedling alders, birch, hawthorn and apple.

By the time I got ready to start *my* gardens, in 1980, this classic edge had become a scrub wood twenty to thirty feet tall, mostly full of popple and alder, with an occasional baby oak and quite a few stripling birches (both paperbark and black birch) and tons of chokecherry (most of it full of black knot, which the remnants still sport). I had a backhoe come, after everything but the birches and a group of apples at the edge of the lower garden had been chainsawed down. The earthmover removed most—though far from all—of the larger stumps, and a similar percentage of the bushel-basket-and-larger-size rocks.

So I started out with the gardens basically the same size they are now, only full of small-to-middle-size stumps and rocks of all sizes galore. Soil was and is extremely sandy, not as acid as might be feared (there's a lot of limestone nearby) but not what you'd call sweet, either.

Along the road, to the west and north, there is a narrow band, about thirty feet wide, of hackamatack (Eastern larch) and spruce, with an occasional white pine. These were already respectable trees when I came and now have achieved an authoritative height of 30 to 50 feet.

That's it for structure. Both upper and lower gardens are pretty much flat, because until three or four years ago I was sure I was about to move someplace more permanent. It seems so silly now, but I spent years refusing to plant even perennials, never mind shrubbery or trees, because I was afraid of losing them when I left. And now that I know I'm not moving and that in any case you can drag a lot of this material along? Well, every year I do plant more perennials, shrubs and trees, but I've gotten so involved with the ephemeral stuff there's scarcely room for anything else.

Or time, either, especially at this time of year, when the mushrooms take—or usually take—more than their share. This year's drought has been catastrophic though, for the mushrooms even more than the garden. We haven't had damn-all. Not even those straw-mulch-infesting, conical-capped, bright yellow deliquescers whose name temporarily escapes me, or the *Lepiota naucina* that usually infest the lawn in front of the upper garden. Have you had better luck? Of course, no mushrooms does leave more energy for tulip planting.

Being that boresome classic, an impoverished writer, I have to watch garden expenditures very closely. This has not kept me from ordering almost a hundred bucks' worth of spring bulbs. Generally gaudier choices than yours as my few scilla (sibirica) and "Thalia" narcissi are almost lost in a host of the weirder sorts of tulips. Do you know the red parrot ones called "Wonder"? I can't stay away from them. Immense flowers of great substance about the color of blood with greenish-maroon brushstrokes. They are not nice even a little and quite strong smelling with that peculiarly sexual, grassy, slightly-burnt smell of tulips. Great showerings of pollen, too, dark purple velvet fairy-dust courtesy a Tinkerbell from hell.

Thinking of bulbs leads me to ask what you do about hyacinths? Got to be one of the ugliest flowers in all creation no matter where you put them or what you do with them, but then there is that perfume, without which there is no spring. Are yours in England by any chance any better looking? (Can't see how they would be but in ignorance there is hope.) It has always seemed an enormous shame to me that the graceful little wood hyacinths have so little scent. In my garden, the big waddy Dutch ones are finally all right just before they give out. In the last two or three years the flowers are sort of mingy and attenuated, just an occasional bell here and there along the stem. Still a less than ideal arrangement but at least not such a sock in the eye, and the glorious fragrance persists undiminished. Can't help wishing there were an easier way, though . . .

And that I had more time to write. I'm looking forward to telling more, hearing more, all sorts of more, soon.

Leslie

Eccleston Square,
London

28 September 1989

Dear Leslie,

I loved your letter.

One of the things our correspondence throws up is the plants that grow in one country and not in the other. You wrote about your *Acidanthera,* a plant I have never grown although I saw some in a lovely garden at Abbey Dore Court just a few days ago. Next spring I will order some and see if I can get them to bloom before winter.

This weekend I have been lionized at a mushroom weekend in the New Forest, the largest tract of preserved English woodland, 100,000 acres, untouched since Neolithic times. The epithet New was acquired in 1077 when William the Conquerer made it into his royal hunting preserve. The word 'forest' meant royal hunting wood, as opposed to 'chase' which means a hunting wood not owned by the king. Torres Spanish Wines invited top chefs from England and Paris for a mushroom banquet (Saturday night), mushroom foray with me as guide and identifier (Sunday morning), *gran paella* in the woods (Sunday lunch). The lunch was sublime – the paella pan was over three feet across. The dish was black rice – *arroz negro*. José Puig (pronounced putch), the European sales manager organized the whole thing for publicity. Apart from being a wine expert he has two other overriding interests, wild mushrooms and cooking *al fresco*. He did the cooking. The cuttlefish ink and the pan had both been carted over from Spain. Building the fire was my contribution — no paper and only one match — this is my one and only party piece. José went away a very happy man. From memory here's how it was done:

3 lb onions
10 sweet red peppers
3 cloves garlic

all chopped, fried in 2 pints of real olive oil (slowly). Then add 6 lbs of chopped squid (half-inch cubes) and cook slowly for 20 minutes, then 6 lbs rice and stir for 3 minutes, then most of 12 pints of fish stock, the rest added as it cooks. Then the important thing, the magic touch, the ink from the squid which instantly turns the rice black. The result got a standing ovation! It is a primitive fisherman's dish eaten when times were bad: I suspect if times were really bad they would sell the squid and make it with only the ink! It comes from the district on the Spanish coast between Tarragona and Alicante, where Spanish rice is grown.

Back to the garden. Yes, Eccleston Square is right in the centre of London, in Pimlico, roughly the area between the Thames, the Houses of Parliament, Buckingham Palace and Chelsea.

Many garden squares are neglected, usually the fault of the old dodderers on the garden committees. (There are 461 squares in London — or were at the last survey.) What happens is that the big trees keep going, taking all the water from the soil which gradually ends up a dry powder. For the first couple of years I spent about half my time mulching with peat, with spent hops from our local brewery, with bark mulch and finally with our own leaf mould.

We are allowed to use the hoses again now. The ban has been lifted after six weeks so I am trying to bring back to life the sad, weakened, unhappy plants. The azaleas, rhododendrons, pieris and hydrangeas have fared worst – five or six have had it – but the camellias have gone through with hardly a leaf lost. They are ten times as drought tolerant as I had thought.

We have a new quality Sunday newspaper in Britain, the *Correspondent*. The gardening column is written by Victoria Glendinning, who is a biographer. She kicked off her column by talking about the thick skin on the soles of her feet from going barefoot all summer and how she picked it off with her nails and ate it. Perhaps my way of telling you about the garden and my thoughts is too mundane! Tell me something about you – what happened to your husband, what caused you to go it alone? . . .

10 October

Since I started this letter all *hell* has broken loose. At ten to eleven on Friday night, 29 September, I had a gardener's nightmare. The telephone rang and a Professor Lovejoy, who represents the company who own the freehold of the square garden, told me that they have a plan to dig up the whole three acres and put in a three-storey nine-hundred-car underground car park – afterwards covering it up again, ostensibly as we  wished. I spent the whole night pacing up and down planning and plotting every form of objection and action right up to and including murder.

Churchill lived in the square at the turn of the century and we are going to use his drawing room for the meetings of our war cabinet.

Life is too chaotic to say more – I will write again soon with more garden talk.

Love,

Roger

P.S. At the weekend I went out mushrooming and found four perfect condition giant puffballs. I made an ordinary batter and cut two in slices and dunked them in it, then fried them in shallow oil in a frying pan. After one side was nicely brown I turned them and sprinkled grated Cheddar cheese on top. By the time the underside had cooked the cheese on top had melted. The whole thing was mouth-wateringly good.

Cushing,
Maine

(Postcard)

October 19, 1989

Just got your letter OmiGod what appalling news. May it turn out to be a threat and nothing more. I'll write very soon at greater length but wanted you to know I'm thinking of you and your garden (and the wickedness of the world) very nearly nonstop.

Leslie

Cushing,
Maine

October 22, 1989

Good grief Roger how can the man's name be Professor Lovejoy and where is Nabokov when we need him? I keep having this fantasy that the whole thing is some awful dream, or a scam you have thought up to give your letters a bit of potboilerish pizzazz. But I suppose it's all too true: this kind of shortsighted idiocy usually is. Any chance of help from official agencies? There sure as hell wouldn't be here, but we do have a brand new private organization set up—I think—to deal with just this sort of thing. Actually, I have a feeling they're more worried about neglect-at-death-or-financial-reversal-of-owner, but they might be able to suggest something or at least give you some U.S. publicity. It's The Garden Conservancy, Box 219 Main Street, Cold Spring, N.Y., and the contact would be Frank Cabot, a major American garden honcho whom I've never met but recently had a nice phone chat with as I may be writing up his white garden for a magazine piece. Your name is likely to be more useful than mine (I don't know if he'd even remember me, though we talked for quite a while) but feel free, etc. . . .

Your woes do put mine into perspective. Somehow Nature's blows are easier to support, even when they get help from humankind. It *did* frost in my absence, and my helper, who is game but inexperienced, didn't recognize the warning signs, as a result of which much produce and annual floriferation was lost that needn't have been. In fact it's probably just as well as I'm too busy to do much putting-up, cooking or even eating if it requires more than washing something off. Still out there plugging along are the usual hardy vegetables: lettuces, carrots, beets, leeks, and the like. Perhaps I should mention here, *à la* Glendinning, that although I adore braised leeks and cook them frequently (usually in butter, with browned shreds of lime zest and the lime juice), they make me fart like a bandit and I can only enjoy them when I expect a full day of solitude in which to toot unabashed.

Of flowers there is little left—Korean chrysanthemums, which every few years I spend major energy extirpating root and branch and then I realize nothing else blooms so late, so reliably and I go find some tiny escapee of my wrath and encourage it and by the next year they are again the rampant weed I can't bear and the whole drama starts again. Also still at it are the white California poppies (*Eschscholzia californicum*), possibly my favorite plant. In spite of their name they do splendidly here, reseeding so reliably as to be perennials for all practical purposes. They are the first flowers of spring as well as the last of fall, their feathery gray-blue foliage and pale cream-primrose-fading-to-white flowers welcome in every situation. Most sources I've read describe them as low and matlike in habit, but here they top out at about eighteen inches and spread just about as far as you'll let them—lots of graceful arching and Japanese attitudes. And they're dandy cut, too—last forever and you don't even have to burn the ends. Obligingly, the roots are shallowish and they don't seem to compete with the things they're right smack on top of—I let 'em go under the roses in the white garden and they get all tangled with the equally-obliging alyssum (a plant I adore in spite of its unhappily plebeian associations). *Calendula* of course still hanging in. Do you know the variety "Touch of Red"? It has strokes of dark brick-rust color up the backs of the petals that makes the orange ones especially glow like neon (much better than the "Neon" variety which, at least in my garden, produces small flowers that refuse to open flat in the correct calendulesque way although, credit where credit is due, even the partially-expanded buds of "Neon" are pretty spectacular). And of course there are pansies. Most of the pansies are in the blue border, ribbons of varieties called "True Blue" and "Black Devil," as well as assorted sports of the latter. Would that there were other flowers as black as the blackest of these, but that deep, velvety, light-sucking *true* black is unique in my experience.

Needless to say, I no sooner sent my drought-complaint letter than it commenced to rain . . . and rain . . . and rain. Where no mushrooms were there is now abundance, so I have to switch my complaint to one of having no time to go and pick. The people down the road who always call me when the horse mushrooms (*Agaricus arvensis*) start on their lawn called again to say something strange was spreading in the sheep-manured strip by the edge of their woods. Bingo! *Lepista* (*Tricholoma, Clitocybe,* when did *you* learn to call their name?) either *saeva* or *irina,* the not-blue blewits in any event, in good numbers and grand condition and, eventually, soup. There's still about a pound of them in the fridge awaiting—little time to cook and no one to share them with. My easy to be with sans social production nearby good friends, an otherwise sensible couple, don't like mushrooms.

What I eventually did was to cook the last lepistas and horse mushrooms together with onion in butter and then braise them in some ancient duck stock I found lurking in the freezer. This I made into some assorted sauces. The best: reduce the whole thing to a paste, add cream and reduce again, then pour the intense charcoal-gray mess over a pile of steamed cauliflower and shower lightly with grated Parmesan. It turned out quite handsomely black and white and although no one saw I found the hardship endurable as I was thus able to pig down the whole thing by myself.

Driving to town I see troops of shaggy manes taking over the front yards. The woods called madly just yesterday, the first dry day though it was blowing a gale, so I went—telling myself it would probably be the last time because once hunting season starts (next Sat.) the price is way too high. Some hunters here are most cavalier and "blaze orange" clothing is no protection against fools who know there's little chance of trouble even if they do screw up. Last year a woman was shot and killed in her own backyard, less than two hundred yards from her door. She was a stranger "from away" and the man who shot her—he insists he had a deer in his sights at the time though no sign of one was found—was a local fellow, scout leader and all around good guy. General opinion seems to have been that it was her own fault because she wasn't wearing any orange and she had on white mittens, which might have been mistaken for the nether end of a white-tailed deer. Everyone knows that's the wrong end to shoot even if it *is* a deer but that seems to have carried no weight. Neither did the fact that the hunter was illegally too close to a house—the victim's neighbor's house—when the shooting took place.

Life in the country. I love it. Especially when it's not hunting season. (In the still safe woods I found rather a lot of inedible *Cortinarii*, not very many almond and pine *Hygrophori* and a whole charge of something that's almost *Tricholoma portentosum* but not quite I don't think. No help from my admittedly small collection of the usual guides—Gary's, David

Arora's, and an Italian item by Rinaldi and Tyndalo called (sigh) *The Complete Book of Mushrooms* that's actually the best of the lot as far as the pics go. The illustrations are water color and—no offense, but—as far as I'm concerned paintings beat photos going away for ID purposes. I shall document it, take a photo with my inadequate polaroid and maybe dry a couple for later identification from someone who, unlike me, knows something.

The mystery items came from the mostly oak-canopied spot by the river where I lived in the summer before I came here year round. It was a very special place, a fairytale cottage down a dirt lane a third of a mile from the main road, fully equipped with splendid views, electricity and phone, no running water (pump in the yard), lots of eccentric architectural embellishment from the hand of the sculptor whose cottage it had been for decades. It finally biodegraded and had to be torn down. The cellarhole and burnt ruins of the studio (the owner gave the place to the fire department to practice on) are still there, as are the lilies of the valley in spring and the mushrooms in the fall.

My former main garden (a roughly thirty- by one-hundred-foot rectangle plowed out of the sloping field just up the hill on the other side of an alder brake) has gone back totally, though the three-foot-deep drainage ditch I dug (by hand, ain't youth wonderful) all around the perimeter has remained, a trap for the unwary. I'd built a tiny thyme garden by the path to the river and that lasted longer than anything else but I thought this time it was finally gone. After all, it's been nine years. There was no sign that I could see of anything but mosses and lichens—the spruce next to it is tall now—assorted expected weeds, bare patches. The soil is pure clay. I stepped right into it to look more closely and saw nothing, felt a sighing sadness, then caught the fragrance of thyme triumphant, bruised but not crushed underfoot. It really is tough stuff. Won't be long now, though, I expect, and all else is so much changed I don't know that I won't be glad when my last traces are erased. What will I hunt then when I walk in those woods?

An academic question, actually, as development is fast encroaching and those woods are unlikely to remain for many more years. They are already much diminished from when I first knew them.

October 29

No time now to go on as it's gorgeous out: sunny and seventy degrees, "unseasonably warm" with bells on. It's probably global warming or the end of the world or something but it's such a novelty to be cleaning up the garden, planting the bulbs, etc. in a tee-shirt that even the mosquito bites (!) are a small price to pay.

Best love,

Leslie

P.S. This is from a recent column—thought it might give you an idea or two.

East-West Mushroom Soup with Mushroom Dumplings

For 6 servings:

1¹/₂ tablespoons butter

1 tablespoon olive oil

2 cups chopped onion, 1 very large or 2 medium

1 lb. firm mushrooms, wild ones such as horse mushrooms or king boletes or blewits, or 12 oz. commercial mushrooms mixed with 4 oz. shiitakes

1 large clove garlic, quartered

1 small carrot, chopped fine

6 cups water

1 egg white

1/4 lb. ground pork

a heaping teaspoon fresh ginger, shredded on the fine holes of the grater

1 large garlic clove, minced fine

1 teaspoon soy sauce

36 fresh wonton wrappers

2 tablespoons marsala or medium-sweet madeira

salt to taste

2 tablespoons snipped chives

Combine butter and olive oil in a large saucepan over medium heat. When the butter melts, add the onion, turn the heat to low and cook *very slowly* until the onion is dark golden and caramelized. This may take as long as 45 minutes but little stirring is required until close to the end.

Save one or two of the firmest mushroom caps to slice for the garnish later and chop the rest into roughly 1/3 inch dice. When the onions are ready, add the mushrooms, raise the heat to medium high and cook, stirring, until the mushrooms have lost their liquid and begun to brown. This will take anywhere from four or five to ten or twelve minutes, depending on the moistness of the material.

The pile of mushrooms will seem enormous at the start, and it may smell a bit odd during the cooking down part. But the quantity will reduce enormously and the funny fragrance—if there is one—will quickly vanish.

Once the mushrooms have started to brown you'll soon have something that looks like rich, lumpy paste. Remove and reserve a scant 2/3 cup of it. Add the garlic and carrot to what remains in the pan, pour in the water, cover and simmer over very low heat for an hour or a little more.

Strain the soup, pressing to get all the flavorful juice, then discard the solids. Return the liquid to the wiped-out pan.

Meanwhile, as soon as the reserved mushroom mixture has cooled off, combine it with the egg white, pork, ginger, garlic and soy. Set out wrappers on the work surface and put a teaspoon-sized dollop of the filling on each one. Dampen the edges with cold water, then fold into triangles and seal. Press the long ends together in the center and set the finished dumplings aside.

When the soup base is almost cooked, bring a large kettle of salted water to the boil. Gently drop in the prepared dumplings and cook for 5 minutes, or until they are swollen and appear to be almost done. Strain the soup while they are cooking. The idea is to transfer the dumplings directly, using a slotted spoon, from the boiling water to the soup, where they should finish cooking in another 5 minutes or so. Stir in the wine and salt to taste.

Slice the reserved mushroom caps quite thinly and set aside. When the soup is ready, divide it among the bowls and float a few slices of mushroom in each. Sprinkle with chives and serve at once.

Eccleston Square, London

8 November 1989

Dear Leslie,

Thanks for your letter full of support and ideas. I have formed a Society for the Protection of London Squares and I am busy (apart from producing three or four books) contacting other squares and gardens to gather together an unstoppable landslide of garden lovers to overwhelm our city planners and the awful Lovejoy and his masters.

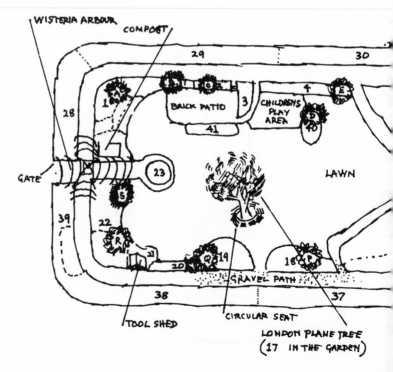

When I think about it you probably have no real idea of what our square looks like — so here goes with a plan, so you can follow what I drone on about.

Eccleston Square Bed Plan

Notes on the most interesting beds and plants

Bed 1 Is kept by Beryl Pye who is a terrific woman devoted to
   gardening. She keeps up the whole area, probably the
   equivalent of a normal back garden, buying
   everything for it and planting
   out to make it her own
   cottage garden.

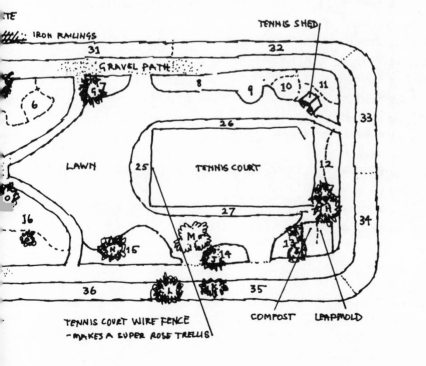

Bed 2 Is our herb garden. It is actually a series of tiny beds about one pace square, each planted with different herbs.

Bed 3 Is a small rather shady area which is looked after by Dierdre Pratt, who goes to a great deal of trouble to keep it going.

Bed 5 The main ceanothus bed, although there are loads more ceanothus dotted around the garden.

Bed 6 The main camellia collection.

Bed 7 Is underplanted with a collection of Dog-Toothed Violets.

Bed 10 Arthur the gardener has created a delightful scree garden here.

Bed 11 The fern garden: this whole area is kept rather damp, and wild irises and other damp-loving things flourish here.

Bed 12 Is our old rose collection.

Bed 13 Is kept, designed, gardened or whatever, by Di and John Goulden who are busily turning it into a collection of interesting variegated shrubs.

Bed 14 Is our winter garden mainly planted with hellebores but also with a few early flowering comfreys.

Bed 15 Has a small collection of flowering cherries and lots of hydrangeas.

Bed 16 Has lots of shrub roses including big Nevada and Marguerite Hilling.

Bed 17 Here a great bank of *Viburnum plicatum Mariesii* is backed by lovely clumps of swaying bamboo.

Bed 22 Is a collection of mainly deciduous azaleas, especially varieties of Exbury azaleas which do by far the best in our rather neutral soil. They are mixed with and given some shade by four or five different Japanese maples.

Bed 23 An evergreen magnolia is underplanted with tulips which are followed by ground-cover roses.

Bed 24 Features a tulip tree underplanted with a mixture of lavender and ground-cover ceanothus.

Bed 25 The yellow bed which has yellow-leaved shrubs and predominantly, though not exclusively, yellow flowers.

Bed 26 Climbing roses underplanted with daylilies.

Bed 27 Climbing roses are underplanted with Tall Bearded Irises.

Bed 30 Old roses, especially Chinas.

Bed 31 Annuals and perennials.

Beds 33/34 The main planting is peonies.

Bed 39 A massive planting of some 200 different irises.

A few of the more exceptional plants have been sketched in to give you an idea of their size and position.

A = *Parrotia persica* the Persian Ironwood Tree. A wonderful mixture of autumn colours.

B = *Exochorda* 'The Bride'. A lovely pendulous shape with the white blossom veiling it as a bride in the early spring.

C = *Callistemon citrinus,* the Bottlebrush. In July it is a delight just bordering on the patio where we have 'barbies'. Very appropriate.

D = *Paulownia tomentosa,* the Foxglove Tree. This will be its fourth season and I hope it will make it into flower for the first time.

E = *Clianthus puniceus,* the Kaka Beak shrub from New Zealand. Its common name comes from the Kaka bird which has a vicious hooked beak for tearing flesh.

F = *Senecio rotundifolia,* the Muttonbird shrub. This shrub, also from New Zealand, is supposed to be tender but it has survived a couple of harsh winters without any problems. Its botanical name has now changed to *Brachyglottis rotundifolia*.

G = *Liquidamber styraciflua* 'Worplesdon'. This is the form of Sweetgum that gives the best autumn colour.

H = Three Japanese maples in a loose group.

I = *Rose filipes* 'Kiftsgate'. As far as I know this is the biggest growing rose you can get. Anyway, I am trying – with some success – to grow it up one of our giant London Planes.

J = *Prunus mume,* the little Japanese Shrub Almond. This is one of the five principal plants of Japanese gardens because of its stalwart ability to fight its way into flower in the snow at the end of January. It is superbly scented too.

K = *Pittosporum tobira,* from China and the east. Again this is thought to be a tender thing but frost has caused it no damage and the scent is terrific in April.

L = *Crinodendron hookeranum* from Chile. Its flowers are lovely little red lanterns.

M = *Betula jacquemontii*. A group of five Himalayan Birch. It has super peeling pinkish bark.

N = *Davidea involucrata,* the Handkerchief Tree.

O = *Morus nigra,* the Black Mulberry, was planted by Colin Lowry who has been on the garden committee for yonks. It is a cutting from a very ancient plant from his parents' garden. Mulberries are one of my all-time favourite fruits although beating the birds to it is a task and a half.

P = *Corylopsis sinensis,* delicate catkins, in March.

Q = A group of deciduous magnolias.

R = A fine specimen of *Liquidamber styraciflua,* the Sweetgum.

S = *Callicarpa bodinieri* variety *giraldii*. This has masses of violet berries all through the winter.

Last week I went up to Nottinghamshire to visit a very grand country house at Flintham which had wonderful walled gardens and parkland (not to mention a giant conservatory). David who took me round (in the company of Elizabeth Luard, a fine cookery writer), ended up by giving me a box of medlars and a box of quinces. How did these garden marvels ever fall from grace? I now am desperate to get both for the garden.

The medlar *Mespilus germanica* makes a lovely specimen tree turning a superb golden sunset colour in the autumn. When I was a child I was told the word medlar meant 'open arsehole' in Anglo-Saxon! Presumably from the appearance of the fruit 'with its broad open eye, surrounded by the persistent calyx . . .' (Bean). Anyway they are picked at the end of October and allowed to start to decay – 'bletted'. I just boiled them up in sufficient water to cover them, for one hour, until they had turned to a pulp, then I strained the mush through an old baby's cloth nappy and added 1 lb of sugar to each pint of liquid, simmered this until it started to set on the saucer and then bottled it. It is a little low on pectin I think and it benefits from the addition of a few sour apples, but whichever way it is a great concoction.

The quinces, *Cydonia oblonga,* I chopped up and boiled for about forty minutes, just floating in water, then strained it through the nappy. Again 1 lb of sugar to a pint of the liquid reduced to setting point, makes a fantastic jelly with a lovely clear pinky cerise-red colour. And then you put the mush in a saucepan with a little of the liquid (1 lb of sugar to 1 lb of mush), simmer for twenty minutes, making sure it doesn't catch – then you pot it up. A great jam with the texture of a thick marmalade is the result. All my friends have gone wild for all three concoctions and almost all has already been eaten.

Now I begin my search for the plants. Quince by the way has wonderfully scented flowers and also good autumn colour. Hillier's, our great tree and shrub people, have in their manual a special fruit tree list with named cultivars of both – presumably with large fruit, good colour, reliable quantities, etc. Half an hour later after phoning round I have raised both *Mespilus germanica,* a form called 'Nottingham', which apparently has the best-flavoured fruit, and *Cydonia oblonga* 'Portugal', large fruit, light orange in colour.

Incidentally, your leek story reminded me of a biography I read years ago of one of the Sioux chiefs who said that when they started to eat and drink the food of the white Americans their 'air' became bad. This suggests two things to me: a) farting was not a taboo subject, and b) a very natural diet doesn't cause such a pong!

Some 'trendy' did a series on TV called *Mushroom Magic* in England this autumn, and it proved very popular. I had nothing to do with making it, but the people who did said that wherever they went my name cropped up – i.e. in France, when the French collectors found a mushroom they couldn't identify, the cry would go up *'prendre Le Phillips'* and my book would be dragged out to help. Anyway they rang my publishers and, having ascertained that I was not dead, they came and filmed me in my room just rabbiting on about mushrooms. They then hacked up the film and put a few minutes in each of the six half-hour programmes.

The result has been that my Mushroom book sales have rocketed: October 1988 sales 252, October 1989 sales 2,004! All of which leads me to believe that the only way for the likes of us to make any real cash is to get on telly. So I have been chatting to TV production companies and as I know nothing about that world I have now got myself an agent.

Leslie, your Californian poppy is a revelation. Having seen it beside the roads right across Arizona I presumed it would be useless in my garden in London. Thompson & Morgan have seeds of eight different cultivated forms only one of which is white – *Eschscholzia caespitosa* 'Milky White'. I hope this is your one. Anyway I have ordered seed and some of the other colour forms as well. I shall put most of the seed out on to the beds when I get it and see if I can get a late natural germination. My cosmos has seeded all over the gravel path but I expect they will all be killed when the temperature drops. I can only hope.

10 November

The cold weather continues. I am thinking of ways to protect my tender plants if we start to get temperatures of below –5°C (24°F). I expect this is a nightly occurrence for you.
Love,

Roger

Cushing, Maine

Roger my peach,

What a lovely present. (Book on white gardens.) How kind of you to think of me . . . and in the midst of such troubles, too. How goes the good fight? I keep trying to track down a song for you that might be helpful in the campaign. It's called (I think) "Big Yellow Taxi." It's by Joni Mitchell, and the refrain is "You don't know what you've got till it's gone—they paved paradise and put up a parking lot."

I'm frantically busy but will write soon—I kiss you and feed you mushrooms & say thanks so very kindly much again.

L

Cushing, Maine

Dear Roger,

Do forgive me for being so long in writing and no excuse really except a severe attack of Life.

Plus the weather has been inconvenient in the extreme—giant snow-storm on November 21, the earliest in my experience here. Followed, not as usually happens even in December and January by rain, but instead by ongoing record cold—it's 6°F as I write this (10 p.m.) and supposed to get colder as the (endless, I long for solstice) night wears on. Mercifully the one day of rain and above freezing temperature we had last week was not enough to completely melt the snowcover and I can only hope it'll be enough to protect the brand newly planted peonies. I finally sprang for four: "Elsa Sass," "Florence Nicholls," "Nancy Nicholls" and "Ray Payton"—two whites, one pink and one red—all of them set in the ground a bare week before the storm and of course I had the *best* intentions of mulching them but . . . The roses thank heaven were already earthed up around the crowns, but I have not yet wrapped the protruding canes with reemay (spun polyester, do you know about/use it?) as I intend to do for an experiment. Each year except for the rugosas my roses die back almost to where the earthing ends, even the floribundas and the hybrid perpetuals which shouldn't do any such thing. So this year I drove stake cages around each plant, intending to fill them with leaves and wrap same with reemay. Leaves at this point clearly out but I may yet get to the wrapping and perhaps do the stuffing with straw if I can find some to buy.

Not all the bulbs had gone in pre-storm either, but I went out the other day and scraped aside the snow and sure enough underneath it was still diggable if not exactly toasty so I've buried the stragglers quite deep with lots of lovely bonemeal and will hope for the best.

At least the snow is beautiful. It's always such a relief to see the landscape smoothed out, simplified, made whole. Went skiing over last weekend and found the woods very calm and harmonious in their white cladding. Spiders evidently as surprised by the weather as the rest of us: their webs were still everywhere—little silken laundry lines with perfect snowflakes hung out in rows to dry.

Interesting about your new/old fruits. According to the excellent *Fruit, Nut and Berry Inventory* put out by our Seed Savers Exchange, medlars are "botanically somewhere between a pear and a hawthorn." The former do okay here, though it seems to be the northern end of possibility for them and fire blight is a problem. Hawthorn thrives (I live on a spit of land called Hawthorne Point and though that's for a person—distant relative of Nathaniel—it might as well be for the tree). Five different medlars are available, though only two—the species and "Nottingham" (guess it really must be the best) are described. Of quinces we can get quite a lot; the *Inventory* lists eight, but none of them are your "Portugal." Portugal *is* named as a parent (along with Orange, a "very old variety") of something called "Van Deman," introduced in 1891, hybridized by— who else?—Luther Burbank.

Quinces I know do grow in these parts. My friend Carol Lundquist has access to a tree, makes jelly that sounds like yours except that it's more apricot/carnelian color; and years ago I came across a fine old large tree some little distance from an abandoned road in the woods where I had gone to look for mushrooms. I filled my jacket with the fruits, which were completely sound and quite plump in spite of their comparatively sunless situation, but foolishly failed to take sufficiently careful notice of the spot. I've never found it again.

Some earlier inhabitant must have planted that quince, they don't grow wild here. I didn't search for more evidence at the time but I usually do. There's something about these obscure vignettes of former lives that's very powerful. Our woods are full of old cellar holes, tumbled-down chimneys, ancient scraggly lilacs absurdly tall still stretching toward the light. Cushing, for instance, though it's now close to entirely tree-clad was cleared bald as the proverbial egg a century ago. All those farms have grown over and gone; their farmers fled West to land that brings forth something other than rocks.

Only we gardeners persist, plus our one farmer—Gerald Smith—who grows sweet corn and squash on exquisite land overlooking the river. He'd have lost the place long ago were it not that Maine has an easement system whereby agricultural land can be exempted from being taxed at its full development value. His son David is a farmer too, but does not live on or seem to have hope of inheriting his father's place (too many kids?). David was in dairying until the big "whole herd buyout" of three or four years ago and he now grows hay, hauls gravel and makes do. Still young (I think in his early thirties) he'll probably move to upstate New York, where land is still cheap enough (and good enough) to permit dairy farming. So the story continues to repeat itself.

I won't go on at length about the unfortunate effect of onions, but do want to say that your Sioux chief's observations are suggestive of what I know about the problems encountered by those unfortunates who, convinced by the health and morality pundits, suddenly begin eating lots of dried beans. It should be a gradual process; you have to slowly build up your population of the appropriate intestinal flora (and presumably, fauna), the ones that digest the unaccustomed saccharides before the ill-wind situation begins to correct itself. Soaking the legumes overnight and then throwing out the soaking water is also efficacious but you probably already know that.

Haven't been cooking much lately myself, too busy with both work and chores: another storm has meant much hauling of firewood, shoveling of snow, etc., leading me to reflect that whoever said "all a woman needs to be happy is a cat and a cucumber" sure as hell didn't live in the country. But I did make a nice duck with wild mushrooms at Thanksgiving time.

Double Duck (Stewed and Grilled) with Wild Mushrooms

Carve the breasts from a four-pound domestic duck and set aside in the fridge. Skin and joint the rest of the bird and refrigerate legs, thighs and meaty sections. (Render out the fat and cracklings for other uses i.e. gingerbread, the fat makes great gingerbread).

Put the carcass, neck and outer wing pieces in a shallow pan with an onion (trimmed but unpeeled) and a few chunks of carrot and roast hot until well browned. Break everything up, cover generously with hot water (use same to deglaze roasting pan) and make strong stock, aiming to end up with about three cups of fairly fat-free broth (omit usual aromatics).

Brown the legs, thighs, giblets and heart in a bit of the duck fat, add *a lot* of dried boletes (about two lightly piled cups of pieces, a couple of ounces) and the broth. Cook until the meat falls apart, by which time the mushrooms will be thoroughly cooked and there will be only enough broth left to be a sauce. Season very lightly as needed—I used only a pinch of salt and about one tablespoon of port.

Score the skin of the duck breasts crosshatch and broil/grill about six minutes without turning to get crisp skin and rare meat. Slice breasts across the grain and arrange in the center of a shallow serving dish surrounded by the stew. I served it with boiled potatoes at least partly because I wanted to show off my all-blues (they're a lovely lavender clear through when cooked and have a special, slightly smoky taste that I think is more than psychological) but I can't think of *any* saucemop that wouldn't suit. Wild mushroom pasta would be especially nice. Can you get it there? We have a tasty brand of dried, Gaston Dupre, and some speciality stores—not here, of course—sell it fresh.

World Going To Hell in a Handbasket Department: can you believe my duck didn't have a liver (rare bird indeed)? What it had, to my great disgust, was an obscenely large, very squidgy packet of "Orange Sauce" full, according to the label, of sugar, additives and orange flavoring. Directions advised heating this up and then sloshing it over the poor creature after it had been roasted for about three and a half years (or until the plastic thingummy it had been impaled with popped up) by which point it would undoubtedly need all the help it could get. Phooey.

Enclosed find a copy of the song I mentioned. Joni Mitchell is big for good causes so I'm sure would give permission if there was any way to use that oh so appropriate refrain in the fight to save the garden.
Work calls,

Leslie

P.S. I'm sure my California Poppy is *E. californicum*. *E. caespitosa* is supposed to be fragrant, which mine ain't, and very short, ditto.

Eccleston Square,
London

20 December 1989

Dear Leslie,

I am horrified at the temperatures in Cushing. It at last brings home to me why gardens in America are so different from ours. (Our low has been about 22°F in London so far this year.)

I tend to think of a garden as a collection of shrubs; the perennials provide low cover and some summer flowers but really only augment the shrubs. I think of *Choisya,* Mexican Orange Blossom, as a quick-growing, dark background evergreen with lovely scented leaves and flowers which come out at any old time of year (often twice) but now your letter has brought home to me that you could never grow it. The other thing that I cannot get through my thick head is that you are over five hundred miles south of me — by my map you come out on the same latitude as the French Rivieras, and to boot you are near the sea. How can it be so cold? In England, anywhere around the coast, you really don't get frost at all yet we are on a latitude that runs just north of Newfoundland. All this is down to the Gulf Stream, otherwise we would not even be able to survive here never mind garden.

For the moment we have seen off the car park plan. The developers have shown us their weakness — they hate publicity. The *Daily Telegraph* did a big article on the story taking them to task for their thoughtless greed. Shortly afterwards the developers sent me a letter confirming that they were not planning to proceed with the car park.

We have won the battle but not the war. That will no doubt creep up on us in a much more underhand manner sometime in the future. One of my ideas for future publicity if it is needed is to stand on the steps of Churchill's house and do the 'V for victory' sign for the camera. My main line for future resistance is our Society for the Protection of London Squares. As soon as any developer sticks his neck out we will bury an axe in it with the combined force of perhaps four hundred squares (100,000 residents).

As we are a conservation area our trees are automatically preserved with a TPO (Tree Protection Order) on each but, as I suspected, the council tree maps were extremely out of date. So I got the council tree man round and we mapped every single tree in the square down to the very smallest. This means that any future horrible desecrators would have to overturn in the region of forty TPOs to do their dirty digging.

Reemay sounds interesting. I have been starting to put in rather tender things over the last two years as we really haven't had a winter. This year I have cut long bamboos and made wigwam frames over the tender shrubs. Then when the weather gets cold I wrap clear plastic over them and staple it on, the thought being that light can get through whilst af-

Flowers December—January scented like marzipan

The leaves come as the flowers die

Petasites fragrans Winter Heliotrope

fording some protection from the cold and especially the cold wind. But it looks dreadful.

My mimosa, *Acacia baileyana,* is about ten feet tall and dropping with flower buds. I hope they will open in January but maybe I will have to wait until April. It is much too tall to build a wigwam over so I have just given it a roof over its head; my latest theory is that this will give it a 5 to 10°F advantage over an open-grown plant.

Do mahonias survive in your temperature? My *Mahonia* × *media* 'Charity' is in full flower and has been for about a month with still three or four weeks to go. Although the leaves are barbarously prickly it is wonderful to cut a piece and bring it into the house, the scent of the sweet smelling yellow flowers pervades every corner. Another plant I grow that is just coming into flower is the perennial weed *Petasites fragrans*, winter heliotrope, which flowers all through January and has a delicious marzipan scent. It probably would grow in your garden but perhaps it would be best not to try as it propagates itself at an amazing rate through its underground shoots which even when they hit a wall will go down a foot or two to get beyond it. My soil is a black friable loam and when it spreads too far I can just spend ten minutes pulling it out to keep it under control. Friends who have clay soil never get rid of it and cannot believe that I persist with it.

By the way 'Big Yellow Taxi' by Joni Mitchell is definitely my theme song from now on. She's certainly got her finger on the desecration pulse.

> Took all the trees and put them in a tree museum,
> And they charged all the people twenty-five bucks
>   just to see them.
> They paved paradise and put up a parking lot,
> With a pink hotel, a boutique and a swinging hot-
>   spot,
> Don't it always seem to go
> That you don't know what you've got till it's gone.

3 January 1990

I can't continue without first mentioning eastern Europe. The changes have been so vast and yet so quick that we all have ended up not knowing which way is up. Romania was inspiring, seeing the students taunting the security police to shoot at them so that the army could locate and then ferret them out. Literally using their lives as bait. A Romanian expatriate on

Tuber
life size

cream
with dashes
of bright red

English radio asked people to burn candles in their windows to support and commemorate them. We did and I hope every Christmas to make it a special feature to remind us all of their bravery and sacrifice.

A super surprise in the garden. Last year Martyn Rix, who is a great bulb expert, gave me a couple of tubers of *Tropaeolum tuberosum*. I planted them under some large dark *Euonymus japonica* shrubs and they rapidly ran right up through the shrubs and then burst into flower in midsummer and didn't stop until November – little red and yellow trumpets like a narrow flowered aquilegia – a real joy, especially for the late season. But this is not what surprised me; when I went to dig them up for the winter I discovered that each of the tubers now had progeny – thirty or forty new tubers! If that is not propagation it's certainly multiplication. The garden next autumn will be draped in the things and will look like some wonderful Andean mountain in Peru. The year after? Love,

Roger

Cushing, Maine

Dear Roger,

It's snowing, about 11 degrees, inconvenient in some ways but in others a great relief. We needed snow. The January thaw (we do always get one) arrived in the rain on New Year's Eve and has proceeded intermittently ever since, so by this week most of the old snow cover had melted off. Poor ol' plants were naked (and getting heaved) and the landscape was ugly you bet, a dispiriting wasteland of dirty old snow, mottled ice, and mud dotted here and there with three months' worth of the beer bottles and fast food wrappers our local punks casually discard from the windows of their cars.

This has actually been a much snowier year than usual. Being on the coast we're much more likely to get sleet, freezing rain and just plain cold. I'll be very interested to see what spring brings since the surprise snow of last fall meant I put on a lot less winter protection than usual. Can't wait to see who survives and who don't and whether the perennially failing but never quite dying tree peony makes it through. It's Lois's, so I can't quite wish its demise, but the damned thing is such a tease—it never gets more than about eighteen inches tall and always has one flower bud, which blasts—that I can't quite wish it a long life either.

The Christmas camellias you told me about on the phone live in my head (the only thing blooming here is the heliotrope in the sunroom, flowering its fool head off and smelling like grandmother). Also alive in my head is your request to hear about the Christmas tree so here it is. Please bear in mind that Christmasness is already half-faded from memory, the object itself now whacked up into boughs and covering the bed of *Fragaria moschata* at the edge of the upper garden. (I went through huge gyrations to get these "classic wild strawberries of the European continent," only to find them highly overrated. I was hoping for an improvement on *F. vesca*, but moschatas have the same awful—reminds me of fake grape flavoring—taste, dammit.)

For years I got my tree from an ill-managed planting of Scotch pines (*Pinus sylvestris*) in a large tract right here on the Point, carefully justifying my theft by taking trees that were crowding others. I get a tree that requires no pruning to fit against the wall and in turn the owner gets her stand managed, was how I always saw it. But budworm (and I think acid rain) stopped me where conscience probably never would have. Each year the poor trees, never seen, never tended, are a little more sickly and yellowish. So now I am an upright citizen and buy one from the tree farm up by the highway. They have pines but I've switched to balsam fir (*Abies balsamea*), Maine's Christmas classic for its dark color, fine fragrance and soft flat needles that cling to the branches for a long time after the tree is cut. Absent Christmas, fir is a trash tree around here, a fast growing opportunist of recent clearcuts, good only for pulp. You have to prune patiently for about a decade to get the lush conicality demanded by the Yuletide trade. This year's selection—a seven-footer, as tall as the little living room will take—was so thick with branches I forewent the tinsel as there was nowhere and no way to drape it.

I always have a decorating party to get the thing up and trimmed, baking a humongous assortment of cookies and inviting my closest friends Alan and Monika Magee and Chris and Rosee Glass. Sometimes others come as well but this year it was just us. Chris always puts up the lights, something he once made the mistake of being very good at so now he's stuck. Everyone jokes because I am *quite* the martinet and explain for the umpteenth time in a stern voice exactly how things are to be done so the tree looks just so. (Start near the trunk with the plain ornaments, wire on the antique ones very firmly, one piece of tinsel at a time, no throwing the tinsel, etc.) Chris says I missed my calling and should have been a first-grade teacher.

But first there is the gingerbread. Before the party I make lots and lots of disks of hard gingerbread, $3^{1}/_{2}$ or 4 inches in diameter, hole near the top edge for hanging up. Also what I call iron icing (the decorator frosting made of eggwhite and powdered sugar) which is put in small plastic baggies. As soon as the guests show up and before things get too merry I slice a tiny corner from the bags so they act as icing cones and everybody decorates several cookies. Alan, being a painter, surprises no one by doing marvelous drawings—usually of vaguely sinister Christmas characters like evil elves. But the year Chris and Rosee went to sing in Russia (a Rachmaninoff liturgy that hadn't been performed since 1911) Chris, who's an architect, did a bunch of Eastern Orthodox churches and views of Moscow that were really a treat. (It's easy-psychology time when those two show slides of their trips. Her pictures are always of people, markets, gardens, landscapes, his are just as invariably of walls, stairways, windows, occasionally whole façades or entire buildings.) The icing hardens while we eat and drink and get the basics on and by then the cookies are dry enough to hang (gingerly) with the other ornaments.

All this seems mighty far away from the garden but that's one of the great pleasures of gardening where it gets seriously cold. (A friend once sent me a book on "cold climate gardening" written by a woman in ?shire. Can't remember exactly where and the book is at the summer house.) It is to laugh. In a place like this, where it's well below freezing for weeks on end and not infrequently well below zero for several days at a stretch, there is actually about a month when you don't have to even think about the whole subject. At all. But that's it. Seed catalogs used to come in late January but now they overlap Christmas, the first of them coming right before the holiday then a deluge starting right after it. I used to resent this, same as I resent the ubiquitous Christmas decorations arriving earlier each year. Don't know how this works in England but here it just keeps getting weirder. When I was a kid the tinsel and Santas didn't go up until December. About fifteen years ago they started appearing before Thanksgiving; now they're in place side by side with the pumpkins and witches of Halloween.

Anyway, this extended Yuletide still drives me nuts but I've come to appreciate having to think about seeds right away while the eggnog is still in the glass and the wreath hanging at the door. It makes the transition back into daily life not just okay but a pleasure. There speaks the fanatic, I suppose. The thrill of seeing those little brown bits of nothing eventually emerge, after weeks and weeks, as little *green* bits of nothing is pretty sedate as thrills go. And you have to be a real gambler to appreciate the crapshoot aspect: will these tomatoes turn out to be as delicious and productive as the catalog promises? (Probably not.) Will these exotic perennials germinate before the turn of the century? (Possibly, but don't count on it.) Will these special white variants of standard flowers actually be white? (Only about half the time, usually the half where it doesn't matter. White poppies (*Papaver somniferum*) in the vegetable beds are more or less gratifying, it's true, but a really lush, two years in the making, 5′ tall, 4′ wide, 20′ long ribbon of white foxgloves at the edge of one's white garden that turns out to be the usual assortment of foxglove colors is—well, you may imagine I was less than pleased, the more as of course nobody viewing its admitted gorgeousness understood why I was so put out.) But there keep being things like this year's white *Venidium fastuosum* (from Thompson and Morgan) so I keep coming back for more.

They have a black and white dianthus, too, that looks stunning in its cover photo. I'm a total sucker for black and all approximations thereof and this latest snare and delusion would have snagged me anyway because I have some lovely black and white columbines that although needless to say are more of a dark purple—the spur petals—and cream are nevertheless among my favorite plants. Don't know their name or variety

Camellia Adolphe Audusson
Sirst flower January 17

except that they're certainly not hybrids—got the seeds from Monika who doesn't remember where she got hers. The plant is refined and compact and the foliage is very dark with a definite blue cast. Want some? Lord knows it sets buckets of seed if permitted and as I keep not getting around to moving the gone-wild tall white columbines from the opposite end of the property over near these where they belong there are no other colors to cloud the issue and they should breed more or less true.

Offering the columbines, telling of my latest entrapment by the catalogs I am reminded that I am that most *déclassé* of gardeners—the random collector. Something looks good, I buy it. Somebody offers me a treat, I take it. *Then* I figure out (or try to) where the hell to put it. As a result my garden is about four-fifths holding plots for experiments and only one-fifth proper garden. Makes me ache to start anew. I have fantasies alternately of bulldozers and moving—preferably to a warmer climate—

but that fades once the spring's flowers start blooming and the garden that already grows starts needing attention . . . Afraid what needs attention right away is work, so will close. Promise to write again soon.
Love,

Leslie

P.S. Here's the gingerbread recipe; I bet it would be a hit at your house too. Forgive the somewhat didactic style—it's from a column.

Ornamental Gingerbread

This stuff is perfectly edible, containing no weird chemicals, stabilizers or shellac. But it smells a lot better than it tastes, and if you want to crunch a thick cookie you'd better have tough teeth.

For approximately 5 pounds of dough, enough for at least 60 large Christmas Ball disk cookies, a family's worth of assorted sculptures, or a few cookies each for every holiday in the year (it keeps forever in the freezer):

7 to 9 cups all-purpose flour

1 tablespoon plus 2 teaspoons ginger

1 tablespoon cinnamon

2 teaspoons *each* mace and cloves

1 teaspoon *each* baking soda, salt and cardamom

1²/₃ cups solid shortening or 2 cups butter (butter smells and tastes better but doesn't keep as long)

2¹/₄ cups unsulphured molasses

1 cup *each* white and dark brown sugar

baking parchment for the cookie sheets

Combine 5 cups of the flour with the ginger, cinnamon, mace, cloves, soda, salt and cardamom. Set aside.

Put the shortening, molasses, white and brown sugars in a large, heavy kettle over medium low heat. Cook, stirring, only until the fat has melted and the mixture is smooth. Don't let it simmer or the finished dough will be dry and tough.

Remove the kettle from the heat, stir in the spiced flour, and allow the mixture to cool until it is barely tepid. Slowly stir in additional flour until you have a smooth, soft, slightly greasy dough that does not stick to your hands when manipulated. Be sparing with the flour; the dough will stiffen as it cools.

Allow the dough to cool to room temperature before use, and keep wrapped tightly in plastic to avoid drying out.

Cookie sculptures should not be more than $1/2$ inch thick, and thickness should be fairly even as little pointy parts tend to burn. Build the sculptures right on parchment, always moisten two parts to be joined, and don't forget to leave a place or two for the hanging thread. Bake thin pieces as below, thick ones at 325 for about 25 minutes.

Christmas ball (or other flat, cut-out) *cookies* Roll dough $1/8$-inch thick between sheets of waxed paper. Peel off a sheet, reverse dough onto baking parchment and remove the other sheet. Use a coffee can for large round disks, whatever other cutters you like. Remove and reroll excess dough. Slide parchment onto cookie sheets and bake in a 350-degree oven for about 14 minutes or until color has changed slightly and surface looks dry.

While the cookies are still warm and soft, use a matchstick to make a hole for the string. Remember to keep the hole at least $1/3$ inch in from the edge of the cookie. Cool on racks and decorate with Iron Icing (below).

Decorative embellishments Raisins, red hots, colored sugars and silver and gold dragees are the most common, but don't forget whole cloves, whole star anise, dried rosebuds and lavender flowers (available at some florists and hobby stores, if you forgot to dry your own last summer). Pictures to paste on to the icing can be cut from magazines or wrapping paper, but the easiest thing to use are paper stickers.

Iron Icing

Is made by beating an egg white until loosened, then stirring in confectioners' sugar until icing is achieved. The mixture will be lumpy at first, then smooth out. Keep it on the flowy side to coat cookies with an even sheet of white. Continue to add sugar until the lifted spoon leaves a thin trail on top of the mass if you want decorating icing that won't sag or run.

Plastic sandwich bags are ideal decorating bags, inexpensive and disposable. Use the kind with square corners and don't fill more than one-third full. Snip a *tiny* triangle from one corner, twist the top of the bag securely and squeeze out a line of icing with which to draw, write, squiggle or dot as the Christmas spirit moves you.

Eccleston Square, London

12 February 1990

Dear Leslie,

Food still fights its way to the forefront. Last time I wrote about the tubers of *Tropaeolum tuberosum*. Since writing I have looked it up and found that it is called Ysano in Peru, Chile and Bolivia where it is eaten like a small sweet potato. My book adds that the flavour is said to be disagreeable (they hadn't tried it). The challenge was irresistible; boiled or roasted I found it quite palatable. Perhaps my powers of self-deception are well developed for the other three people I tried it on were not impressed. Next year I shall have loads and will try serving it in various ways.

My other food event came about like this. We have invested in a leaf shredder to help us get rid of leaf-mountains that build up at the beginning of winter. The main purpose is to stop us burning off leaves and so causing yet more damage to our long-suffering environment. The results of our Kemp (American made) shredder have been excellent – a fine mulch of thumb-nail-sized bits of leaves, but (and at last I come to the point) the pile heated up in two days to what felt like a terrific temperature. So I resolved to try an experiment. Years and years ago my uncle Frank cooked a ham in a hay box and we duly ate it for Sunday lunch at a massed gathering of the cousins. What hot hay can do cannot hot leaves achieve? I went to our local butcher and bought a ten-pound piece of ham, or more properly bacon as it had already been salted and a little smoked. It was in a plastic bag. I buried it two feet down in our heap, having first made a couple of small holes in the bag to stop it exploding.

My uncle had told me that it takes about two weeks to cook a ham in hay, but my patience ran out after about four days and I dug it up. *It was cooked.* In fact I think it was chronically overcooked by the way it fell off the bone.

It was very good. Daughter Phoebe (seven) was full of praise. Amy (four) was not so keen: I suspect it was much too salty for her virgin palate. I had a moment's panic after we had all eaten it, remembering all the publicity about salmonella and the way things should be cooked to a very high temperature, but all was well.

21 February Late-night musings:

I've just seen Sylvester Stallone's mother of all people on the dreaded box. She said that her son came to her when he couldn't make it with a woman and that she counselled him. I feel that for sex to work there must be a fundamental desire, and although the desire is instinctive I have always presumed that it is really a desire towards procreation, a desire that usually masquerades under the name 'love', that is the essential ingredient for sexual compatibility. I accept that there is also lust in the simple sense, otherwise how could one explain prostitution? Maybe this sounds a bit moralistic, but it's the way it strikes me.

Back to the garden. Camellias are one of the corner-stones of our garden; we have more than a hundred different cultivars. From October to April there are always plants in flower — starting with the rather tender *sasanquas* which go through until Christmas. Then in January the *japonicas* start up. They make a terrific mass of colour more and more coming into flower week by week. If there is a frost they just go dormant: the flowers that are out are burnt but the buds just wait until it warms up and then start again. The main area that I have the camellias in has a carpet of wild primroses as an underplanting. They also have been in flower for months and look like going on and on. Primroses love it in our city atmosphere, each year I split up the clumps and get about twenty-five new plants from each. Three years ago someone gave me two plants, so now I have hundreds and hundreds. I love them and as they love the garden there is total compatibility — of course linked to fecundity.

Bed 6: The Camellia Bed

Shrubs

A = *Acer japonicum*

B = *Acer negundo* 'Elegans'

C = *Acer saccarhinum* 'Lacinia-tum'

D = *Arundinaria fortunei*

E = *Arundinaria murielae*

F = *Arundinaria nitida*

G = *Berberis darwinii*

H = *Buxus sempervirens* 'Elegan-tissima'

I = *Camellia* 'Adolphe Audusson'

J = *Camellia* 'Adolphe Audusson' (a white blotched sport)

K = *Camellia* 'Ama No Kawa'

L = *Camellia* 'Apollo'

M = *Camellia* 'Arejishi'

N = *Camellia* 'Ballet Queen'

O = *Camellia* 'Betty Sheffield'

P = *Camellia* 'Bob's Tinsie'

Q = *Camellia* 'Christmas Beauty'

R = *Camellia* 'Citation'

S = *Camellia* 'Contessa Lavinia Maggi'

T = *Camellia* 'Cornish Snow'

U = *Camellia cuspidata*

V = *Camellia* 'Dear Jenny'

W = *Camellia* 'Debutante'

X = *Camellia* 'Donation'

Y = *Camellia* 'Emmet Barnes'

Z = *Camellia* 'E. G. Waterhouse Variegata'

AA = *Camellia* 'E. G. Waterhouse'

AB = *Camellia* 'E. T. R. Carlyon'

AC = *Camellia* 'Francis Hanger'

AD = *Camellia* 'Grand Slam'

AE = *Camellia* 'Guest of Honour'

AF = *Camellia* 'Inspiration'

AG = *Camellia* 'Kramers Supreme'

AH = *Camellia* 'Lady Clare'

AI = *Camellia* 'Lasca Beauty'

AJ = *Camellia* 'Margaret Davis'

AK = *Camellia* 'Mathotiana Rosea'

AL = *Camellia* 'Matterhorn'

AM = *Camellia* 'Melody Lane'

AN = *Camellia* 'Miss Universe'

AO = *Camellia* 'Nagasaki'

AP = *Camellia saluenensis*

AQ = *Camellia sasanqua* 'Hugh Evans'

AR = *Camellia* 'Snow Goose'

AS = *Camellia* 'Tiffany'

AT = *Camellia* 'Tiptoe'

AU = *Camellia* 'Tomorrow's Dawn'

AV = *Camellia* 'Vittorio Emmanuelle II'

AW = *Camellia* 'White Fishtail'

AX = *Caryopteris × clandonensis*

AY = *Ceanothus dentatus*

AZ = *Ceanothus* 'Frosty Blue'

BA = *Ceanothus impressus*

BB = *Ceanothus* 'Italian Skies'

BC = *Ceanothus verrucosus*

BD = *Chaenomeles speciosa*

BE = *Euonymus japonicus*

BF = *Euonymus* 'President Gauthier'

BG = *Forsythia* 'Lynwood'

BH = *Hamamelis* × *intermedia* 'Jelena'

BI = *Hydrangea* 'Kluis Superba'

BJ = *Hydrangea* 'Lilacina'

BK = *Mahonia* 'Charity'

BL = *Populus alba* 'Richardii'

BM = *Pyracantha* 'Watereri'

BN = Rose 'Chinatown'

Rose 'General Schablikine'

Rose 'Mme Edouard Herriot'

Rose 'Morning Jewel'

BO = Rose Nevada

BP = *Senecio greyi (Brachyglottis greyi)*

BQ = *Senecio rotundifolia (Brachyglottis rotundifolia)*

BR = *Spirea thumbergii*

BS = *Viburnum tinus*

Perennials

I have not drawn the plants in but just marked the spots

CA = *Agapanthus umbellatus*

CB = *Campanula lactiflora*

CD = *Chelidonium majus*, the wild Greater Celandine

CE = *Crocosmia* × *crocosmiiflora*, the common montbretia

CF = *Hemerocallis fulva*, the common Day Lily

CG = *Echium pininana*

CH = *Hosta sieboldiana*

CI = *Impatiens glandulifera*, the Policeman's Helmet

CJ = *Lamium galeobdolon* 'Variegatum'
CK = *Macleaya cordata*, the Plumed Poppy
CL = *Tropaeolum* 'Jewel Mixed', the common nasturtium
CM = *Tropaeolum tuberosum* 'Ken Aslet'
CN = *Phygelius aequalis*
CO = *Primula vulgaris*, the common primrose
CP = *Pulmonaria*

I've got a yellow area in the garden, but as yet it is not a great success. It is mainly foliage – golden philadelphus, spirea, hops, berberis and maple, then patches of flower – roses, gladioli, broom, etc. This year I am trying to improve it and make it really work. I have gone mad on lilies almost all yellow but with a few whites as well to break up and thus show off the yellows: 'Connecticut King' and Citronella strain for the yellow, with *Lilium* 'Mont Blanc' and *Galtonia candicans,* the summer hyacinth, for the whites. I am also planning on some perennials, when the plants become available: a patch of *Coreopsis verticillata* which I hope will stay in flower for months, also *Campanula* 'Dickson's Gold', and then poking through them some *Crocosmia* 'Solfatare'. I am not convinced that even this lot will be an unbridled success. Do you have any favourite yellow perennials that come leaping to mind? All help gratefully received.

By the way do you remember months ago you wrote about *Acidanthera?* Well we now have some in the garden but it wasn't me who planted them. Beryl Pye (she really is a sweetie pie) planted them: she has a corner of the garden that she completely looks after herself – a sort of cottage garden within the garden.

Sorry to be so long replying but I am invaded. *Herbs*, the next book, has just been pasted-up – the colour proofs went back to the publisher yesterday – and now we are already deep into doing the paste-up of the *Mushrooms of North America* for Little Brown. A thousand pictures!
Love,

Roger

Cushing, Maine

February 15, 1990
11 p.m.

Dear Roger,

I've spent the last hour or so starting the first seeds, am dead tired but thought of you keenly as this is the official start of my garden year. It's too

Leslie

early to do the bulk of it, but leeks, onions, pansies and a few other items (such as cardoons and *Salvia patens*) must be begun now if they are to perform well when the time comes.

It's completely quiet, hasn't been a car by since dinner time, the phone silent. Peace. Outside the back door the snow is pale gray and smooth. Just stopped coming down a little while ago after falling for two days, most of the time right at the edge between snow and freezing rain. It has built an almost lacquered surface, glazed and shining rather than fluffy and sparkly. Shadows are deep, blue and charcoal and near-on black. From the chicken house to the back door, one pure diagonal line of dots—courtesy someone's little cat feet—each dot brilliant, an almost painful silvery white in the lamplight from the windows.
Sweet dreams,

Leslie

$Cushing,$
$Maine$

Dear Roger,

Right drove up just now so can't truly answer your wonderful letter/packet of goodies but did want you to know they'd arrived. (I'll pass on the *Sutherlandia montana* seeds to somebody in a warmer climate. "Hardy to –5°" means "won't winter over" around here.)

Don't know if the enclosed catalog of hot and ornamental peppers by "The Pepper Gal" will be of interest as you can see she's rather haphazard—but it does give an idea of what's available. Is all your research for the vegetable book already done? (that's my speciality, you know).

Or maybe you don't know. My flowers get photographed a lot, and most of the garden writing I do is about ornamentals these days. But I came to gardening out of pure hunger—two decades ago the only way to get good produce here was to grow it. Now the slant of light on a leaf and the fragrance of night-blooming flowers are as important to the taste of an heirloom tomato, but my first Maine gardens were purely utilitarian enterprises.

I did do a lot of carpet bedding with the vegetables; perhaps by way of compensation. There were zigzag borders of leeks, with the triangular patches filled by assorted lettuces. Beds of fennel were ringed with rhubarb chard, and I got a lot of mileage out of seaweed mulch—the black is very effective.

There's a fellow on our road who is a perfect carpet gardener of the old school. His whole front yard is filled with patterns and (except for the sunflowers) flat as the proverbial pancake. Plastic doodads are minimal, he does it all with flowers: zinnias, snapdragons, impatiens, petunias, dusty miller—the year before last he spelled out HELLO! in yellow and orange marigolds (yellow on an orange ground). Rather like an Escher in that you didn't really see it until it was pointed out to you then you couldn't *not* see it. This year yielded no similar splendor but I have hopes for next. Doesn't do to be snobby, though—I think we all start out as naive painters and only move to Impressionism after a bit of practice.

Truth be told, I sort of miss carpet bedding, but not as much as I miss my mother's Pennsylvanian gardens, where I played as a child and which I can see from the few pictures that exist were very gracefully designed. All I can remember directly are the hollyhocks against the silvery rail fence, the stream that flowed down one side of the vegetable garden in a rock-lined channel, and Japanese beetles which I "helped" by picking in hundreds from the roses. The roses I don't remember at all, but those beetles are as clear as yesterday.

And so is the quality of the food—simple salads of sliced tomatoes, sweet, tender corn on the cob, lettuces of astonishing crispness and depth of flavor. I missed vegetables like that my whole adult life, but I made do with what the markets offered until I came to Maine, where pure necessity forced me back to the garden at last.

When I moved here in 1972 the only way to get eggplant was to grow it. Ditto fresh herbs. Twenty years ago the way to cook with fresh basil, dill or coriander was to grow your own; the only way to get a summer squash smaller than a baseball bat was to pick one from your own plants. Farmstands were few, far-between and ill-stocked.

They still are, when you think about the riches available through seed catalogs. For the first few years, I just went to the local nurseries and bought seedlings. Then I caught on to starting from seeds, began running tomato trials, comparing the different breeds of bell peppers, ordering exotic potatoes. So if you need some pictures of or information about weird edibles, maybe I can help.

Off tomorrow a.m. for Philadelphia to be a visiting luminary at "the Book and Cook," a big restaurant promotion they (the city) put on every year.

As soon as I get home, copy editing of *The Modern Country Cook* for work, and for fun writing to Roger. Hope all's well with you and yours. X X Leslie

P.S. "drove up" is Maine slang for totally busy.

Cushing,
Maine

April 5, 1990

Well my dear I scarcely know where to start so I will start at starting, since that's pretty much what's going on around here. There's still a bit of snow in the shady places and heavy, wet snow is predicted for tomorrow, but the catkins are silvery velveting out on the pussy willows, the first crocus are blooming and assorted early narcissi have buds. Tulips are still pretty low to the ground. Greening-up has just begun. The lawns are still more brown than otherwise and there is mud everywhere.

Spring as usual: it's cold and raw and highly suggestive of going to Florida except that you have to be here so you can get going with the seedlings. Our season is so short even tough things like asters and snapdragons are best begun at least eight weeks before planting out. March and April mean a fridge top paved with pots, crowded babies awaiting transplant lining every windowsill. I rent space to grow stuff on at a greenhouse in Camden (about half an hour up the road) but the house is still littered with seedling impedimenta because I do most of the actual work in the kitchen—employing the shining hours of early morning when I'm still too fuddled to write.

A greater concentration on perennials and shrubbery would certainly alleviate the burden; our climate limits the options less than you might think. Mahonia, for instance, is I believe quite hardy in most of its varieties even in Maine. But I got started this way as a result of being a renter and have remained a real sucker for annual flowers. And since

I'm also more or less the vegetable queen there's not really much help for it.

This year I'm trying a new datura, *D. suaveolens*, which is supposed to be extremely tall and very fragrant. Alas, germination looks doubtful. Also a new salpiglossis called "Kew Blue," to be known as "Salpiglossis Last Chance." For several years now every kind of salpiglossis I've tried has failed to produce the gorgeous dark browns and violets that are the whole point of the plant. Instead, I mostly get dingy mustard yellow flowers in which the characteristic gold veins are lost. If the "Kew Blues" don't perform I'm going to admit salpiglossi are nothing but uppity petunias and say the hell with it. Will spare you further annuals list; there are *dozens* even though each year I swear I'm going to go in for something recherché and difficult in a different way (like species clematis) instead.

I'm also trying to cut down on vegetable varieties, but new enticements make that hard. This year's flings will include—just started the seeds today—"Evergreen" tomatoes, still green when ripe. They should go well with the proven "Lemon Boy" (yellow), "Zapotec Pink" (an heirloom that's actually a rather creepy green-flashed pale magenta) and White Beauty (which really is). The "Beauty" is also one delicious tomato you bet, and a very long keeper. By the time they're fully ripe they've turned a lovely shade of creamy ivory and they encourage me in the matter of the "Evergreens," proving as they do that odd color doesn't preclude fine flavor. Speaking of which, allow me (in case I haven't already done so) to recommend "Brandywine," unquestionably the tastiest tomato I grow. Of course, that's the extent of its virtues—it's late, shy bearing, prone to cat-facing . . .

April 12

But maybe I shouldn't go on about tomatoes (perhaps one thing that does better here than there?), since among the seedlings in the garden there are a lot more flowers than food. Many are perennials I either can't afford or have trouble finding in nursery catalogs, things like the yellow delphinium, *D. zalil,* and tree dahlias (from J. L. Hudson Co., no Latin name supplied, seed claimed to have been collected from the wild in Mexico). Tree dahlias are supposed to eventually reach six or seven feet and have dangling clusters of pink and purple bell-shaped (!) flowers. I will believe it when I see it which to date I have not done. (Catalog not illustrated.) They make gorgeous foliage plants, so far about five feet tall, with huge, tropical-looking but fundamentally dahlia-shaped leaves and serious trunks, complete with the appearance of bark. But they don't set much in the way of tubers, just one or two paltry lumps per plant, so although I started two years ago—this will be year three—I don't seem to be getting ahead on them. It's maddening since conventional dahlias do, if anything, too well, increasing madly like your nasturtiums. (I'm jealous of those *Tropaeolum tuberosum,* can't find a source, do please send seed if your plants set any.) There are always millions of giant dahlia tubers at the end of the season, reputedly (ahem) edible by someone besides the mice. I confess I haven't tried it yet. They're so damned prolific I can't help feeling that if they were tasty we'd know it by now. Wheelbarrows full of them, "Free, Help Yourself," are a fairly common front-yard decoration around town in the early fall. I was going to say something about how thrifty Yankees would never give that much food away if it were any good, but wheelbarrows full of free cucumbers are also a regular feature (and almost nobody collects mushrooms).

I have given some thought to your yellow corner, an idea that struck a familiar chord. Two years ago I started building a pink and yellow "border," actually the front section of the right hand side of the lower garden. This was inspired by the acquisition of a large, vaguely Chinese-flavored Minton bowl, enamel yellow outside and the color of raspberry sherbet within and not even a little hideous as by rights such a combination should be extremely.

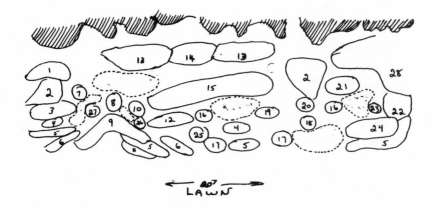

Minton Bowl Border, Lower Garden

1. *Althea* (peach colored) from Beth
2. *Thermopsis caroliniana*
3. *Hemerocallis* "Hyperion"
4. *Dianthus knappii*
5. *Dianthus plumarius* "Old Laced Pinks"
6. *Heuchera sanguinia* "Bressingham Hybrids," selected for paler shades
7. *Phlox* "Rosalinde"
8. *Papaver orientalis* "Princess Victoria Louise"
9. *Korean Chrysanthemum* (pink) from Olive
10. Lily "Parisienne"
11. *Allium roseum*
12. *Hemerocallis* "Raja"
13. *Helianthus* from Paul
14. *Astilbe* from Paul

15. Bearded Iris (yellow) from Lois
16. *Heliopsis* "Golden Glow"
17. *Alchemilla mollis*
18. Rose "Amber Queen"
19. *Echinacea* "Bravado"
20. *Phlox paniculata* (pink) from Paul
21. *Dicentra spectabilis*
22. *Monarda* (deep pink) from Bruce
23. *Ligularia* "The Rocket"
24. *Hemerocallis* "Stella d'Oro" and two peach-apricot mid-season bloomers whose names are lost in the mists of time
25. Lily "Pink Perfection"
26. Lily "Yellow Blaze"
27. *Filipendula* (pink) from Lois

The dotted lines are Tulips: "Yellow Parrot," "Apricot Beauty," "New Design" and "Baroness."

In between, self-sown: *Digitalis ferruginea, Linaria purpurea* "Canon J Went," *Digitalis purpurea* and *Malva sylvestris* "Mauritiana."

Still to come: a pink landscape rose, a test specimen from Jackson and Perkins that as yet has no name, more Echinacea plus an experimental Forsythia from plant breeder friends of Paul's.

So, in addition to the plants you mention, what about our dooryard staple forsythia and what about witch hazel? And *Clematis tangutica* (love them yellow bells). Things like Welsh poppies (*Meconopsis cambrica*) and Lady's Mantle (*Alchemilla mollis*) probably are such a given that they're not worth mentioning but they sure put out a lot of yellow down there in the lower regions. You didn't mention iris but the yellow ones here (nameless gift from a friend of Lois's) look very good with the bleeding heart and pinks, and the foliage stays a nice bit of pale orderliness as the summer blowse progresses. Ligularia? My garden is too dry and sunny for this wide-leaved wonder to flourish but I seem to remember you saying you had some. I can't grow Japanese iris, either, to my everlasting regret. *Dianthus knapii,* on the other hand, is very happy here. Bloom season isn't as long as the pink pinks' but they will rebloom in full if cut back hard.

Do you know *Thermopsis carolina?* It's a pea-relative with lupin-like, pale yellow fingers. Blooming period is pretty short but the foliage is dainty, pretty and long-lasting, a nice bright sort of poison green. And I'm a big fan of *Digitalis lutea,* happily perennial here and a mad self-seeder (but easy to weed out). The foliage is very unlike regular foxglove foliage, almost strap-shaped, dark green and shiny. The flowers are quite small, somewhere between gold and brass with a dusting of brown spots. Height seems quite variable, so far I've had 'em anywhere from three to five feet. One of the best things about them is the bee-bump. Bumblebees love them but can't quite get inside, so all summer there is reliably a chance to view the flowers looking like sacks-of-something-that-wiggles, with bee-butts barely protruding from the open ends.

Speaking of splendors given to self-sowing, I can't find that winter heliotrope in any of my catalogs. It certainly sounds delightful and might well be less rambunctious in our harsher climate (probably, knowing my luck, it'll be one more thing to "treat as annual" and start in a little pot every spring).

And thinking of self-seeding brings me to your story about Mr. Stallone (great name, under the circumstances). Rather a wow that he brings his impotence problems to his mother—and perhaps indicative of why he's got 'em. Can't read a crucial word here. Did she "counsel" him, "console" him, or something else entirely?

A complex problem, and as you mention, quite a difference between long-term compatability ("love") and the simple desire loosely defined as "lust." Speaking for myself, I can't say the latter feels indissolubly tied to the former. It's hard to know for sure—in my case both suitable partners for the one and likely targets? objects? recipients? of the other have been scarce unto nonexistent for years—but as far as I can tell, desire is just

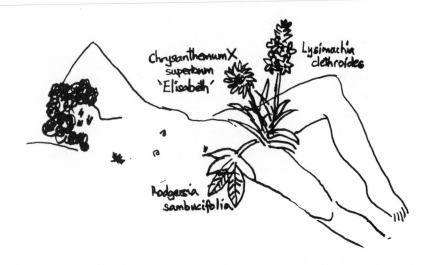

linked to general mood (I'm horny when I'm happy) and that, in turn, is linked to all the usual cues (accomplishment, affection, etc.) and also very importantly to light. There's an enormous need, especially about this time of year when there has been long deprivation, to feel the sun on my naked body. Usually, thank goodness, at some point in April there's finally at least one day when it's warm enough to take off all my clothes and go lie on the back porch, legs open, getting everything bathed in/by those rays ... Not something I'd want to try in lower latitudes but sunburn is seldom a problem in Maine even in high summer.

Just looked up from the page: it's snowing, so I guess it's still sublimation-in-food time. I'm trying to eat up the last of the summer garden stuff from the freezer. Yellow squash with sugarsnap peas and basil, stewed tomatoes with grilled peppers and coriander and baby purple onions, harvest stew full of snap and shell beans, zucchini, peppers, squash blossoms and cream. A funny diet as the first asparagus comes into the stores, but the first asparagus won't come into the garden for at least a month and when it does I want to face the new season with a clean slate (and a clean freezer).

More soon, the Easter baking is calling. Feel like it would be nice to send fancy egg breads to the folks of Eastern Europe, especially Russia, where they've still got such a long, weary way to comfortable abundance (and such a long tradition of festive baking for this holiday). Come to think of it, I wish I could send a nice plump, fruit-studded Kulich to *you,* and hope all is well in (good grief, a head tax!) your part of the world. Love,

Leslie

Eccleston Square,
London

Leslie,

A great letter, lots of things I must respond to, but first the realization has finally hit me that you are the queen of vegetables and a princess of annuals!

Three volumes are already out in the series of books on garden plants I am doing with Martyn Rix – *Bulbs, Roses* and *Shrubs. Perennials* we are just finishing off for delivery in May. This will be followed by *Vegetables, Conservatory Plants* and then *Annuals,* hopefully one a year over the next three years. We are and have been working on all three for the past couple of years so now it is down to (in the case of vegetables anyway) finding the exciting rarities. You sound as if you have lots! Exciting! We need photographs!

I'm going to be boring and tell you how I do my shots to ensure success.

HERE BEGINNETH THE FIRST LESSON:

Do a bracket on all exposures. Do what the meter tells you to do, i.e. f11 at 1/60th of a second, then do a half stop lighter, then a stop lighter, i.e. f8/11 at 1/60th and f8 at 1/60th, then half stop and whole stop darker, i.e. f11/16 and 1/60th. This may sound a bit tricky but in fact once you're set up you can just crack through by using the aperture ring. In fact I do it by feel and so the shots only take about as long as it takes to wind on.

When choosing transparencies (it must be slide film) it is often the case that a darker exposure is better for reproduction. This is especially true in the case of white flowers; the only sort of tranny good enough to reproduce from has to have detail in the whites. This will almost certainly mean that the foliage will be on the dark side. When taking dark objects like black flowers the opposite will be true. The meter in your camera is a mindless moron and must be kept under control: all professionals do brackets as they *know* they can't take a perfect exposure, only amateurs can do that with one frame. Although it sounds expensive (film costs go up by × 5) it means you will get usable results every time.

LESSON THE SECOND:

Use a slow colour film like Kodak Ektachrome 100ASA or Kodachrome. The slower the film the more body there is in the colour, known as colour density or saturation. This slower film will mean that the exposures will be more difficult so in some instances you will need a tripod. A still like a bunch of potatoes can then be shot with a longer exposure time, say 1/8 or

Fill the frame as this

1/4 second. This sort of exposure time will of course be no good for flowers growing as you will get wind movement, but when doing flowers growing you will need all the depth of field you can get (this is achieved by stopping down, i.e. f16 in preference to say f8). So you will still be helped by a tripod so that you can shoot at say 1/30th second or even (in low wind conditions) 1/15th.

Please will you shoot some of your wild-sounding vegetables for us? They should be done on a background of clean earth or stone or something very simple and kitchen gardenish. If there is a detail that does not show, say pink-fleshed potatoes, could you just shoot say half a dozen but cut one in half to show the flesh? They should not be small in the frame but nearly fill it so that there is greater detail to reproduce from.

LESSON THE THIRD: LIGHT

Harsh sunlight is too contrasty, especially for still life, best shot on a day with thin cloud cover. If the sun always shines in Maine a help would be to use a white card as a 'fill-in'; this is to reflect some light back into the shadow areas so that you don't end up with a shot that has bleached high-

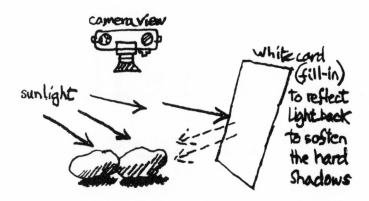

lights and black shadows with no detail — even Rembrandt with his extremes of *chiaroscuro* had detail in the shadows. With flowers growing, however, this need not apply. If they look great in the natural light they will look great when shot. Again though, if you shoot against the light, i.e. with sunlight coming through the flowers, make sure to do the darkest of the bracket as the sunlight will tend to flare the film and make the result lighter than the meter tells you. (I am presuming that you have a camera that you can operate manually.)

Now the difficult bit, how to pay you. The sums we get paid are pretty measly, somewhere in the region of $20 a shot (I'm not complaining of the deal), so I won't insult you by offering that; but can I pay for film and buy you a tripod if you need one? I stress paying for the film as doing loads of shots is really the way to get good ones; each time you look over what you have done you think of new ways of getting better pictures. Also if you tackle the same subject again it pushes you into finding a new angle/viewpoint or trying a different time of day or a change of light. Basically doing lots of shots gets you in practice. Taking photographs is just like playing the piano: the more you practise, the better you shoot. (When I say I will pay for film I don't mean only film that might be of use to me in a book, I mean all the film you need.)

My yellow flower bed backs on to the tennis court so it has twelve-foot-high netting at the back up which run roses, clematis, golden hops, etc. It is a very sunny spot overlooking the main lawn where people sit in summer. (We are having summer now, the temperature goes up to around 75°F every day and only down to about 52°F at night.) Anyway, my system is that in the beds that you see from the lawns in summer I try to plant things for summer effect, and the beds seen from the outside and the main path I plant more with spring things. The above is my explanation of why no forsythia or witch hazel, but *Clematis tangutica* is a lovely thought. Also, I haven't put in Welsh poppies (I have some seed). Ligularia is also a good idea although, like your garden, it may be too dry; but

I shall add them to my list. I have just done a plan of the bed so that I have a record of what is there. As you will see I have gone very strongly for yellow foliage plants and to break up the yellows I have put in quite a few white flowered things. The annuals tend to be self-seeded or otherwise scattered about so that they come up naturally through the shrubs and perennials. Inevitably I have blue larkspurs and other mismatches arriving by accident that don't fit into the scheme, but so it goes.

Bed 25: The Yellow Bed

1. Rose 'Maigold'
2. Rose 'Handel'
3. Rose 'Mme Isaac Pereire'
4. *Humulus lupulus* 'Aureus'
5. Rose 'Casino'
6. *Clematis alpina*

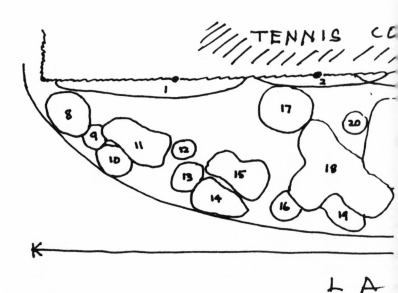

7. Rose 'Autumn Sunlight'
8. *Spirea thunbergii*
9. *Ribes sanguineum* 'Brocklebankii'
10. *Phlomis fruticosa*
11. *Euonymus fortunei* 'Emerald 'n' Gold'
12. Rose 'Graham Thomas'
13. *Melissa officinalis* 'Variega'
14. *Phlomis fruticosa*
15. *Berberis thunbergii* 'Aurea'
16. *Abutilon* 'Canary Bird'
17. *Acer japonica* 'Aurea'
18. *Berberis thunbergii* 'Aurea'
19. *Melissa* 'Variegata'
20. Rose 'Yellow Charles Austin'
21. *Physocarpus opulifolius* 'Darts Gold'
22. *Melissa officinalis* 'Aurea'
23. *Artemisia lactiflora*

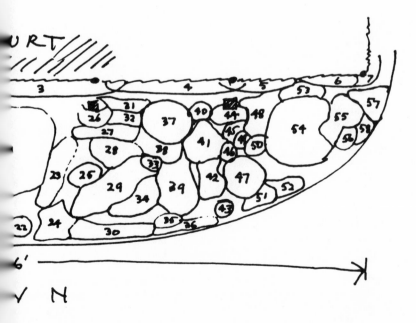

24. Tuberous begonias (yellow)
25. Rose 'Yellow Charles Austin'
26. Rose 'Lady Hillingdon' Climber
27. *Lilium* 'Connecticut King'
28. *Anthemis tinctoria*
29. *Lilium* 'Sunray'
30. *Calendula*
31. *Alstroemeria* 'Ligtu Hybrids'
32. *Lilium* 'Citronella Strain'
33. *Filipendula ulmaria* 'Aurea'
34. *Lilium* 'Mont Blanc'
35. Tulip 'West Point'
36. *Calendula*
37. *Weigela Looymansii* 'Aurea'
38. *Helichrysum* 'Sulphur light'
39. *Coreopsis verticillata*
40. *Lilium* 'Citronella Strain'
41. *Lilium* 'Connecticut King'
42. *Lilium* 'Connecticut King'
43. *Melissa* 'Aurea'
44. Rose 'Lawrence Johnston' Climber
45. *Gaillardia* 'Aurea'
46. *Filipendula ulmaria* 'Aurea'
47. *Spirea* 'Gold Flame'
48. *Galtonia candicans*
49. *Lilium* 'Connecticut King'
50. Rose 'English Garden'
51. *Origanum onites* 'Aureum'
52. *Sagina glabra* 'Aurea'
53. *Lilium* 'Connecticut King'
54. *Philadelphus coronarius* 'Aureus'
55. *Catalpa bignonoides* 'Aurea'

56. Tulip 'West Point'
57. *Calendula*
58. *Cytisus* × *kewensis*

There is a yellow leaved Fuchsia which I want for the gap above 12/15

Annuals in Between:

Cosmos 'Sunny Gold'
Cosmos 'Candy Stripe'
Eschscholzia 'Sundew'
Oenothera
Chrysanthemum parthenium 'Aureum'
Consolida ambigua
Physalis alkekengi

On 2 May I will be giving a lecture at the London Museum. They are having a History of London Gardens exhibition all summer and I'm to do a talk on Eccleston Square. (Pay £60, cost of me making slides about £120.) I must be mad but I am quite looking forward to it and it gives me another chance to moan on about the ruddy car park developers. Also I am driven to crystallize my thoughts and philosophy on gardening (too big a word for having ideas).

Loved your thoughts on love in the light/lust in the dust. Hot sun, I agree, is the great aphrodisiac, but then close runners are good food, and of course drink. But after all that there has to be something special there doesn't there?

Love,

Roger

Cushing,
Maine

Dear Roger,

Thanks for your letter. The diagram of the yellow border is fascinating and the photographic encouragements just that. I'm still camera-shopping (like computer-shopping it's quite the undertaking and could easily eat up a person's life if she weren't so pressed to do six thousand other things, most of them equally expensive and even less gratifying).

I am, it's true, the queen of the annuals and vegetables, a title of dubious desirability given that there is this longish period in the beginning of the summer when a) the work-pressure is beyond belief, tray after tray of babies to plant *Right now! Yesterday! Hurry Up!* and b) the garden looks—not exactly like hell, but not exactly like a garden anyone in their right mind would be proud of. There is gorgeousness in the perennial beds—right now the columbines, pinks, coral bells and iris are blooming, foxgloves are just about to do it, delphiniums hard on their heels—but most of the garden is brown earth and weeds, with hundreds of little plants set doinkety-doinkety-doink . . . not in rows, it's not *that* dreadful, but not in close enough proximity to look anything but paltry in the extreme and as many now have their first flowers it's somehow even worse: a three-foot area with two screaming orange calendulas in it, a scattering of zinnias, here and there a white venidium (they really are going to be gorgeous, by the way, one of those rare instances where the catalog didn't lie) and just the beginnings of lushness from the alyssum, which at this point is not a "carpet of snow" but a scattering of loose threads.

Oh well.

Do you have raccoons in London? They do splendidly in suburbs here and are sometimes seen in cities . . . Come to think of it, I don't even know if you've got the damned things in England whatsoever. If not, be joyful. They're most notorious for rooting around in garbage and for eating all the corn two days before the ears are ripe, but they also dig up any newly-set plant that sits on the faintest raccoon-nosable hint of bone meal.

So one way and another, not much gratification just yet, especially in the edibles department. Asparagus and rhubarb (this year's recipe discov-

ery is rhubarb and dried cherries—terrific!) are over and now it's pure leafy green—lettuces, cress, rocket, and of course lamb's-quarters, an exquisitely tasty weed *much* easier to grow than spinach since not growing it would be the trick. Other People's Strawberries are starting to come in, my newly-planted "Tristars" are looking very promising but also like at least another two weeks off.

As you describe your choices in the yellow border I realize how public your garden is, how important it is to please your fellow square-dwellers, the multitudes of passers-by, the Guardians of Ancient Trees, just about everybody except the Queen (and for all I know, her, too). Leads me to think on the meaning of the garden as an enclosure. That's where the word comes from, after all, and for me that sense of a protected place is vital. In my case the boundaries are more psychological than physical—there are no fences or sidewalks or hedges, both of the main gardens more or less bleed off into the woods and fields—but there is a clear sense of something-within-borders because all the plantings are oriented toward the central paths. The gardens have obviously been built to be viewed from within, and this inward turning is as effective in its way as walls. You can tell right away when you first see the property that the gardens are not for public display.

And as soon as you're in either garden you can tell one vision—if it can be called that—is in charge. Some areas are very utilitarian, others quite formally designed, and not a few of the transitions are on the rough side. It's really a sort of private dialogue between myself and the plants, with classical design aesthetics relegated to the back seat.

I *do* care what Lois thinks (after all, she owns the place). It's nice to have friends in and around. And I'm vain enough to be pleased when painters want to immortalize the joint even though easels set up in the narrow paths present problems of their own.

Considering how haphazard the place is, it's gotten quite a lot of painterly attention. Lois has mostly been resistant—gardens are not her sort of landscape—but Nancy Wissemann-Widrig has become a regular

When it rains,
Nancy takes refuge
in the greenhouse

10-10-14

Nancy Wissemann-Widrig

visitor, her husband, John Wisseman, paints here from time to time, and so do others from the area.

After a while, they add up. A few years ago a gallery called Maine Coast Artists had a show of garden paintings and so many (6 or 7 out of about 60) were done here they had me come and give a talk about "Art in the Garden." Big mistake on my part. Everybody who came to the talk wanted to come see the garden. I told 'em it was better in the paintings and they shouldn't mess with their illusions.

Nancy is such a fixture at this point that, like Lois, she's part of the garden and welcome whenever. But other than that, well, "secret" isn't at all the right word, but I tend to be very close with the place, have never (and don't intend) to be part of the garden-club tour circuit and was *livid* the other day when a woman I'd never seen before came strolling right into the garden, about a hundred feet (through a field) from the nearest public right of way. She announced, in tones implying she expected me to be grateful, that she'd admired it (walked through it, from the sound of her) many times previously, asked a whole bunch of questions in spite of my extremely frosty responses, and then blithely announced she'd be back when it was further along, since not much seemed to happening just yet! I was too nonplussed to suggest she wait until she was invited into the equivalent of a stranger's living room. Fervently hope my coolness will be enough to discourage further intrusions. We shall see.

I still boil in retrospect, realize my attitude probably sounds churlish, if not absurd, especially to an urbanite. But as you will see when you visit, this is a very quiet, little-traveled place. During the busiest part of the day a car goes by, maybe once every twenty minutes or so in the winter, once every two or three minutes in the summer. And in both cases said car is almost always being driven by someone who lives or works or is well known on this two-mile stretch of dead-end road where there are not more than thirty-five houses *if* you count numerous summer places. People pretty much keep to themselves by unspoken but widely-understood agreement and while they feel free to do things like come to the door and ask for donations for the Cancer Society, they don't just drop in on strangers. Thank God. The woman, who has a summer house on the main road, is undoubtedly "from away," a phrase that of course also applies to me, and to anyone else not born here. In fact, there is a famous Maine joke about the subject that I've always liked: Seems an outsider had occasion to be at the funeral of an elderly resident, a man much loved in the small fishing community where he'd lived ever since his birth. The outsider remarked to a native:

"Guess you'll really miss old Joe, he was the very best type of Mainer, wasn't he?"

"We'hnt a Mainah," replied the native, "his folks were from New Jehseh."

"But I thought he was born here," the outsider protested.

"So 'e waas," replied the native, "but that don't make 'im a Mainah. Yer cat can have kittens in the oven, but that don't make 'em biscuits."

This is perhaps a bit extreme, but the basic idea is okay with me, one of the local customs that seems a bit limiting but makes its own kind of sense.

As does—to return to the garden—the local habit of planting practically the whole damn yard to lilacs and to hell with the other forty-nine weeks of the year. There's a certain sameness once the season is over, but that's actually quite restful, and during lilac time it's an overpowering intoxication. On some stretches of road—the ones lined with old farms—there are such masses of pale purple bloom the fragrance pours through the car windows even at sixty miles an hour. Nice to reflect that New England lilacs were already emblematic when Lincoln died, that they're one of those imports that has flourished here as nowhere else. I've read that the collection at Harvard's Arnold Arboretum is the largest in the world, and everyone I know describes it as a proper wonder, but lilac time is planting time and somehow I have yet to get up there and see it.

What we have here are generally the common purple kind. *Syringa vulgaris.* Most well-maintained older properties have hedges of them along at least one border and some right-thinking homeowners who don't have them to start with go ahead and plant them. Lois set a row between the house and the road when she moved here thirty years ago, along with a short hedge at her Western boundary, but I have been remiss. Currently have only one, a "Miss Ellen Willmott" in the white garden. I've long had in mind a nice Maine-style hedgerow running down the hill between the upper garden and the lower, and just today my friend Sam, his chainsaw still running from the whacking-down of a couple of extra birch trees, pointed out that lilacs would be just right in a spot currently occupied, *faute de mieux,* by a couple of undistinguished chokecherries.

Sam has been setting his own lilac hedge, using sprouts from the property originally settled (and lilacked) by his great-great-grandfather. In Sam's case, the distance between lilacs is only a few thousand feet, but lilacs grow all over this country, a wave settled westward with the pioneers, for just Sam's good reasons. Not only are they long lived, handsome, easy to transplant and care for, they're symbolically loaded: a sprout of lilac is a coal from the home fire—guess I'll get mine from Lo's place.

I've gotten a lot of my plants from friends, a realization brought home with special force when I made the diagram of the yellow/pink bed. Compared to your elegant yellow border, it's filled with the nameless— or, more accurately, the name-unknown-to-me. It's frustrating, but names aren't everything, and when I think of things like how a rose's color may change depending on the light, the importance of pH to hydrangeas, the effect of soil fertility on plant size and vigor, documentation of the garden takes its place with musical notation, recipe-writing and choreographer's diagrams. The representation conveys such a small part of the real thing. I can't, for instance, send the baby phoebes having discussions in their nest under the eaves (they sound like they need oiling), can't send you the fragrance of night blooming stock as evening comes on, can't send the velvet feel of mullein planted too close to the path as it brushes against my bare calf. Can't send you the mosquitoes, either. Count your blessings.

Pan-Fried Shad
with Rhubarb Compote

(From a column once more. Compote is also tasty with pork chops or other fatty meat—or plain, eaten with a spoon, though it's a bit intense in that mode.)
For 4 servings:

$^3/_4$ lb. young rhubarb, trimmed but unpeeled, cut into $^1/_3$ inch dice, about 2 cups prepared

$^1/_4$ cup sugar, or slightly more

$^1/_8$ teaspoon salt

1 large garlic clove, split into 4

a one-inch piece of cinnamon stick

2 slices fresh ginger, each about 1 inch in diameter and $^1/_8$ inch thick

$^1/_4$ cup dried cherries, about 1 oz., available in natural food and gourmet stores

1 small, barely ripe cooking pear, such as bosc, peeled, cored, and diced slightly smaller than the rhubarb

8 slices bacon

4 medium-sized shad fillets, about $1^1/_2$ lb., or the same weight of herring fillets

cornstarch for dusting

Begin with the compote. Combine the rhubarb in a non-reactive bowl with the sugar and salt. Stir well, cover the bowl and let sit, stirring from time to time, for about $1^1/_2$ hours or until the rhubarb has given off roughly $^1/_2$ cup of juice.

Put the garlic, cinnamon, ginger and cherries in a heavy non-reactive saucepan big enough to hold the rhubarb in no more than three layers. Strain in the juice, reserving the fruit. Simmer over low heat, stirring occasionally, for about ten minutes or until the cherries are plump and the liquid is reduced to a couple of tablespoons of very thick syrup. Remove and discard garlic, ginger and cinnamon.

When the syrup is ready, add the rhubarb and pear, stir well and raise heat to low-medium. Cook, stirring often, for about eight minutes or until the rhubarb is barely softened and there is little or no free liquid in the pan. Remove from the heat, let cool a moment, then taste to see if extra sugar is needed. Puckery-sour is too sour, but don't forget this is a relish, not dessert. It will keep in the refrigerator for about two days.

To complete the dish, fry the bacon until it is crisp and drain it well, reserving the fat. Right before serving, pour enough of the clear, residue-free bacon fat into a wide frying pan to make a very generous layer, about ¼ inch. Heat until it is very hot—almost but not quite smoking.

Pat the fillets dry with paper toweling, then rub lightly with cornstarch. Slide the fish into the pan skin side down and cook, turning once, for about three minutes a side. Fillets should be lightly brown and slightly crisp on the outside, just done within. If the fat is both deep and hot they will not be greasy, but they should be briefly drained on absorbent paper to wick off any external oiliness.

Serve at once on warmed plates, garnished with the reserved bacon and accompanied by the compote. Parsleyed new potatoes go well with this.

So would a parsnip and potato purée.

Historical note (possibly apocryphal): some sources mention a Micmac Indian legend concerning the origin of the shad, an extraordinarily bony fish. Seems there was a porcupine discontented with his lot who asked the

Great Spirit Manitou for a better situation. Ever obliging, the Great Spirit turned him inside out and threw him in the river.
Love,

Leslie

Eccleston Square, London

21 May 1990

Dear Leslie,

French gardening is thriving and blossoming. In fact, after a three-day trip to Paris I am still in shock at the enthusiasm and effusiveness of *Ses Horticulturistes*. I had to go to do a talk about shrubs at a chateau called Courson about twenty-five miles south of Paris. Martyn, my co-author, went with me. (Martyn is a fantastic botanist who loves most of all searching the mountains of China or Africa or wherever for rare, new or lost plants in the grand manner of the old plant hunters.) Anyway, our French publishers, Flammarion, put us up in the Hotel Trianon on the Left Bank about three metres from the 'Boule Miche'. I was in slight trepidation of the hotel as years ago I stayed in the Hotel Petit Trianon on the Left Bank, which was incredibly cheap and incredibly itchy—the walls of the entire room were covered in squashed fleas and bugs!

The flower show was terrific. There is a whole new generation of French plantsmen; young, vital, keen and most of them specializing in one area of rarities or another. Of course lots of southern tender plants (I bought three Bougainvillea to see if I can get them to grow outside); but also I met a world expert on Japanese maples, a man with hundreds of carnivorous plants, a man with ancient roses, a man with more than two hundred different scented geraniums (not pelargoniums) and there were also lots of daturas. Then I met a man from Vallauris, where Picasso lived, who gave me some super things to pop in the garden – all incredibly tender. There was an artist who had made the most fantastic pots I have ever seen – very large terracotta and decorated all over with patterns in relief that reminded me of Arab jewellery. They cost about £700 each! so I didn't actually bring one home.

The next day I went to see the recreation of the Claude Monet garden at Giverny. About 10,000 other people had the same idea, but it is such a special place for me that I was able to walk around without even noticing them. Years ago I did some experimental photographs in different light, i.e. shots of the same view every hour from dawn to night. The changes were amazing and it showed how accurate Monet was in his subtle observation of light and colour. I think it would make a super project to go back to Monet's garden (on the closed day) and try to make a series of studies in different light.

After Monet we went on to a garden in a little valley near Dieppe, the 'Parc Floral des Moutiers'. The house is by E. L. Lutyens and Gertrude Jekyll acted as consultant on the garden, but I gather that her plans have become too expensive to keep up. As you approach the house there is a series of garden rooms divided up with lovely walls so that they continue the architecture of the house into the garden, thus making a natural transition between the architecture and the wooded garden that runs down to the sea. The point of all this is that one of the rooms is a white garden; and thinking of the articles you spoke of that you might have to do, I have done you a few photographs. The problem was that the garden was packed with visitors. There is a view showing the walls and arches that lead through from room to room: the walls have *Hydrangea petiolaris* and on the house, a climbing rose, and in the beds there are your favourite 'Iceberg' roses and masses of *Centranthus ruber* 'Albus'. I also enclose one shot taken down the valley from the house where wonderful rhododendrons were planted by the grandfather of the present family. As you look out from the terrace at the back of the house you see only lawns and woodland falling away down to the sea but hidden in the woodland are magnificent forty-foot-high rhododendron specimens planted in vast groups.

11 July

Back to 'Blighty' and the Square. Your (I think of them as 'your') Californian poppies are fantastic in different spots all around the garden. I have all the different colours I could get, but I think in the end I prefer the yellowy-orange and the reddish-orange – they look more natural. I have another great self-seeder packing out the spaces, and sometimes burying the camellias *Chelidonium majus* the greater celandine. Although it's very different from the California poppies they are closely related, it also makes a mass of blue-grey foliage. The genus is known for the bright orange latex that bursts out of every stem as you break it – just like a *Lactarius deliciosus* – but the whole plant is poisonous. It was an old cure for warts though – not eating it, that would be too permanent – just rubbing the 'milk' on them. Jean Palaisul wrote in his book *Grandmother's Secrets*: 'He who carries it (greater celandine) upon his person together with the heart of a mole will vanquish his enemies and win law suits.' Very useful in America that would be. The other well known use for the red milk is as a reviver of flagging sexual capabilities – how administered I leave to your imagination.

My *Rosa* Nevada are flowering like mad again. Looking back in my diary I find that they were at their height around 17 May. Do you grow it? Do you like it?

I had a letter from Rod Tulloss, the Amanita man. Apparently there were two bad poisonings in New England last season and he had been trying to identify the mushroom. After months of work he was able to prove that it was *Amanita crenulata* described by Peck. – I had photographs of two collections that I had made in the Eastern states over the years but of course I could put no name to them. The information arrived

Above: Eccleston Square in winter. I have lived here for seventeen years and only remember it looking like this three times.

Below: The children, especially Amy, go mad when it does at last snow in London.

Above: Maine, looking toward the house from the trees by the ravine. Tall dahlias, cosmos and echinacea grow at the back of the lower garden, masking all that lies before them (including the steep sweep of lawn between the garden and the house).

Below: The very first thing I did when I started replanting in the Square was put in lower canopy trees; this is the Japanese cherry *Prunus* 'Shirofugen'.

Above: In Cushing, "kniola's black" morning
glory, purple sage, artemesia, agastache. Soft
pathways of wood chips and straw smother
weeds, quiet the sound of footsteps.

Middle: Hidden paths run all through the
main large shrubby beds in the Square. This
one is lined with plain wild primroses.

Below: The secret paths are getting more
and more elaborate
– the children love them.

Left: Looking into the garden from the north (house) end in Maine. In a foggy dusk, the black iron arch is flanked by fragrant trumpets of *Brugmansia*.

Below: The azaleas just coming into flower in London; they are underplanted with *Dicentra eximea*.

Above: One of my favourite roses, *Rosa soulieana,* on the Square railings. This plant was grown from wild seed from China and given to me by James Compton.

Right: At the edge of the blue border looking north toward the house in Cushing. Delphiniums star in early July, set off by the dark leaves of *Rosa rubrifolia*. The gray pompom in the foreground is a sea buckthorn, slow-growing, needle-leaved, impervious to cold and wind.

Left: Poppy border, early July. Self-sown Shirley poppies line the west side of the central paths. *Clematis pannicu-lata* climbs Bill's new alder and cedar arch.

Below: Ceanothus 'Cascade', one of the most free-flowering amongst our collection at Eccleston Square.

Next page, below: The fern garden in Eccleston Square. In summer it is a cool scented haven.

Above: Two of my favourite roses in the Square in the foreground,
just going over, 'Fantin-Latour', in full blast behind *Rosa
californica* 'Plena'.

Tall pink feathers of *Filipendula*, yellow dots of *Oenothera*
and the white lace of cow parsnip glow in the lower garden in
Cushing at dusk.

Amanita
crenulata

from Rod the day I had to send the proofs of my mushroom book back so I was able to crush it in. I think it will be the first time a photograph of it has ever been printed.

No we don't have raccoons in London, or England for that matter. They look sweet but they sound like a disaster – everything in my garden lives on bonemeal so please don't send me a sweet little raccoon pup? kitten? calf? My worst pests this year are snails. They are having a field day amongst the hostas and ligularias that are supposed to give foliage variety to the fern bed.

I planted a few seeds years ago of a thing I was told was Crispy mallow, *Malva crispa*. As far as I can now ascertain in my reference works it is now a variety of *Malva verticillata*. Well, whatever the botanists decide its name is it's good to eat! It's used in an Egyptian dish, melokia soup, flavoured with ground coriander and cayenne, pepper and salt.

I have loads of it in the garden now and I think the only way I can keep it from taking over is to eat it. I forgot to look up the real recipe so I made up a soup. I cooked three cloves of chopped garlic in olive oil and added it to three potatoes and three big handfuls of mallow leaves that had been boiled for three-quarters of an hour in a weak chicken stock. I flavoured it with salt and pepper and then liquidized it in the wizzer. The mallow leaves have a mucilaginous quality which thickens the soup very nicely. The children were crazy about it.

Off to Cornwall for one week tomorrow – all rocky cliffs and big waves and lovely gardens full of blue hydrangeas.

Write *soon*. Love,

Roger

Cushing,
Maine

July 24, 1990

Well Roger you tease! All this about the flea-bitten Petit Trianon and your understandable trepidations and then zip about the Trianon proper. Was it Grand I hope? Must say one of the nice things about my extremely *petit* celebrity is the occasional opportunity to stay in nice hotels on somebody else's nickel. When I go to Philadelphia to do the Book and Cook celebration they put me up at the Four Seasons which is very *grand luxe* (as America goes), and even though I get the low end of what's available the rooms are nevertheless always the sort of rooms where I feel a bit abashed as I put my ratty old nightie in the *très élégant* bureau. Life in the lane of the expense account—it's all business travelers natch, deducting their brains out; but I don't think I'd better get involved in politics just now.

Come to think of it, those travelers may not be entirely fixed on business if the interesting discovery I made during my last stay is any indication. I was lying on the floor next to the bed, getting ready to do the assorted exercises that help to keep vastness at bay. Happened to turn my head and look under the bed and there was a pair of extremely scanty scanties—black, with lace. I suppose I should have turned them in to housekeeping, in case they had sentimental value for somebody or were perhaps immensely expensive designer scanties or something but instead I kept 'em (though I haven't yet found any occasion suitable for their display).

To return to your letter: Those young vital keen plantsmen (and women?) and the conference itself sound very stimulating. Frustrating, though, for those of us for whom bougainvillea is strictly the stuff of fantasy. Are you sure those scented geraniums aren't pelargoniums? I ask because I have a fancy geranium catalog that lists over a thousand varieties, seventy of them scented, and they're *all* pelargoniums of one sort or another. Can't say I'm much tempted by any of them, though "Banded coconut" (*P. patulum*) sounds kind of engaging: "white flower, coconut scent, rounded, pale green leaf with distinct zone; trailing." Oh well, can't buy everything . . . Please tell more about the daturas, I think they may have possibilities here—at least more possibilities than bougainvillea. My *D. suaveolens* of course failed to germinate; all I've got again this year is plain old jimson weed (*D. stramonium*), known as "stinkweed" for very good reason. (I keep thinking I've got it extirpated but I keep being wrong.) *But,* my neighbor has something else, she knows not what—it's a very handsome low bush, the leaves gorgeous and trumpets immense, but it doesn't seem to be fragrant—and last spring I noticed some yet-another-kind being started by a local professional; so the genus (I notice on looking it up there are a *lot* of species) must offer a fair amount that would survive this far North.

The white garden you describe sounds glorious beyond words—can't wait to see the photos and am meanwhile reminded of so many things, among them a garden up north of here (near Bar Harbor) that was designed by Beatrix Ferrand. Lawns leading down a gentle slope to the sea have been planted with wild rose (*rugosa,* actually) hedges that look very natural but were actually carefully placed to enhance the perspective, making the sweep look far longer than it is. This architectural element is all that's left of the original, in all probability because this garden too was too expensive to keep up. Another aspect of the ephemerality that is such an essential part of gardening, for good or ill. Even Gertrude Jekyll's work not immune! This should point up the importance of learning to make those charts and diagrams as descriptive as possible, but there's still a bit of nagging doubt. You do say—or did you?—that you feel Monet in his garden. The restoration there *sounds* very successful yet I wonder. Without the guiding spirit of the original designer, how can the care-takers/recreators copy or cope with the inevitable glitches and splendid surprises? What did Monet do when the snails wasted his clematis and he had to stick something else in the hole, quick?

At least with him we have the paintings. Much better than diagrams, apropos of which I must tell you mine of the yellow border is already in-accurate. Once the heliopsis started blooming they turned out to be all wrong—*way* too orange—and I had to get them out right away. Or sort of right away. They announced their unsuitability at the start of a killer dry heat wave and I had to keep patiently making bouquets with the about-to-open buds until the weather finally broke. They've settled in happily between a big bunch of very tall goldenglow and some squatty but indomitable *coreopsis* "Early Sunrise" at the edge of the vegetable patch, where the three make a satisfying sweep of gold that leads the eye right to the edge of the woods (where it stops dead and blinks in disap-pointment. Design improvement there is definitely called for, a project for the fall).

I love *Hydrangea petiolaris* and it had been neck and neck with Dutch-man's pipe (*Aristolochia durior*) for the place upon the wall where I need a vine and then I'd just about decided against (it takes quite a while to get established here and I need a more immediate show) when you bring the whole thing up again.

Don't know *Rosa* Nevada at all—looked it up in *Roses* where it doesn't seem to be listed in the index and went thence to Beales, where I saw a very nice picture and read on the same page "Given the choice I would never exchange one bloom of Mme Hardy for an armful of Iceberg." He goes on to add: "Nor would I plant a bed of Mme Hardy in the middle of my lawn." Reminds me that I really must get some of Madame, no matter how hard it is to figure out where to put her, and how is one to make the garden smaller, hence more manageable and less full of weeds and gener-ally lovelier and more civilized, if there is all this stuff one keeps wanting to plant?

And how, when it comes to roses, is one to be noble in the matter of the environment when one is plagued with thrips? Even assuming one had the time and it was environmentally wise to apply rotenone daily, it wouldn't work. Neither does insecticidal soap, garlic, sabadilla dust (which is in any case hell on the bees) . . . Organic gardening manuals inevitably advise you to plant resistant varieties when all else fails, but they never talk about how the things you *want* are always the most vulnerable. This year I was sent a sample of something called (approximately) "Meidiland everblooming carefree landscape rose" which indeed it seems to be, big clusters of faintly fragrant little very double flowers and nice dark green leathery foliage on a good sized, spreading, healthy plant apparently unbothered by thrips, blackspot or the evil birch leaf miners that drop from above and devastate all other roses in the vicinity. But is it lovely? Is it noble, graceful, poignant, *interesting?* It is not. Pretty is about the kindest thing I can think of to say, damning with faint praise when you're talking about a rose.

August 10 . . . Already, so I think I'd better get this in the mail, although there's much else to tell and I will any day now. Do want you to know the photography is finally under way. I got the camera about two weeks ago, have used some film and am having a dandy time. After years and years of asking photographer friends, "Please, would you memorialize this totally weird eggplant for me?" and "Could you get a shot of the hollyhock—the way the light is coming through the petal?" etc., it's a great relief to finally be doing it (or at least trying to do it) myself. Still very frustrating as I don't yet know what the hell I'm doing, which is to say don't know how to set the images I see in the garden on the film. With my naked li'l eyeballs, for instance, I see quite clearly the way some pink *Limonium suworowii,* serendipitously planted beneath a group of common foxgloves (*D. purpurea*), echo not only their eccentric arches but also the tone, in a different shade, of their rather plummy color. *However,* getting this amusing juxtaposition nicely framed, correctly lighted, properly exposed, etc., has so far eluded me. I *see* a patterned tangle of spires in multiple, subtly various pinks, unified by a broad band of bright green leaf, but I seem to be photographing something between a bunch of pink moosh and the very worst sort of seed-catalog illustration. Oh well, "perseverance furthers," as an old I-ching-enamored friend used often to say. And as another friend has turned me on to a much less expensive film-processor than the one I started out with, your seed money should go a bit farther.

It does go, though, doesn't it? The old saw around here is that "a sail-boat is a hole in the water into which one pours money." I think the same could be said of the garden excepting it's a hole in the ground and you have to dig the damn thing before you can pour the money into it.
More soon,

Leslie

Cushing, Maine

August 14, 1990

Dear Roger,

Just gave a little talk at the local historical society, title: "Ecology in the Kitchen," a benefit for the Cushing Recycling Project. We're working on getting teaching materials for our school and a few neighboring ones, and the committee has decided to buy special bins—one for each of Cushing's roughly six hundred households—to make it easy to set out glass, plastic, etc. for the garbage man to collect as part of his regular rounds.

Our town landfill is now closed and you must drive about fifty miles round trip if you want to discard-your-own without paying a fee. A big change from when I first came here, and I rather miss Sunday At The Dump, a congenial source of local news and gossip if a bit gamey fragrance-wise, but the new regime has been very instructive. Now that we have to pay attention to where the trash goes we can really see where it comes from. In our case, it comes from the mailbox. We use very little packaged or canned food, the garden debris and kitchen scraps are composted, beer bottles are returnable and newspapers are used as mulch. What's left? Wine bottles and junk mail, roughly 450,000 times more of the latter than the former.

So, in keeping with the general theme I talked a lot about using leftovers, storing same in glass refrigerator containers or old yogurt tubs, composting—and eating weeds. Big hit. Almost all in the audience are country dwellers and most had heard of dandelions, but lamb's-quarters, pigweed, purslane, the usual lot, turned out to be revelation. I passed around a bunch of lamb's quarters and purslane for tasting and the best part was seeing the converts work on convincing the reluctant. Now, if they all just go out and tell their friends.

Weeds in my opinion don't get nearly enough respect and neither does the accidental landscape. We have for instance a whole field of milkweed between the so-called orchard and Lois's barn. It was in full perfection the middle two weeks of July: fragrance to beat any jasmine and in the butterfly blue twilight a multitude of fireflies to replace the monarchs of afternoon. I suppose that's the ultimately comforting thing about life in the country—most of its greatest delights do not come (except inadvertently) from the hand of man.

Respect notwithstanding, I've had a hard time restraining myself from weeding out all the purslane. Had to pay special attention to be sure there'd be enough for the talk. Usually there's plenty no matter how hard I try but this has been a good year for tidiness on account of it's so dry that anything weeded *stays* weeded. The problem is compounded because I seem to have cleverly planted my garden in a drought pocket. On more than one occasion it has remained rainless here when it was pouring a mile down the road. The soil, as I have probably already complained, is sandy, and to top it all off (or not top it all off) I have a dug well only eleven feet deep. The water is pretty much all for the garden but even all is not enough.

Not my idea of a good time, but this is the plot I'm allotted, and over the years I've learned a lot, duress the teacher, about xeriscaping (our current vogue term for designing gardens that use minimal added water). The gray-leaved plants, especially the needle-leaved ones, really are much more drought-tolerant. I'm appending a list, though don't know how much good it'll do. I've also learned a bit about rationing: to water the potatoes when they first set flowers, the peas when the flowers are in bud, then again when the pods start to fill. And tomatoes produce very tasty fruit when the plants are a little bit stressed. The skins are on the tough side, but that isn't too big a deal. Same goes for peppers—in fact I think many fruiting plants produce better when not too lush and green.

Not too lush and green won't do this year, unfortunately, because the garden is about to be infested with photographers. I'm doing summer entertaining pieces for *Metropolitan Home* and *New York Times* magazines, pieces that will have Eating From (and In) the Garden as their themes. Both shoots are scheduled for early September so I'm madly mulching, praying and washing everything up to and including my teeth over at Lo's, so as to save every drop of water for the garden.

Which is looking pretty good as a result, rainlessness notwithstanding. Old dry gardener's tricks like setting out baby plants in little water-catching bowls scooped from the soil (and of course heavy reliance on mulch) are paying off. But things still look a little less full than they do in damper years, especially since around here you can't cram things in the way you could in a drier climate. How can we have drought and damp at the same time? Being English you will know the answer is Fog. Every third summer or so we get wall-to-wall fog for weeks on end and the mildew reaches epic proportions. Or would if permitted. So I keep the perennials at arm's length from each other and let the annuals fill in more or less each summer, depending on conditions.

What I do about the lawn is nothing and this year I'm paying the price. I have what's called a yachtsman's lawn—"he mows what grows"—so it's always a bit discouraged by summer's end, more like an advertisement for clover than a rolling greensward. But this year *Ugh!* and I've got about two weeks to make it look like something you'd want to have a romantic picnic on. We have had one big thundershower (just the other day), but that's the classic day late and a dollar short. Lawn paint (yes, Roger, there really is such a thing, which its seller proudly claims is "lifelike" and non-toxic to plants or people) is out of the question so I think I'll just spread a number of Persian rugs and runners over the offending stubble and hope it looks artistic.

The food I feel more confident about. Heavy on the gorgeous vegetables. I'm planning a large plate of sliced tomatoes, showing off the colors of "White Beauty," "Lemon Boy" (hideous name but a fine bright yellow and very nicely balanced flavor), "Evergreen" (thick-skinned but very sweet as it turns out and "Nepal" (have I mentioned it? bright red slicers, not too large, good true tomato flavor and breathtaking uniformity for an open-pollinated fruit, each one baseball size and shape, big red peas in a pod).

Also a similarly colorful assortment of potatoes, simply steamed, partially peeled and piled in a shallow basket. "All Blue," actually a fine deep violet, "German Lady Fingers," which are a pale primrose yellow inside; "Red Gold," the inside of which is a deep gold; "Caribe" for its very white flesh. I may throw a few beets in here too, haven't made up my mind. The hot item in that department is "Chioggia," candy-striped red and white and offered by more and more chic catalogs as "an old Italian variety." They really are lovely, though not too much to write home (or to Roger) about in the taste department. And you have to serve them raw if you want to preserve the color. *But* the color really is spectacular. So far the best thing I know to do is to slice them very thin, like chips, and serve them with dips the same way.

There will be lots of thick green herbal sauces, natch. Basil is one place I have put the water and although the coriander has of course bolted in the heat, I'm planning to wow the folks by sprinkling the fish with soft green coriander seeds. They're delicious. Not sold in stores. Same like radish pods and rocket flowers. In the U.S., by the way, nobody knows what you're talking about when you say rocket. You have to call it *arugula* since only Italian communities have had anything to do with it for about the last century. Funny to wonder how this and other old English herbs, so popular with the colonists, seem to have vanished until just a few years ago—lovage, burnet, chamomile, tansy. Well, they're coming back now.

And I'm going—to deadhead what is this year a positive sea of white cosmos. It's very impressive at the moment and I want it to keep on plugging until the photographers come. After that, the goldfinches can have their field day eating the seeds. I intend to let the garden hang and go mushrooming instead.

Love,

Leslie.

*Garden plants that have done well in Cushing garden
when rainfall was below average*

Achillea—all varieties except *A. ptarmica*

Armeria maritima

Artemesia—all except *lactiflora*

Calliopsis

Coreopsis—*grandiflora* does better than *verticillata*

Centaurea cyanus

Cerastium tomentosum

Convolvulus (Ipomoea) purpurea

Eschscholzia Californicum

Gazania rigens

Hemerocallis—the "wild" orange (*H. fulva*) types do better than the fancy hybrids

Lavendula angustifolia

Liatris spicata

Limonium latifolium

Nicotiana affinis

Oenothera missouriensis

Origanum vulgare

Papaver—all varieties, esp. *P. rhoeas* and *P. somniferum*

Portulaca grandiflora

Rosa Rugosa—depends. "Blanc double de Coubert" languishes. Lois's nameless magenta ("Roseraie de l'Hay"?) is unfazed

Rosmarinus officinalis

Ruta graveolens

Salvia—most varieties both culinary and ornamental but not *patens*

Santolina chamaecyparissus
Senecio cineraria
Thymus—every blessed one I've ever grown has been very drought-tolerant
Tropaeolum majus
Yucca filamentosa
Zinnia haageana

VEGETABLES: Forget it, except melons which taste better if not watered once fruit has sized up. Best seed source for drought-tolerant vegetable varieties is Native Seeds/SEARCH, a non-profit organization dedicated to preserving the Native American agriculture of the Southwest, 2509 N. Campbell Ave. #325, Tucson, AZ 85719 U.S.A.

Garden plants commonly recommended as drought-tolerant that have not proved noteworthily so in Cushing garden

Cleome hasslerana
Cosmos bipinnatus
Echinops ritro
Helianthus annuus
Stachys byzantina (lanata)
Tagetes erecta, T. patula. (T. tenuifolia does OK but still not great)
Verbena rigida
Zinnia angustifolia

Eccleston Square,
London

Dear Leslie,

We have been having temperatures here that I associate with Florida or Texas; about two weeks ago it was up in the high nineties with an all time record of 98.5°F. A friend recorded 105°F in the shade of his garden on that day. I picked that day to go off to the south of France where it was even hotter. But the vineyards were in fine shape and I expect it will be a good year for French wines although the droughts that they have had will no doubt mean a small crop. Virtually the only other plant showing any sign of life in France was your jimson weed, *Datura stramonium* (we usually call it thorn apple because of its horribly thorny fruits). This grew in profusion all around the converted barn we had rented for our trip, though it had some assistance: every evening just at dusk when we were playing *Boules,* the 'Gardener' Gerard would arrive to water. He watered the lavender and the hedge that had been planted to shield the pool from the enquiring eyes of the passers-by – totally ineffectual as any full blooded Frenchman or woman will stop the car and get out for a good substantial stare – and after the new hedge he then watered the jimson weed. The result, as you can imagine, a stinking forest.

The aubergines looked so good in the markets I thought I must have a go at a dish that I ate in Paris about a hundred years ago. A friend of mine from school, Ann Wigzell, married a French actor called Grégoire 'Coco'

Aslan. Actually he was an Armenian. His mother was a terrific cook and she made us this very simple but most wonderful Armenian aubergine dish. I think the proper name for it is caviare d'aubergine. I allowed one large aubergine per person. Burn the aubergine skins over a naked flame and peel them, slice them and liberally salt them leaving for a few hours to sweat. Wipe off most of the salt and fry in really good, first-pressing olive oil for about ten minutes until absolutely soft. Take off the heat and squeeze over it a liberal amount of fresh garlic, tip the whole lot into a flat dish and mash it all up together. Fork over the surface and then leave it to go cold. It sounds so simple yet all the flavours – the oil, the salt, the burnt surface of the aubergine and the quarter-cooked garlic – are a perfect combination.

Coco was a fascinating man who told super stories of the great French beauties like Bardot and Mylene Demongeot, but what interested me most was that he had started his career as a swing drummer. Years later I was listening to a record programme and the disc jockey played a record by Roger Roger et son Orchestre featuring dans les batteries the great 'Coco' Aslan.

Back to daturas. My big tree one has failed to flower again this year so I still don't know what it is. Three years ago a plant of belladonna, *Atropa belladonna* appeared in the garden and I encouraged it for its lovely purple bell flowers and terrific shiny fruit. It was a mistake. This year I have young plants all over the garden. What I have succeeded in doing is finding the most fecund weed of summer. I must have pulled out over a hundred already. The rate of growth is incredible; it seems to be about fifteen inches high in a week and also to come into flower that quickly. I have decided to keep the original plant. It is well tucked away from children's prying hands, as it's so poisonous. Each year I will cut it back before the birds start to eat the berries – if I remember.

The Society for the Protection of London Squares is developing apace. I have had to research the history and legal aspect of squares and this led me to a fascinating book called *Report on London Squares* by the Royal Commission of 1928, a gigantic work which led to an Act of Parliament in 1931. It is a most thorough work with details of 461 London squares telling you who owned them, what the condition of the garden was, how they were financed, etc. I am now attempting to re-examine all the squares to see what has happened in the meantime and what the modern problems of financing them and, of course, protecting them, might be. A gigantic task: so far I am in contact with about fifty or sixty squares and am in the process of getting details out of the various garden committees. We had a drinks evening in Eccleston Square and about a hundred turned up. It was fascinating to hear of all their problems. One square has only the legal right to charge £1 per house per annum garden rate. This generates £37 a year, enough for one gardener for one day a year! One of the techniques of the developers is to buy a block of houses together and then leave them to fall to bits. After five or ten years of neglect the damage is terrific, so they go to the local planning authority and propose to turn the whole site into offices or a hotel or whatever. The planning authority normally tells them that they must remain as private houses whereupon the developer says that the cost of repairing them would be greater than any possible income he might gain. Then the whole thing is left and the buildings degenerate and degenerate. Next time round the developer puts up a new plan, perhaps with some sweetener involved, and so it goes until he gets his way, unless the residents stay diligent and keep up their objections.

We have these marvellous green areas in our city that make it human and liveable in. It is ergo the actual inhabitants who must fight for every square foot that is left. The office worker or even the hotel visitor looks for convenience in the short term and might well support developers trying to build car parks or whatever. This means that we have to fight the incursion of businesses into the private houses of the squares. The other awful prospect is that any city planner wandering around looking for sites for amenities like electrical, gas or water substations or new underground railways buildings naturally first looks at the open spaces – the poor old squares, again. At the moment there is a plan to build a new underground railway building on Parliament Square right opposite the House of Commons. The rotting houses ploy seems to be in practice in Stanhope Gardens, a lovely large square which has derelict houses on two complete sides and is causing horrible problems for the remaining residents.

My historical research on our square has also been fascinating. Pimlico (our district) is a triangle about one mile by one mile by one mile bordered on the south by the River Thames. Up to 1828 the majority of it was a market garden which grew vegetables for London. The land was incredibly fertile, giving three or even four crops of vegetables a year, first peas then turnips then potatoes then cabbages. Our little corner did not in fact grow vegetables but was part of a reservoir system that supplied water to London as it then was. This consisted of a wonderfully balanced ecological system of allowing the incoming salt tide on the river to push the down-flowing fresh water up into the reservoir system and at the same time use the weight of water to drive a massive wooden pumping system which lifted the water to an even higher level so that there was a head of water to service the customers who lived at a slightly higher level. The pumping engine was a marvel of its time and was visited by the elegant ladies of the late eighteenth century. The main reservoir area is now Victoria Station and the canals that fed it provided the land to build the railway tracks out to the river – then over it and on south.

One of the other elements of this water system was an area of tiny canals about twenty feet apart into which the new water from the river was run to let it settle and clarify. Between and around these mini-canals were planted willows or more specifically sallows to grow the 'withes' to make the baskets for the vegetables grown on the rest of the Pimlico area. Eccleston Square is on the site of these canals and 'withe' beds. So my latest project is to have a small demonstration bed of sallows in the garden. I have spoken to the chief dendrologist (tree historian) at the Forestry

Commission and he is looking into the plant history of the area to see if he can find exactly which of the hundreds of forms, hybrids, cultivars or whatever would have been the ones originally grown.

In reply to your letter, the geraniums that I referred to are pelargoniums; not geraniums in the botanical sense but of course in the vernacular both are geraniums. Have you seen the new book *Index Hortensis* by Piers Trehane? It is referred to as the authoritative guide to the correct naming of perennial plants (more volumes may follow eventually). It has become our bible. Trehane lists 152 geraniums proper many of which are just cultivars. Pelargoniums he doesn't list as they fit into the tender or bedding plant category, but as you say there are at least 1000 different cultivars in commerce.

I misled you a bit over *Rosa* Nevada – it is not a species and should therefore not be *Rosa* Nevada but just the Rose Nevada. A pedantic point but if you now look it up in our *Roses* book you will find two pictures of it (p. 104/5) – one a lovely specimen at the Savill Gardens in Windsor Great Park. My plants still have quite a lot of flowers, it's such a wonderful vigorous thing, I feel reasonably sure that it would be hardy in Maine.

They have plants of it at Pickering Nurseries Inc., 670 Kingston Road, Hwy 2, Pickering, Ontario, and also at Historical Roses, 1657 West Jackson Street, Painsville, OH 44077.

As far as the photography is concerned, keep at it, and then keep at it again. Remember you need constant practice to keep your hand in.

I am still grappling with understanding your complaints about the woman who wandered into your garden. On a fine day we often have as many as a hundred people in the square garden. Privacy is at a minimum but lots of opportunities for chats. What we don't have we don't miss!
Love,

Roger

Cushing,
Maine

Dear Roger,

Your letter was a delight and will be answered . . . not right this minute. Another major food shoot in the garden tomorrow and the next day, book MSS overdue back at the copy editor's *already* and . . .

Yours in haste,

Leslie

Cushing,
Maine

October 13, 1990

Dear Roger,

Your letter proper is still in process but I wanted to get these photos to you so you could critique them before I do the potatoes and beets. I'll be doing the peppers while these are in transit but might be able to redo them if I heard from you soon enough, so please call if these are all wrong. I've already noticed that doing everything with the same background may not be such a bright idea and will seek others that are similarly unobtrusive—it ain't easy!

And neither is getting the color right. Most of the stuff was done with Ektachrome 100, which seems to make everything a bit yellower than it should be (cloudy days or shadowy places employed almost throughout, by the way). Fuji 50 on the brandywines doesn't seem to have helped; they're still the wrong color. Can this be fixed in the printing? Should I be using some kind of filter?

Still too much to do. Such as be inspired by your historical delving into the London squares. It made me wonder as I did when I first came about the history of this place. Cushing itself is fairly old as U.S. settlements go; we had our bicentennial two years ago, I think it was. As far as this specific plot is concerned I know almost nothing except that the potato farm would have been in the 1920s or 30s.

Cushing has always been primarily a fishing village—it's all lobsters now—and I do know there was a clam factory (actually a processing plant where the clams were shucked and packed) about three thousand feet from here as the crow flies, on a spit of land above the river. The factory and the farm that followed it are now gone, the land strewn with modern houses. But I've seen a photo of the factory workroom, taken in 1903, that shows long trestle tables piled with clams. There are about a dozen women in whaleboned shirtwaists and long skirts, most of them seated at the tables. Their hands are temporarily idle, they are valiantly facing the camera. I have been told they came to work from all over Cushing and also, in rowboats, from Tenants Harbor across the river.

I know the main road to the point used to run right through the field that is now our orchard. It ran on a diagonal down the hill and by the creek below the lower garden. When the state paved and widened the way they moved the road to its present location on the northwest side of the property. You can still see the track of the old road, in part because I occasionally drive down it in the truck, to bring manure to the lower garden.

Your eggplant dish sounds delicious, *baba ghanouj* without the complication of *tahini*. I make similar dishes all fall; eggplants take a long time here but when they start producing they come all at once and you have to think up ways to eat lots. I used to put them up by making *caponata*, doing it the old-fashioned way, individually deep-frying in olive oil first the celery, then the onions, then the salted and drained eggplant, *then* simmering everything a good long time in a spicy, thick, sweet and sour tomato sauce. The result is canned and is, as they say, of long conservation, a dark, intense, velvety sort of eggplant jam for which I was (if I say it myself) locally famous. It has been some time since I made any because each year I try another short-cut in hopes of finding a modification tasty enough yet mainstream enough to be put in a column.

Alas, all of the short-cuts are dross compared to the labor-intensive real thing.

A lesson there, but we knew that. Stay well.

October 21, 1990

Last night was the night of doom. Today it's all black frost under the still-flaming leaves, an abrupt end to all but the hardiest. Usually I've got everything covered but this year has been just too topsy turvy and to tell the truth I'm glad. When I first started gardening in Maine, there was always frost in early September and serious cold by October, but the last few years have had long slow warm falls, and I have had squash plants that died of old age, ancient annuals that dropped with exhaustion, a garden that ungracefully decayed instead of getting slammed while still in vigorous bloom. No question I've gotten higher yield and at least six more weeks of cut flowers, but at a considerable price.

What I like, I've decided, is sudden early death, the kind of frost that brings sight of the end while there's still plenty of blue sky and crisp apple left to enjoy. I want to clip off all the old stalks, weed out what I can and move a few delphiniums around while the sun is still strong enough so you can work in thin summer clothing. I really like cleaning up a lot better than planting. All that spent stuff piled on the compost, the soil—or at least patches of it—smoothly dark brown. The raised beds once more almost formal in their rectangular geometry.

Finally (for about five minutes) I can *see* the garden whole. It's the history of art all over again. A suffocating Victorian jungle of overgrown summer is swept away into smooth earth. Weed-free, indeed very nearly plant-free, it's like the fresh breath of modernism, the recurring triumph of structure over detail.

There's also, of course, a very agreeable sense of completion. When all the potatoes are in the cellar, the leeks and swiss chard hilled with straw.

When all the bulbs are planted, all the tools cleaned, when the garden is hidden by the all-forgiving snow, I get a chance to lie fallow myself for a while, resting body and mind before the growth cycle starts again. You, on the other hand, have something happening in the garden all year round, which at this point in my life I'm no longer sure is a blessing.

Cushing, Maine

November 12, 1990

Dear Roger,

The hard frost on October 20 was a real whammer—it probably went down to around 28 and stayed there for several hours—so only a few of the hardiest things are left. Calendula endures, of course, there's still a pansy or two here and there, and second-crop spires of delphinium, along with a very pretty slightly lavendered-blue annual salvia (*S. farinacea*, "Blue Bedder") that's turning out to be unexpectedly tough. Leeks are doing fine, also the chard, carrots, beets, lettuces and a gratifying plenitude of rocket. The parsley all bolted long ago; perhaps because of drought, perhaps because I was so slow planting it out that it got disgustingly potbound.

Each day as I walk over to the mailbox (I'm still in the summer house) I think, well, time to make the annual diagram of what went where (the one I should have done in midsummer) so I can yank up the assorted corpses and do some planting before the ground freezes. But what with this and what with that I have of course done nothing and the giant box of spring bulbs mocks me six or seven times a day. So do the little pots of *Onopordum*, which I can't quite decide where to put in view of those monster thorns. And there are all these tiger-lilies I want to move from the lower garden to the hot-color bed near the greenhouse. But the other day I *did* manage to do some seed gathering, feeling now or neverish since frost means rot, scattering, and the attentions of the birds. Late fall now, the trees mostly unleafed and it's getting brisk, but seed day was sunny and blue, warm enough to go jacketless. It's a fussy job but I love the architecture of the pods. What a fine collection of cunning boxes they are.

This year's revelation in the seedcase department was the portulaca, which I've never collected before. At the end of each stem is a cluster of shallow cups, each with a perfect onion dome lid, each filled brimming with tiny seeds. Did it this year as the variety, "Swan Lake," was both extraordinarily lovely (a pure but soft white) and extraordinarily expensive. Might as well give it a go, though I hope I can get it going early enough so it starts blooming before transplanting time, in case I have to rogue out any throwbacks. Which will be throwbacks to what, I wonder. Will they be some kind of wishy-washy pink, like everything else in creation that isn't yellow? Never until this minute wondered what the wild form of portulaca looks like (the ice plant that grows wild on the coast of California blooms in cheap baby-blanket colors, gutless pink and blue), but purslane's white, as I remember it. I've put a lot of energy into removing the blinking purslane *before* it flowers—we mostly eat it in salad though Lois, who has a high slime-tolerance, likes it cooked, too—so I can't quite imagine the flowers at the moment.

Really cleaned up in the morning glories, trying to be sure of a good supply of one of this year's happiest finds, a deep royal purple variety called "Kniola's Black," supposedly a wildling noticed and perpetuated by a farmer in Iowa. Regardless of origin it was splendid, rather smaller than the common Japanese type, with hairier vines and earlier, much more prolific bloom. Mixed with old standby "Heavenly Blue" it made a splendid screen at the edge between the blue border and the white garden, so I tried to collect up enough to spread around by giving little packets to deserving friends for Christmas (do you want some?)
Love,

Leslie

Eccleston Square, London

Dear Leslie,

God, it's months since I wrote. First the tomato photographs were superb. You put me to shame. They were so good I felt like giving up! You ask about colour film Ektachrome 100 versus Fuji 50; there is no answer to the question which is best. There are slight differences of emphasis — you pays your money and takes your choice. Also film changes a lot every time they make a new batch. The batch number is overprinted on the box next to the use-by date. If you get a roll you like the colour of, go back to the shop with the number and buy all the rest of the stock they have.

Now to your second letter. Thanks for another set of fantastic photographs, I am knocked out with the 'Yellow Ruffled' tomato and especially the Hyacinth Bean which we had tried to get hold of and failed. A couple of points on the shots: focusing becomes a problem in two ways, one when you shoot smaller objects and thus have to get in closer and two, as the light gets weaker in the winter. There are two solutions and by combining them you will be able to sort it out.

(1) Make sure you do not need to focus from near the lens to far away all in the same shot, by keeping the vegetables nearly in the same plane rather than spread out away from the camera. The depth of field is the area that is in focus as seen from the camera — as the lens is opened up to compensate for poor light it gets less and less.

(2) Do not let the camera's tiny mind think for itself; you must use the

manual override to make sure that the lens stops down. Left to itself it will shoot at say f2.8 at 1/60 of a second, but to get your depth of field you may need f16. This means setting the shutter speed at $1/2$ second, and of course this means mounting the camera on a *firm* tripod.

Another critical element is deciding where to focus. Providing you are going to stop down at least 3–4 stops the place to focus is about a quarter of the way back from the front of the shot. This will then mean that the front vegetable and the back ones will pull into focus. If, however, you are not able to stop down – say you are hand holding the camera for some reason – then you must get the front vegetable in focus. It will look crummy if only one middle one is in focus. End of lecture. I hope I am not being too pedantic.

I told you about our Kemp leaf shredder – it really is a marvel, the ground-up leaves are halfway broken down in a couple of weeks. This year I am trying a new ploy; where we have cleared out old shrubs and are putting in a new planting, once the shrubs and bulbs (if any) are in I am putting a 6″–8″ layer of the two week old half-rotted leaf choppings on to the bare earth. The idea is to keep the new shrubs a bit warm in the winter and then in the spring I hope it will keep back the weeds. Our worst offender is chickweed, it goes mad from the beginning of March onwards. I am also hoping that by April it will have started to rot well down, because I then plan to seed it with annuals which I am hoping will be able to germinate through the mulch. If it works it will be brilliant so cross your fingers for me. The only disadvantage is that if it does indeed hold back the weeds it will also hold back my self-seeding annuals. And so it goes.

Portulaca oleracea is India's contribution to the salad world – the flowers are yellow and about one-eighth of an inch across. In England they hardly ever come out as they need really bright sun – not like my beloved osteospermums that obediently open with good light rather than strong sun. Osteospermum has been a revelation in the garden over the last two hot summers, flowering from mid May to December. In November I took loads of cuttings which I keep in a small tunnel made of bent bamboos covered in plastic, so if we do get a bad frost I should at least have new plants for next year.

Over the last few years I have been getting more and more interested in ceanothus. They do very well in London, they positively thrive on the drought and the summer heat we have been getting and they are hardy down to about 15°F below which we don't get (in ten years I haven't lost one). The collection has now built up to thirty-six different entities, eleven species and twenty-five cultivated forms. We have an organization that has been set up to save garden plants called the National Council for the Conservation of Plants and Gardens. They have a scheme under which certain gardens hold what is called the 'National Collection.' There is already a National Collection of ceanothus at a place over near the west coast, Cannington, but the Council think it would be worth having another registered collection in London. I have talked to the people at Cannington and they have given me cuttings of all that they have that I don't (about twenty) and I have given them cuttings of all that I have that they don't (about two). When I have plants of all these I will have nearly sixty entities. Apart from these I have been in contact with two nurseries in California and am now attempting to get the customs clearance to bring to this country another twenty or so that can be found in the U.S.A. If I solve all this I then have to find room for eighty to ninety giant plants in the garden. I'm enclosing my current list. In England they are almost always grown as wall plants but this is only to give them winter protection – I have no walls so I grow them all free standing, or, as they are easily blown over, free propped would be nearer to the truth but nevertheless they grow in a much more natural way than up a wall.

Ceanothus Collection

Held at Eccleston Square Garden London S.W.1. Open twice a year under the National Garden Scheme or on application to: The Eccleston Square Garden Committee, c/o Roger Phillips, 15a Eccleston Square, London S.W.1. Tel: 071 834 8654

Plants are listed in alphabetical order, the key number in front of each plant is the number marked on the bed map on the garden, the number/s after each name tell you which of the beds it is planted in. Date of planting is in ( ), approximate age at planting 1–2 years.

 1. *C. americanus* 5 (1989)
42. *C. arboreus* 7 (1991)
25. *C. cyaneus* 7 (1990)
 9. *C. dentatus* 6/17 (1990)
38. *C. dentatus* var. *floribundus* 17 (1990)
51. *C. divergens* 38 (1991)
11. *C. impressus* 6 (1989)
46. *C. incanus* 31 SICK (1991)
50. *C.* × *lobbianus* 38 (1991)
40. *C. maritimus* 24 (1991)
49. *C. megacarpus* 1 (1991)
53. *C. papillosus* 6 (1992)
24. *C. purpureus* 17 (1990)
29. *C. rigidus* var. *pallens* 15 (1990)
27. *C. spinosus* 31 (1990)
16. *C. thyrsiflorus* 1 (two)/5 (two)/13/28 (two) 30/32 (1982)
17. *C. thyrsiflorus* var. *repens* 35/41 (1986)
30. *C.* × *veitchianus* 36 (1990)
26. *C. verrucosus* 6 (1989)
 3. *C.* 'Autumnal Blue' (*arboreus*) 16 (1990)
 2. C. 'A. T. Johnson' 17 (1988)
23. C. 'Blue Cushion' 17 (1990)
 4. C. 'Blue Mound' 5 (1987)
28. C. 'Brilliant' 15 (1991)

5. C. 'Burkwoodii' 5/40 (1987)
41. C. 'Burtoniensis' 1 (1991)
6. C. 'Cascade' 35 (two)/36/37 (three) (1984)
22. C. 'Chelsea Blue' 17 (1990)
21. C. 'Concha' 17 (1990)
7. C. 'Delight' 5/40 (1987)
37. C. 'Dignity' 7 (1990)
44. C. 'Eleanor Taylor' 31 (1991)
35. C. 'Emily Brown' (*gloriosus*) 15 (1990)
43. C. 'Frosty Blue' 6 (1989)
8. C. 'Gloire de Versailles' (✕ *delileanus*) 16 (1990)
10. C. 'Henri Desfosse' (✕ *delileanus*) 5 (1988)
34. C. 'Hurricane Point' (*griseus*) 17 (1990)
12. C. 'Italian Skies' 6 (1989)
36. C. 'Joyce Coulter' 15 (1990)
48. C. 'Louis Edmunds' (*griseus*) 17 (1991)
13. C. 'Marie Simon' (✕ *pallidus*) 37 (1989)
39. C. 'Mount Vision' 23 (1991)
14. C. 'Perle Rose' (✕ *pallidus*) 17 (1989)
15. C. 'Puget Blue' 32/37 (1986)
31. C. 'Sierra Blue' 15 (1990)
47. C. 'Sierra Snow' 7 (1991)
52. C. 'Snow Ball' (*rigidus*) 5 (1991)
45. C. 'Snow Flurries' (*thyrsiflorus*) 7 (SICK)/13 (SICK) (1991)
32. C. 'Southmead' (✕ *lobbianus*) 17 (1990)
20. C. 'Thunder Cloud' 17 (1990)
18. C. 'Topaz' (✕*delileanus*) 16 (1990)
19. C. 'Trewithen Blue' (*arboreus*) 5 (1987)
33. C. 'Yankee Point' (*griseus* var. horizontalis) 37 (1989)

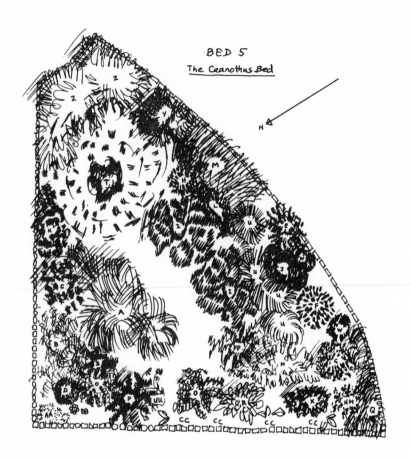

Bed 5: The Ceanothus Bed

All the areas between the plants are deeply mulched with bark and chopped-up leaves, giving the appearance of the floor of a dense beech wood. In the centre of the bed there is a small hidden area that the children who play in the garden can use as a secret camp. Also the cherry is a big strong tree with convenient low branches that we let the children climb.

Shrubs

A = *Arundinaria murielae*

B = *Azalea* 'George Reynolds'

C = *Berberis darwinii*

D = *Ceanothus americanus*

E = *Ceanothus* 'Blue Mound'

F = *Ceanothus* 'Burkwoodii'

G = *Ceanothus* 'Delight'

H = *Ceanothus* 'Henri Desfosse'

HH = *Ceanothus rigidus* 'Snow Ball'

I = *Ceanothus thyrsiflorus*

J = *Ceanothus* 'Trewithen Blue'

K = *Chaenomeles japonica*

L = *Corylopsis sinensis*

M = *Cotoneaster salicifolius floccosus*

N = *Fatsia japonica*

O = *Halesia monticola*

P = *Ilex aquifolium*

PP = *Laburnum anagyroides*

Q = *Lavendula spica*

R = *Magnolia sinensis*

S = *Mahonia* 'Charity'

T = *Prunus* 'Kanzan'

U = *Pyracantha watereri*

UU = Rose Alchemist

W = *Rhododendron dauricum* 'Midwinter'

X = *Rhododendron* 'Pink Pearl'

Y = *Skimmia japonica*

Z = *Spirea thunbergii*

The rose 'Alchemist' (UU) sprawls all over the holly with stems well over twenty feet high, at least five feet higher than all the books say it should grow! Of all the roses we have in the garden it attracts the most attention with its very old-fashioned cabbagey flowers that change from having an orangey centre when they open to a pale gold centre as they mature – hence its name.

Perennials

AA = Michaelmas daisy, some form or other of the *Aster nova-belgii:* only an ordinary bluish one but it makes a superb clump five feet round and four feet high, flowering from August to November.

BB = *Actea pachypoda,* the American woodland doll's eyes, but mine is a funny form of it that has a whole clump of eyes bunched together at the end of each of the little red stems rather than the normal one eye per stem.

CC = Hostas. There are about ten rather large hosta plants along the front of the bed, all of them rather late flowering so that I get a good show from the end of July onwards.

Please write soon. Apart from your past life I need more ideas for interesting annuals, especially native American ones.

Love,

Roger

Train to Poughkeepsie,
New York

January 9, 1991

Dear Roger,

I'm currently on the train—pardon attendant wiggles—traveling from New York to Poughkeepsie (two hours north-west in the Hudson River Valley). Outside, a gray landscape in fog: the river, lightly stippled, is the color of concrete. Every trackside tree, each weed, is glazed with ice, grayed with the glazing—in the distance the hills are as soft as spring. Occasionally the fog lifts and gray clouds move across the gray sky.

Bulletin: train has just passed a chain-link fenced hilltop—on the fence a sign: Fantasy acres/MUDBOG.

Not the most inspiring of landscapes, in spite of some noteworthy icicle formations. But I'm told the Hudson Valley is gorgeous; I'm primed for it to be so by famous paintings (the Hudson River School is enjoying a big revival here, by the way) and, I suppose, it had better be, because I'm going to move here to make a partnered life with Bill Bakaitis.

You are perhaps not so surprised. I'm surprised, myself, and disinclined to make predictions about the success of the project, but so far so good. We moved to our present involvement from a phone + mail friendship that grew out of the Rindge mushroom foray. His long-suffering marriage came to an end last spring, when his wife asked for a divorce (not for the first time) and their mutual efforts to avoid that course were unavailing. He came for a clear-the-head-go-mushrooming and general R & R visit this last fall and here I am. I think. My head and most of my heart (the non-Bill part) are still in Maine, and I'll be going back mid-April or early May to get the garden in. Bill will join me for the summer (God Bless Teaching) and I guess from there we'll see.

Ducks taking off. Across the river, many mansions—and several fortress-like constructions that can't possibly *all* be prisons and hospitals but look like they should be.

January 15

Your letters—and my obligations—pile up apace. But as soon as I finish the seed orders you'll be hearing more . . . assuming, of course, that the world does not in one way or another come to an end (feeling very gloomy on that score and couldn't stop crying when the tanks rolled into Lithuania. Can't claim I was surprised; but I sure was sad).

More soon,

Leslie xx

Eccleston Square,
London

4 February 1991

Dear Leslie,

When I heard your news all I could think to do was wander around the garden picking one of every flower that I could find. The pressed results are my best wishes for you — I hope it works out really well for both of you — I have known Bill since the New Jersey Mushroom foray in 1984!

No I am not really surprised. When no letter arrived through December I came to the conclusion you were dead or in love — the arrival of your letter told me you were alive.

I love-love-love your article on the garden; it sounds so enchanting I can't wait to see it, I hope when I get over to Maine in mid-August it will be at its best. Leslie, what a hard decision to make to leave your garden and half your heart in Cushing! I hope it works out that you can be a gardener half the year and a partner for the other half. Will this give you more time to write to me? I hope so. I'm sorry that I didn't thank you for *The New England Epicure*. I have been reading it over lunch, and I am up to Halloween. The chapter that knocked me out was when you had to cook a bath-long salmon and used the bath as a fish kettle by putting hot rocks into the water native-American style. I can't wait to try it, it's so simple, so obvious and I am sure so effective.

I am now fixing dates for my publicity launch for *Mushrooms of North America*. So far Boston is fixed for 16 May then 20 to 24 May the West

Coast, Los Angeles, San Francisco, Seattle, Portland and across to Denver. I will be giving a lecture every night. My current plan is to mix up the slides every night and thus show them in different ways so that I don't start repeating myself and put the audience and myself to sleep.

Why don't you and Bill come over for a pseudo honeymoon? and I can take you on a grand tour of English gardens. I gather you can get round trips USA Europe for about $200. We will put you up. I am going to visit lots of historic gardens this year – I have decided that it is time I made a real study of gardening history. My plot is this year England (plus USA?) next year Italy, Spain and Portugal. To visit gardens in USA I need a really good book on your historic and important gardens. Is there such a book? Title, publisher, please.

This winter is much colder than last year and everything in the garden is much more behind – it's probably better. Last year on 2 February I had flowers on thirty different camellia plants, this year I have flowers on 5 and in fact only one flower on each. I keep telling everyone how much better it will be when the weather finally warms up as they will all flower at once and make a real show. (Maybe you should hop on a flight and get here for the first week in March.)

On 29 January we return willows to their home in our garden. John White (the dendrologist) has come up with a theory as to what plants may have been grown here. Amongst his collection of willows (he holds the National Collection of some hundreds of willows), is *Salix viminalis* from 'Little London', an area of market gardens and small holdings on the River Welland in Lincolnshire, about a hundred miles from London. I quote John's letter: 'It seems likely that market gardeners moved there from London in the nineteenth century (buildings do not pre-date 1850). This was probably associated with the extension of the London and North-Eastern Railway from Peterborough. This willow is unlike the local wild *Salix viminalis* so I suggest it is an Osier of London origin.'

We know that the lease on our land was obtained on Lady Day 1828 and the developer, Thomas Cubitt, started to clear out the market garden and willow growers from the area; it must have taken some time as the

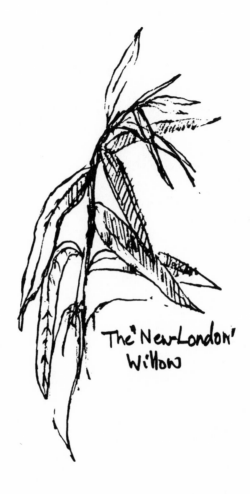

The 'New London' Willow

reports talk of great battles and problems getting them off the land. The first house (number one) was completed by 1836, but then I gather there was a property slump (nothing changes) so that by 1850 only twenty-three houses had been completed. All this backs up John's supposition and until further evidence comes to hand, if it ever does, I am accepting 'Little London' as the best bet.

John White sent me cuttings with planting instructions. Willow cuttings by tradition must not be planted until after the first full moon in January. For sound reasons: if you plant them earlier the soil may be warm enough to cause them to strike – then the frosts of January and February push the cuttings upwards breaking off the juvenile roots. Leaving it until late January means that by the time the soil warms up and the little roots start to grow the chance of a severe frost is over. So, attended by a small group of garden lovers, the cuttings were duly planted and a small libation poured on to the soil, most of the libation descending down the throats of said garden lovers.

Lots of love and fun for you both.

Roger

P.S. Are you of Lithuanian descent?

Clinton Corners,
New York

February 25, 1991

Dear Roger,

More time to write? More time to write? *Ha*! Nevertheless, I will be in touch soon and am meanwhile utterly bowled off my feet by your lovely expression of congratulation. Scheduling now mildly disquieting—my garden best in later summer. How long will you be here? Letter follows.

Leslie

P.S. No, I'm not Lithuanian. My family on both sides came to the U.S. some time ago, from Russia and Hungary, mostly. Bill is half Lithuanian (the paternal half) but doesn't seem to feel connected to the current tragedy that way. Both of us just generally sorrowful as world citizens.

Clinton Corners, New York

Dear Roger,

BILL: What could be better than the arrival of your new book, timed perfectly with the new crop of dark morels? Mushroom picking by day, eating by dusk, and reading in bed till the lights go out!

What a lovely addition to our library. As always the clean Phillips style illuminates many of those dark areas that even classic texts leave behind. "So, that's what a Burgundy-Buff Cap looks like!" I am sure it will be one of those books used quite a bit, and for me a special thrill since I watched you photograph so many of them while at the several forays we worked together.

Congratulations, Roger. I hope you sell a million!!!

LESLIE: Me too, says Leslie, who has yet to give the *opus splendiferous* more than an envious glance. I could blame it on the ol' mega-workload, but the real problem is those morels! Paradise. B. of course knows all the spots and the one we've been visiting is extraordinarily appealing even without the mushrooms. An old estate grown over with woods and scrub, every now and again a huge specimen tree, clump of daffodils. B. found one cluster of black beauties rising through the carpet of yellow petals under a vast forsythia. No camera along, of course. I think I'll get one of those itty bitty numbers like spies have, small enough to shove in a back pocket.

BILL: Chapter Two: other events in our life. Perhaps Leslie has told you that we are about to buy a big old house. Old for the US of A means Civil War stuff. Big as in a ten-room colonial.

Leslie says it is still a bit small, what with this and what with that. An office here, an office there, here a greenhouse, there a laundry, and before you know it we will have to build an addition just to have adequate guest room. You had better come soon, before it all gets eaten up.

The summer will bring with it all the thrills of two homes and two gardens. Grand designs in both places, if you please. Spring is such a nice place from which to dream. Everything here is as tendergreen as it gets, no weeds, just gardens perfect in their plan, stretched out across the imagination of our yards. It is America, Roger. Dreams unconstrained by other nations, other people, creatures . . . As of yet insects do not appear to chew our lettuces, or molest our tomatoes or squash.

LESLIE: The frigging deer, however, have trimmed the ancient yews in the yard of the new house to the most fantastical shapes—hideous beyond imagining, probably irreparable and there you are. My dreams mostly involve chain saws and backhoes.

BILL: Leslie has been frantically packing essential items in boxes even as we write. She intends to hit the road tomorrow. Has been saying that for the past week. She's off to Maine and the gardens hewn out of the wilderness. I am led to believe it is all blackflies and mud there now. Better to send her off to get it all cleared. I'll stay behind and thoroughly enjoy this spring, then get along up north for the summer–spring of mid-coast Maine in July and August. See you then. Chanterelle time, I presume.

LESLIE: Let him gloat, I figure I'll finally have a little peace and quiet (*pace* the blackflies) to get some work done, and, if I plan it right, a second spring complete with lilacs and my many tulips. No one around here—at least no one visible from the roads—seems to be capable of anything except red and yellow Darwins. Handsome enough in their way but a bit boresome after a while. The same cannot be said of the dogwood, at its peak right now and indeed very hard to leave. B. helped clean up the garden last fall, so I'm hoping that getting it going again won't be too difficult, especially since in view of my changed circumstances I was very restrained in the perennial-ordering and annual starting departments. The whole problem of delegating basic garden functions turns out to be a very interesting one and how well I've solved it remains to be seen.

Enough! packing calls (at least it calls me, and I've decided it's not fair for him to have the last word—unless of course he wishes to say something blanket-affectionate, to match the assorted friendly sentiments I send myself . . . !)

BILL: It's a very nice book. One I have been waiting for, for a long time. Thanks again . . . B

Cushing, Maine

Dear Roger,

Here's what I think, now that I'm home:

Narcissus are very nice, the scent of hyacinth is such as dreams are made on, but it is in tulips lies the preservation of the world. I've decided it's humanly impossible to plant too many, assuming, of course, you're not using them to spell out your company logo in red and yellow or something like that. (Poor cannas, by the way, talk about a magnificent flower damned to ignominy by ill-use!)

I have both made and seen any number of effective tulip beds, but I still think they shine brightest indoors and have an old blue mason jar of them on the desk this very minute. A vase of flowers carries an implicit suggestion of order, a suggestion to which said desk has no right, being as it is in very nearly terminal disarray. But the tulips in their incongruity are saviors against madness. For one thing, they're huge—so immense they take up enough space to block out a fair amount of muddle. For another, they're pretty close to terminally disarrayed themselves. A parrot tulip in the last full blown stages is blowsiness personified. Yet even at the edge of decay the fleshy petals are still turgid, their color layered shimmering and satiny. These happen to be "Estella Rijnvel," red, pink and white, with brushes of green. "Black Parrot" is worth the price of admission, too, and so is the dark red "Wonder" I've mentioned before. The paler ones don't do so well; they tend to start turning brown sooner, before they really hit that moment of total relaxed exposure.

The other thing I love is the way tulips are their own arrangement, stems and blossoms slowly turning and bending, changing with each passing day. Greenery, other flowers, all the arrangers' embellishments only confuse the issue. I'm not saying they don't enhance mixed bouquets—vaguely Dutch assortments of peonies, roses and tulips are practically a trademark of *luxe* decor and rightly so—but tulips never need accompaniment themselves and are always prettiest I think without bother or fussiness.

I concentrate on the cottages, Darwins, and super-late types like parrots and lilies, for a good solid six weeks of The Joy of Tulips. I know I could get more if I could bring myself to like species tulips, but I can't. Either, like *Kaufmannianas*, their proportions are all wrong: great big flowers on short stems and a general effect of consummate squattiness, or, like *T. sylvestris*, they are in proportion, hence delicate, hence much more like true wild flowers which are fine but not tulips.

They're about the only ones, on the other hand, that I enjoy seeing sprinkled here and there under the trees. Tulip beds are okay—I guess—in large public gardens and similar well-manicured venues, and a long-lived survivor in a weedy dooryard has undeniable nostalgic charm, but as far as I'm concerned tulips are too intentional to do well as part of the landscape. To me, they're a crop, more like strawberries than snowdrops, and I plant the bulk of them in the vegetable garden.

This has the benefit of forcing me each fall to think a bit about next year's garden, because I put the tulips where hills of winter squash will be planted. At this point it's mostly force of habit; I once thought the spreading vines would hide the ripening bulb foliage. Which they would in a warmer climate. Here spring is usually too cold for any such tidiness. By the time the squash gets lush, the tulips have already been looking tatty for ages. Still, it does keep them nicely out of the way, and the squash vines are over in plenty of time for me to dig up the bulbs, separate, and replant in fertilized ground. Where, of course, they will fail to bloom, having just split in half. It takes *years* for them to recover and I'm not entirely sure it's worth it. Limited income notwithstanding, I think from now on I'll just let 'em go and buy new each autumn as necessary.

It's like hilling up tea roses for winter, which at this point I seldom do. Wind and cold always decimate them at the very least, the hilling is a chore—you've got to get the soil from somewhere and then take it *to* somewhere; and since early planted new bushes usually do splendidly all summer and fall, I've decided that in Maine tea roses should be treated as annuals.

Shrubs, of course, are a different matter. I feel about "La Reine des Violettes" the way I do about sweet peas and old-fashioned tomatoes: come hell or high water, whatever it takes.

Time, mostly. I thought I could just come back and resume but of course the weeds are way out ahead and planting is way behind. So—

More soon,

Leslie

P.S. Suddenly had a horrified thought—*You* don't have tulip beds, do you? Somehow I see yours nicely scattered about amongst the shrubbery *but* . . . Anyway, no offense meant. If you have beds, I'll bet they look great.

The Marquette Hotel, Minneapolis

18 May 1991

Dear Leslie,

I am out in the Midwest promoting *Mushrooms*, a ten-city tour no less – a city a day; New York, Boston, Minneapolis, Los Angeles, San Francisco, Seattle, Portland, Denver, Chicago and then Bernardsville in New Jersey. Three days down and seven to go. Will I make it? God knows. So far I am having fun meeting 'mushroom maniacs' in every city, all with morel stories to tell. Yesterday I did a programme for local public radio here with Steve Benson called 'Talking Sense'. Also on were Lee Mugli and John Ratzloff, author of *A Guide for Rooms,* a whole book of morel mushroom jokes. Anyway, we all told terrible morel stories and

MOREL WHISTLE

BLow acrOss
hard-dried end

had a big laugh – mushroomers are worse than fishermen for telling the tall story. I have made a morel flute – if you blow across *the stem* of a dried morel you get the Morel Hunters' call to arms.

The centre of Minneapolis is riddled with things called sky walks. One floor up from the ground you walk through these glass tunnels from building to building then right through the shops on that floor of the building and out across another street on another tunnel bridge. One of the locals told me that in the winter many people don't go out of doors for months. It all gave me a horrible shock of *déjà vu*. Here I was in Fritz Lang's Metropolis at last.

It seems about a thousand years since I wrote so let me go back a bit. We had a hard winter this year, the first one for four years – all those lovely tender plants I have been nursing along got hit. In fact I kept a record of what happened so that I will know what plants survive what temperature.

Exciting news. Three weeks ago a man called Philip Lloyd rang me up. 'Are you the chairman of The Society for the Protection of London Squares?' he asked. When I affirmed that I was he asked if he could come over, which he did right away.

It turned out that he worked for a Japanese property company called Fujita. Fujita had bought about half the houses in a little square in Bayswater just across Hyde Park from us. On looking into the deeds of the houses they discovered that they owned the square garden as well! After much chat, Philip asked me if I would do a survey of the current square, a plan of what the planting might have been one hundred and fifty years ago when it was built and a third plan of what I thought would be the way to relandscape and replant it to make it one of the best squares in London! Then he gave me about four days to do the lot. But actually this is the way I love to work. I got straight down to it—did the survey at 5.00 a.m. the next morning. The square at present is a dump; virtually no plants, five or six London plane trees and everything overgrown and silted up so that even discovering where the beds and path were was an exercise in industrial archaeology. I drew rough plans, consulted Bean on the dates that plants and shrubs had come into cultivation in Britain to see that the things I suggested were possible in 1850, and was able to get the survey and the spec. 1850 plan done in about thirty-six hours. I then got a trained landscape architect to draw them up for me whilst I continued working on ideas for the way I would like to see the garden look if the money was there to do it.

Philip Lloyd had mentioned that John Claudius Loudon had lived within a few hundred yards of the site, though the garden of his house was destroyed years ago. This started me going. I went over to Vincent Square where the Royal Horticultural Society have their library and heaped a table up with his books and those of his wife. Did you know he only had one arm so couldn't write? – all his books were dictated to his very young wife. After his death his wife continued his great work with the most exquisite illustrated books on bulbs, annuals, perennials (in two volumes) and, finally, conservatory plants. Though she did them in a different order, these are exactly the same volumes that Martyn and I are in the middle of doing right now, down to the detail that we too have had to split perennials into two volumes.

The chance was there so I took it. What I did was move the paths to make a larger area at both ends of the square (it is, of course, a rectangle) so that I could have room for memorial areas for both the Loudons. At the more shady southern end I plan to plant a shrub garden given over entirely to a selection of the shrubs that John Claudius talks about in his major work on shrubs, published in 1825; they will all be grown as single specimens with little stepping-stone paths between them so that you can get amongst them and really see how they grow. At the other end of the square, the northern end that gets more light, I am proposing a Mrs Loudon Flower Garden as a memorial to her and her work, naturally choosing plants and varieties that she illustrates in her books. These two plantings will be mainly hidden from view as you approach to give that element of change as you come upon them. In the centre of the garden I want a small delicate fountain approached through two lateral tunnels of climbing roses. The stepping-stone path that runs down the lawn will have bulbs planted through it so that in early spring there will be a wild area. I will send you copies of all the plans later.

The reason for the rush was that Mr and Mrs Fujita were making a world-wide tour of all their companies and were due in London in a few days. The whole party, about eight or nine, arrived—complete with interpreter—to see Eccleston Square on the Saturday morning. Nicky and my two girls, Phoebe (now eight) and Amy (five) gave them coffee and chocolate Bath Oliver biscuits. They seemed to enjoy the visit, although I think having two children at what could have been a boring old business meeting was what made it. They went back afterwards to the office and saw the plans—all is approved to go ahead with the Loudon gardens.

The Japanese do everything in the most detailed and organized way and already I have had to submit a plan of what my involvement in the scheme would be plus a detailed bit of all the steps involved in laying out and planting a square—it runs to more than eighty steps.

The square, by the way, is called Craven Hill Gardens and was originally part of Lord Craven's estate. Before the houses were built it was designated as a plague pit. Luckily, although the land was held for this purpose for many years it was never used, even plagues go out of fashion.

On the Eccleston Square threat (now much reduced) I have written to the agents of the freeholders, presenting to them the idea that they might get some good publicity by giving the land to the Garden Committee. Reply: 'We are considering your proposal.' – Well anyway I tried.
Love,

Roger, and hugs to Bill.

Cushing,
Maine

Dear Roger,

The reason you haven't heard is that I'm frantically trying to be sure you'll have something to *see* when you get here. Do not be away all spring and expect to walk in in mid May and plant, is my advice to you. Weeds? The word is inadequate. No question that for folks like me, gardening is a constant process of beating back the wilderness. Now I know why Lois, who doesn't get here until June, has always confined herself to a few perennials, a small vegetable patch and an occasional go at pruning.

Lois's vegetable garden is mostly grown over now—my place more than does for both of us—but her splendid rhubarb remains. It was on the property when she bought it thirty years ago and was already well established then. But part of making the place livable was completely rebuilding the plumbing system and when the man came with the backhoe he said, "These giant rhubarb plants are right where I've got to dig for your septic tank. Would you like me to move them somewhere else, would you like to keep them?" She was newly up from the city and just sort of said "Well yes, sure, of course I'd like to keep them. Put them over there," and made a vague gesture in the direction of the barn. The fellow picked up these two enormous clumps of rhubarb with his backhoe and stuck them down near the barn where they have been ever since, thriving like crazy and very delicious. An uncommon kind, no one knows what it is, not bright red at all but green with just a tiny tinge of red. In a good year the stalks will be two and a half feet long and completely tender from end to end and with a lovely flavor.

So, the rhubarb was at one end and then she had just a conventional little vegetable garden, a rectangle where she had planted asparagus from seed, and lettuces and Swiss chard and carrots and beans and things like that, all of which would flourish until they were about two inches tall and then the woodchuck would come in and eat them, over and over and over again and Lois would go out and speak sternly to the woodchuck, which was quite tame, and we're talking years so it was like a family of woodchucks. I would come over to visit and there would be endless woodchuck stories because Lois had this Titanic struggle—or perhaps Sisyphean would be a better adjective. She tried mothballs, for instance, mothballs being an organic gardening device for keeping woodchucks away, one of the many organic devices that don't work very well. So the woodchuck would go through the Maginot Line of mothballs and it went through criss-cross string and it went through bloodmeal and it went past the have-a-heart trap and on one memorable occasion she waited in the garden to whack it on the head with a stick and when she did it just kind of reared back and looked at *her* very sternly and she got scared and left.

The woodchucks continued to be an issue after I came and cleared and began making my garden. For several years I would go next door and borrow Edna's .22 and shoot them. It works in that the one you shoot stops eating but it's not completely satisfactory. Before long, others come to fill the void. Then one summer a family of skunks came to live under my house and the woodchucks disappeared. I don't know if it was the skunks, actually I think it may have been the raccoons, both the raccoons and skunks started coming at the same time. But when the two other creatures came the woodchucks went. I have no proof of cause and effect, and in fact they shouldn't occupy the same niche because they eat differ-ent things but whatever it was I'm glad it happened and I kind of enjoy the skunks.

They did a job, I'm sorry to say, on Lacey (Bill's daughter's dog) when they were last here. Well the dog was barking so the skunks got defensive. They're very tame because they've been living comfortably under the summer house for years. I throw my meat scraps into the woods—there are lots of creatures there who like to eat stuff like chicken bones so what's the point in sending them to the landfill? I just fling out fish guts or fat I've trimmed off the steak . . . whatever bits of carnivore garbage I have and basically what I'm doing is feeding the skunks. It's been live and let live. We've had a couple of meetings in the garden where everybody got a bit scared and backed off but I've never been afraid of them. Unfortunately last fall they got to eating the tulips. Bill when he was visiting had a couple of confrontations when he was standing close to the front door with this arsenal of rocks and throwing the rocks at the skunks and he actually hit them a couple of times and they would kind of amble off. You really would have had to kill one I think. So that was a kind of a standoff.

Apart from woodchuck prevention the thing they do which is quite wonderful is that they love to eat yellow jackets, wasps, any hive of those things gets torn apart. I think there must be sugar in the hives and I think maybe the insects themselves are tasty, insects are what skunks mostly eat, after all. Three weeks ago I was walking by the lower garden when I noticed the most tremendous nest of yellow jackets—they make the same kind of nest as wasps, a gray paper football—just merrily sitting there on the ground with yellow jackets coming and going quite close to the walkway. Then while I was dithering around and not having the time to go to town to the hardware store to buy some kind of ghastly yellow jacket poison, the skunks just came and ate them. Thus in my view skunks are sort of like bats, quite nice to look at, and so environmentally beneficial that I can't see any reason to evict them, besides which I don't know if I *could* evict them.

Regrettably they don't weed. I don't seem to do anything else. There is some revenge in the form of nearly-nightly dinners of lamb's-quarters steam-fried in butter with garlic, but you can't get too excited about eating buttercups and witchgrass (poison and pure cellulose), my principle afflictions. What I do with those (and everything else in the vegetative waste department) is pile it at the southeast side of the upper garden where the ground slopes off precipitously. Under the pile are grocery sacks filled with newspapers, and the end result is (or is becoming) something approaching soil. I've been doing this for about three years, and in another year or two will no longer be in constant danger of falling backwards into the brambles when tending that side of the garden.

One year I piled hay bales there, building a sort of temporary raised terrace so I could plant a row of tall peas right at the edge of the world where they wouldn't be in the way. It was great for a while—I think the Great Wall of Hay kept the ground nicely cool and moist because the peas grew very tall and lush—but then most of the vines got gnawed off at about two inches above ground level because in piling up all those hay bales I had built the world's largest condominium for mice.

I use hay for mulch as well, and to cover the paths. It works very well as long as you keep after it, but it brings in so many weed seeds I'm thinking of switching to straw even though it is more expensive and less pleasant to walk barefoot on. A Pennsylvania woman named Ruth Stout once wrote a terrific book called *How to Have a Green Thumb Without an Aching Back* in which she advocated monster piles of straw mulch year round. She just kept piling it on, replenishing it as it broke down, and parted it, like the Red Sea, in order to plant. I don't remember what she did about the slugs. Pennsylvania is hot enough for year-round cool soil (if you left thick mulch on here that way you'd never see a tomato), and she kept the layer so thick the weeds were smothered before they got started. Not an option in this semi-ornamental establishment, where the weeds have had the benefit not only of my absence but also of weather as warm as late July for most of May.

Dry as late July too. Everything, even the weeds, is just sitting there in the desert-like sand and trying not to die. Is this global warming? We are eating wild strawberries three weeks early, even as the last bits of lilac perfume the air. Bunchberry is still in flower, right next to the pink lady's slipper(!) Must say I've always wondered about that name. Could it be a corruption of something else the way foxglove is really folksglove? My friend Swy (Susan Wysocki) calls them scrotolota, which looks a lot more plausible. Or does slipper have other connotations and I'm just naive to think of shoes?

In the garden, all is fairly chaste unless you count a fair number of mating bugs. The hollyhocks haven't begun to bloom. I have again started some *clitoria* and am determined to find out this year if they really were named for their astonishing resemblance. (Dead ringers, except that they're a fine bright blue.) Common name for the wild form is "butterfly pea," which doesn't sound especially promising. The seedlings are still in the greenhouse as I write, and mysteriously missing on top of that. The feminine form may be grossly underrepresented if they aren't found, because the sweet peas have been totally wiped out by the worst cutworms in years.

This is, in any case, not great sweet pea ground (too hot, sandy and acid) but I usually do okay, especially with the "Floral Tribute" mixture from Thompson and Morgan. I had a fine stand of them coming up when I left for the last trip to N.Y., came home to find just a couple of sprouts, all the rest sawn off. Nothing for it but to replant with standard "Spencers" from the farm store and hope for the best.

Weeds, cutworms, drought, the litany of my woes reminds me this is really more farm than garden in the growth as well as design departments. Being surrounded by fields doesn't help, and neither does having the annuals and perennials mixed in large beds where there is a lot of exposed soil all winter each year. Then I compound the problem by refusing to completely clean up in the fall (actually, not so much refusing as failing, what with this and what with that; but I do it at least partly to be rich in volunteers).

I am in total awe at your speed in researching and designing the Loudon gardens. What a marvelous commission! Let's hope the commissioners are as decisive as you are, since if things follow a normal course you will now get to hurry up and wait for months and months and months.

The plan certainly sounds delightful, a fine mix of aesthetics and education—be sure to keep me informed as the project goes forward. Will the folks whose houses border the square have any say, or does Fujita's ownership give them absolute control? I rather hope so, and not just for speed's sake. Surely after all your vicissitudes you'll agree that art by committee is oxymoronic, in the garden as much as or even more than anywhere else.

June 10

With the lilacs and tulips gone by, shirley poppies not yet started, the show is pretty thin right now unless you count the iris, which every year at this time I am reminded I should plant more of. And there is the hesperis. What a revelation. It's probably as common—and possibly as boring—to you as petunias and marigolds are here. But I had only read about it, never seen, or, more to the point, smelled it when I started the seeds last year. "Dame's Rocket" sounded so enticing, so loaded with lovely cottage-garden associations that I went for it without stopping to think about where to put the plants. They languished in the trays for a while, ended up thrown in together in an out-of-the-way empty space and pretty much forgotten. Neglect didn't bother them, by midsummer they had made handsome green mounds about a foot tall. Then they almost got ripped out because the cabbage worms got to them; by the end of the season they were hideous testimony to the importance of BT (Bacillus thurigensis, an organic pesticide that really *does* work, though you do have to keep at it).

But being me I didn't rip them out and this spring, well ahead of the wretched bugs, the four remaining plants have made a huge bush, almost five feet tall and that many around, covered with purple, pale violet and off-white flowers. The fragrance covers the whole garden at night, a mysterious mixture of lilac and clove.

Looking at a bunch of them on the kitchen table I'm struck by how much they do resemble lilacs, those innocent four-petaled, open flowers, yet everything about them is simpler, simultaneously coarser and more fragile. I'd say, "Why on earth doesn't everybody grow them?" but I know the answer—they're biennials, gratification not only delayed but temporary.

Will close for now to get this in today's mail. Hope all's well, can't wait to see you.

Love,

Leslie

Eccleston Square,
London

Dear Leslie,

Before the other news let me thank you for your wonderful book, it's got fun just leaping about all over the pages. (*The Modern Country Cook* by Leslie Land, Viking 1991)

You went on and on about weeds, brambles, etc. in your letter. Over the weekend I met a gardener who squatted a lovely Victorian house in Brixton (South London). The garden grew only broken-down fridges, old cookers, rotting carpet, broken glass, the whole grown over with a thick layer of brambles. He, Marcus, has a solution, perma culture. Have you come across it? It's an Australian No Dig system. All you do is slash down the weeds and brambles, throw on a small amount of bonemeal and then cover the whole thing with about twelve layers of wet newspaper. On top you put a mulch of well-rotted stable manure about six inches thick, you then plant your annuals or perennials straight into it, the same day, giving them about three handfuls of soil each. If you want to plant shrubs you break a small hole in the membrane and plant the shrub in the soil and weeds below, then replace or renew the membrane right up to the stem of the shrub. Water the whole thing well in and bingo! a garden.

Do you remember I chatted on about sowing my annuals on top of a deep layer of leaf mould? It has worked well and I now have in flower about forty million opium poppies and sweeps of our lovely wild larkspur, *Consolida ambigua*. Next year I am going to put a dusting of blood, fish and bonemeal on top before throwing on the seeds so that the leaf mould will have a better balance of nutrients – but it works and it has kept the weeds right down.

I love dame's violet, sweet rocket, *Hesperis matronalis* or whatever you like to call it. I would love to get hold of a sack of seed, especially the white form. It would be wonderful in forests under the lilac where little grows because of the shade. But no seed merchant has it! Why not? Too common or wild I suppose. A sudden thought: maybe Suffolk Herbs have it? I checked in their wild flower seed catalogue and found it listed not as a wild flower but as a cottage garden flower! I am breaking off right now to send them a cheque for £12 to send me twenty packets.

I have got a most odd plant in the garden (I mentioned it before but this time I have done a sketch of the fruit), it was bought as the American woodland plant doll's eyes *Actaea pachypoda* but instead of one eye (berry) per stem it has a group of eyes – a composite eye like a fly. No book mentions it, what can it be?

All over London this spring there have been problems with London plane trees, *Platanus acerifolia*. There is a fungus disease that attacks the leaves and leaf petioles and causes up to a 25 per cent leaf drop; there are also a great many dead trees, especially on the roadside, possibly killed by salting in the icy weather, or by the very dry summers we have had over

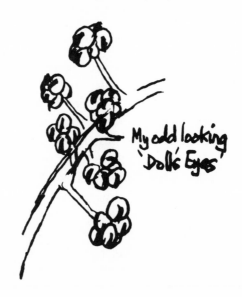

My odd looking
'Doll's Eyes'

the last few years. Possibly it is a combination of all three problems that is causing us to lose so many trees. Anyway I am nervous that in the future the problem may get worse. My only solution at the moment is that people should not plant so many planes: monoculture is at best of times a very dangerous thing, one only has to think of the Dutch elm disease to realize how devastating the results can be. Anyway my advice to people who have asked is: diversity.

When we had our really cold spell at the end of January I kept a record of what I thought might get damaged or killed by frost. Anyway read it through and you will see what winters in central London are really like.

Tender Plants Report February 1991

For four winters we have had virtually no frosts, a matter of down to 28°F (-2°C) at night rising above freezing during the day. This has gradually led to an increase in the number of more tender plants in the garden.

February 2–5 we had night-time lows of 27°F (-2$\frac{1}{2}$°C), with the temperature rising to about 34°F (1°C) during the day.

Feb 6 low 26°F (-3°C) high 31°F (-$\frac{1}{2}$°C), $\frac{1}{2}$" of snow. The wind-chill factor is rather low at the moment; a very slight breeze from the east, perhaps 5 m.p.h.

Feb 7 low 22°F (-5°C) high 28°F (-2°C), 4" fall of snow.

Feb 8 low 22°F (-5°C) high 28°F (-2°C), 4" snow. Wind 5 m.p.h. north east.

Feb 9 low 18°F (-8°C), high 31°F (-$\frac{1}{2}$°C), 1" snow. Some sun.

Feb 10 low 24°F (-4°C), high 32°F (0°C). A little sun.

Feb 11 low 28°F (-2°C), high 37°F (3°C). A few hours of sun.

Feb 12 low 25°F (-3$\frac{1}{2}$°C), high 36°F (2°C).

Feb 13 low 29°F (-1$\frac{1}{2}$°C), high 37°F (2$\frac{1}{2}$°C).

Feb 14 low 25°F (-3$\frac{1}{2}$°C), high 40°F (4°C), a few hours of sun, the wind very slight from the south west.

Feb 15 low 28°F (-2°C), high 44°F (6°C), there has been some light rain and the snow is thawing very rapidly.

Feb 16 low 28°F (-2°C), high 46°F (7°C).

Feb 17 low 31°F (-^{1}/$_2$°C), high 46°F (7°C).
Feb 18 low 32°F (0°C), high 44°F (6°C).
Feb 19 Low 25°F (-3^1/$_2$°C), high 45°F (6^1/$_2$°C).
Feb 20 low 28°F (-2°C), high 44°F (6°C).

At this point I am stopping the records as the cold spell seems to be over. The temperature stayed well above freezing last night 40°F (4°C). When the cold weather started I was able to bring a few pots in from the garden to my back yard where the temperatures would be about 3°F (1^1/$_2$°C) above those in the garden but with no wind-chill factor to allow for. These pots were put back out in the garden on February 18.

List of the Main Plants in the Garden That Are Thought to Be Subject to Frost Damage

Abutilon ('Canary Bird') wire basket full of leaf-mould surrounds trunk up to 2′. I have pruned it back, as I would anyway have done and it is now showing signs of shooting away.

Acacia baileyana wire basket full of leaf-mould surrounds trunk up to 2′. As soon as the weather started to warm up it became apparent that the branches of the Mimosa had all got fine lateral cracks. By March 18 all the leaves have died and the branches have turned from their fresh grey-green colour to a dull brown, I am hanging on in the hope that it will start to break, but it seems doubtful. June 1 dead as the proverbial doornail. July 1, wrong again, thank goodness I hung on to it, I went out and told Arthur to dig it out when we saw that the good wood on the trunk that had been protected with the leaf-mould was just beginning to break!

Albizia julibrissin leaf-mould 1′ high round base, this year even the young shoots have not gone back at all, what seems to happen is that if you get a good hot summer especially with late season hot days the wood matures properly and will withstand any old temperature; however if the late summer is cold and damp the new wood will die back at the first sign of frost. No damage shows at all by March 18.

Alyogyne hakeifolia (Mediterranean) in my back yard, it went back out into the garden at the beginning of March and is fine.

Ballota acetabulosa, in pots on the patio, it has died right back and at March 18 shows no sign of recovery. April 30 pronounced dead and removed.

Bougainvillea in Bed 25, no protection. April 30 looks completely dead but I will give them another few weeks to see if they move at all. Later dead.

Bougainvillea in a large pot on the patio, leaf-mould 6″ high round base. Dead.

Bougainvillea in a pot in my back yard during the very cold spell. Dead.

Callistemon citrinus leaf-mould 6″ high round base, the leaves are a little damaged.

Callistemon pallidus leaf-mould 6″ high round base, the leaves and the tips of the young shoots are slightly damaged.

Camellia cultivars as per list unprotected, I can see no damage and by March 18 many are flowering well.

Camellia sasanqua unprotected, one specimen, 'Narumi-gata' is rather badly burnt, it is in rather an exposed situation, I shall move it to a more protected position.

Camellia cuspidator unprotected, fine.

Camellia saluenensis unprotected, fine.

Cantua buxifolia (Mediterranean) in my back yard, it went back out at the beginning of March and is doing well.

Ceanothus species and cultivars (38) as per list 1st-year plants with plastic bags over them and leaf-mould to about 6″ deep at base.

Ceanothus 'Burkwoodii' is the only one that is damaged, both of our specimens are rather badly burnt although only a few small branches have died back.

Choisya ternata unprotected. No damage.

Choisya 'Aztec Pearl' unprotected. No damage.

Cistus unprotected, no problems.

Clianthus puniceus leaf-mould 6″ high round base. The plant was covered in flower buds when the frost hit; about 75% of which have been killed, otherwise only the top 3–4 inches of the branches have died back. Quite a lot of flowers through May.

Coronilla valentina subsp. *glauca* (herb beds) unprotected, no problems.

Chrysanthemum frutescens (bush daisy), they look very badly damaged, all the leaves and young shoots are black. They are all dead. I have cuttings in the tunnel which have survived.

Crinodendron hookerianum unprotected, the leaves are a little burnt at the tips but the profuse flower buds are looking most healthy.

Crinodendron patagua unprotected, the leaves are a little burned.

Cytisus battandieri (Pineapple Plant) leaf-mould 6″ high round base. No damage.

Cytisus maderensis (Beryl's Bed), the leaves have all been burnt off but by March 18 it is showing new shoots all over.

Datura (*arborea?*) wire basket full of leaf-mould surrounds trunk up to 2′. As the weather starts to warm up a little, some cracks can be seen in the old wood, the young shoots and leaves have all gone completely soft and are just hanging deadly down. Early March I cut it back to just the main stem, all the rest of the wood was already going rotten. March 18 right at the base it is showing signs of breaking. Coming back well June 5.

Ebenus cretica (Mediterranean) in my back yard, it went back out at the beginning of March and is doing well.

Echium fastuosum leaf-mould 6″ high round base, some cracks are showing in the main stems as the weather warms up a little, all the leaves and flower buds are black and very dead. March 18, yes it is completely dead and now gone.

Echium pinaniana wire basket full of leaf-mould surrounds trunk up to 2′. The leaves were badly burned, but a week later it is impossible to judge if the growing tip is killed off or not. Three more weeks later and it is confirmed as completely dead.

Escallonia unprotected, undamaged.

Eucryphia 'Nymansay' unprotected, some of the leaves are burnt.

Feijoa sellowiana leaf-mould 6″ high round base, undamaged.

Fremontodendron 'Californian Glory' wire basket full of leaf-mould surrounds trunk up to 2′, no damage.

Fuchsia (large standards in pots) leaf-mould 6″ high round base. March 18 no sign of life yet. April 30 the tall stems of the standards have been cut back right to the ground, from which new healthy shoots are now appearing.

Genista aetnensis unprotected, undamaged.

Geraniums (scented leaf) unprotected, they have suffered very badly, the stems are all badly frosted, I will not remove them completely in the hope that they will break from the roots. March 18 there seems to be no hope of them coming back, so out they must go. I have cuttings in my little tunnel which have survived.

Griselina littoralis unprotected, looks fine.

Grevillea rosmarinifolia unprotected, March 18 the leaves have died back, but they look as if they will come back OK.

Hebes unprotected, there is some damage on the large-leaved more tender ones.

Hibiscus unprotected, no problems.

Hoheria lyallii unprotected, March 18, a few young branches have died back a bit but otherwise they are beginning to shoot.

Lavatera olbia (the common one) unprotected. Only the very tips of the young growth were frosted. Coming back well.

Lavatera assurgentiflora 'Barnsley' unprotected. Only the very tips of the young growth were frosted. Coming back well.

Leptospermum lanigerum unprotected, no damage.

Leycesteria formosa (Himalayan Honeysuckle) unprotected, no damage.

Lupinus arboreus leaf-mould 6″ high round base, a few of the stems were broken by the snow but otherwise it seems OK, but it is amongst other shrubs and therefore well protected.

Magnolia grandiflora unprotected, no damage.

Nerium oleander (in pots on the patio) wire basket full of leaf-mould surrounds trunk up to 2′ (one), (two) leaf-mould 6″ deep at base. The main stems have died back to about one foot above ground but below that they are coming back well.

Olea europaea (Olive) leaf-mould 6″ high round base. Badly frosted above the protection, the bark is all split and starting to peel off after only a week or so. Despite this damage it all seems to be throwing new leaves; perhaps this sort of reaction to frost is what gives ancient olive trees their wonderful characterful gnarled appearance.

Osteospermum in beds unprotected. The stems have all been killed off by the frost, the question is will they come back from the roots. About half of the plants have been lost including 'Whirligig' which seems the most tender.

Osteospermum cuttings in tunnel. By March 12 they have made terrific roots and I have now potted them up.

Pelargoniums unprotected. Completely killed.

Pittosporum tenuifolium 'Purpureum' unprotected, undamaged.

Pittosporum tenuifolium 'Variegatum' unprotected, undamaged.

Pittosporum tobira unprotected, undamaged. This is a really good plant not planted enough in my opinion.

Senecio greyi, unprotected, undamaged. The cuttings that I put in my tunnel have all made terrific roots and are now (March 12) potted up.

Senecio rotundifolia (*Brachyglottis rotundifolia*) unprotected, just about 6 leaves have dropped off, otherwise no damage.

Tropaeolum tuberosum (tubers about 3″ down in the soil), March 18 a few of them are starting to come through now so obviously they have survived.

Wattakaka sinensis (Climber) unprotected. April 30 new growth breaking out.

Back to early flowering perennials. Have you ever tried woad? I love my great misty yellow mounds in late April or May – this is another thing I will plant more clumps of.

We leave for the States in six days so the next contact will be hugs on your step. So excited to see the garden – keep weeding – keep watering – keep deadheading – keep cooking – here we come.

Love,

Roger

Cushing,
Maine

August 19, 1991

Roger,

We are having hurricane Bob. It's about 7:30 in the evening now and the edge if not the eye is upon us. We have had just buckets, sheets of rain like you can't believe and the winds are very high but I don't think, looking out of the window at everything madly tossing about, that they are anywhere near the hundred miles per hour that everybody on the radio has been talking about all afternoon.

So far damage is minimal. The lattice work tomato support in the center of the upper garden, the one that sits perpendicular to the winds from the west has gone over, although this time it's in the winds from the east. All of the stakes holding up the sugar snaps in the lower garden are leaning at an assortment of crazy angles, and interestingly enough, so far the only big damage is the apple tree that Bill sawed out the middle of so that we could see the shore. The left hand part of the "V" has now bitten the dust, or more accurately bitten the tomatoes and the delphiniums and everything else that was underneath it, and that has cleared a path for the winds to come across the lower garden and do even more damage. All of the trellised cucumbers are, of course, plastered to the ground, and the very very tall pink hollyhock, the twelve-foot one, is now leaning over at about forty-five degrees.

It will be interesting to see the damage. I mean I think to a large extent the damage will be the bruising of leaves. Probably won't know until tomorrow; it'll be abated before long but it's also coming dark. There are a lot of leaves on the grass which will now of course be greener and greener and greener and so far I would say I'm getting more benefit than harm. Bill took the pump out of the pond, cheerfully remarking that I probably would not have any further need of it this year and I think he must surely be right.

So far the little peach tree which isn't in really good condition, which I fear may not make it through the storm, is holding up and the greenhouse is still in place. We had a lot of talk as to whether the greenhouse could survive and if the winds really were a hundred miles per hour I doubt that it could; but I opened the doors at both ends so that the wind could whistle through and that's what it seems to be doing and that's also to some extent what it seems to be doing to the teepees that hold up those hyacinth (*Dolichos lablab*) beans and the teepee that holds up the currant tomatoes.

The central path is impassable, all of the artemisia has gone over and I think I will walk around until I can take a picture of it because it's making a very beautiful shape. You remember that the white phlox, which is now blooming in earnest, had already begun to close that opening under the archway and make a pretty shape against the path? Now there is a folded quality, an almost woven quality, with the bright green phloxes rising behind the gray-green of the artemisia. The alyssum is in full carpet and it leads up in a kind of cream white and then the white is sort of cleansed as it hits the phlox's tops. The thyme is still blooming but the bloom is near the end so there's a grayness under the purple that picks up the gray of the artemisia. Not so pleasing is the sight of the beautiful blooming acidanthera in the window boxes at perilous angles; but so far that shape with all of the white morning glories and the asarina climbing the strings has not broken. All I did was staple the strings to the frame of the house but at this point in mid-storm they are okay. It'll be interesting to see what happens when the wind backs around and comes from the west because that's where it can get a good run-up across the open spread of field. I'm pretty protected from the east by all of that scrub and second growth. So far only old age and the prudence that comes therewith is keeping me from taking a walk because it's beautiful and it's very warm (almost tropical). So far we still have power. The lights flickered a couple of times but on the news on the radio they were saying that one hundred thousand households in Massachusetts have lost power and on and on in the usual litany of hurricane woes so I may be speaking prematurely.

It's now August 27. It's hot, muggy, might as well be the dog days, just thick and wretched and miserable but the garden did in fact weather the storm very well. The entire garden has come a long way since you were here. All of the things that were naked and tiny and not pretty then, encouraged by the rain of the hurricane and just by the passage of time, are now larger and blooming. The central white path, although nothing like its usual self, has the handsomeness that I look forward to each year. The phlox is bloom-city. It's a little shorter than usual, which means it's about three feet tall, but very floriferous and not a trace of mildew. The cosmos has started to bloom in earnest. A lot of it did go over in the storm and I let it lie so that instead of these feathery green bushes with beautiful flat candid flowers, what I have is an intermingling of the foliage with the foliage of the alyssum and the portulaca and these flat white flowers looking up at you from various recumbent positions and that turns out to be very effective.

In addition to all this, there is *piccolino* basil (Bush Basil, *Ocimum minimum*) in the alyssum. I've a friend who calls it Afro-basil because it looks like it's been given one of those bushy haircuts. It has tiny very pungent leaves and right now each bush is maybe about a foot and a half across and the same height, a very tidy little mound. They are just about to bloom, so what you have is the standard main leaves of the bush which are dark green and about a half inch long, then the flowering stems which are a pale chartreuse, with leaves about a quarter or an eighth of an inch long, and presently it will be making white flowers.

Next year, I think I'll put some *toronjil* (*dalea* species) in that section.

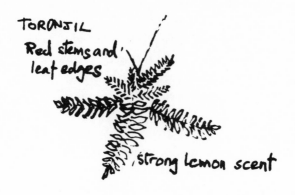

Do you remember the *toronjil,* the Mexican marvel that grows right next to the Joe Pye weed, the thing that looks like mimosa but isn't? It closes at night but doesn't close at the touch. Tiny bluish leaves with a beautiful delicate red edge, and good sized, eventually gets to about four feet though this year I don't think it will on account of the drought. I got it to flower last year for the first time because I potted one and put it in the greenhouse. It made extremely petite flowers which I remember, probably inaccurately, as a kind of purply pink but it did not make seeds. I'm sorry I forgot to put it in anything I cooked while you were here. It has a unique, delicious, lemon/pepper/camphor scent, but only when very fresh. The perfume dissipates within hours and the dried herb is dust. Perhaps that's why it isn't better known. Seed, purportedly collected by Zapotecs in southern Oaxaca, Mexico, is from J. L. Hudson, P.O. Box 1058, Redwood City, Cal. 94604.

The Gaura (*Gaura lindheimeri*) is just beginning, barely, to bloom and its—honesty compels me to say—rather weedy-looking arching arms are reaching out. They do go well with all of those low matty things, though, because they put in a little bit of height. All of the white bee balm (*Monarda didyma* "Snow Maiden") is blooming. The white is not strong, it's not like the white of the lavatera next to it (*Lavatera* "Mont Blanc"), which is a very pure, intense, laundry-line white sheet white that just shines from the bushes. The monarda continues to be dark green on the old growth and chartreuse on the new growth and brown and silver where the painted lady butterflies are all over it. They really are having a good time whereas the bees appear uninterested.

The datura which was so paltry a month ago is now beginning to bloom. It's the nameless one from my neighbor. Very low and bushy, not one of those big majestic items and I'm sorry to say it's not particularly fragrant so I guess it isn't *metaloides,* though the leaves are very blue. Enormous great white trumpety flowers, though, big even for datura, that are perhaps most striking before they open. You get a long calyx, maybe four or five inches, out of which the flower rises and the flower is very long too, a cream color before it opens to white. It's a perfect closed whirl with five sharp points and then very very slowly they unfold and unwind themselves.

The *Nicotiana sylvestris* is also starting; at this point what I mostly have is fragrance and suggestion but the big flat leaves promise monstrous plants; as far as I can tell it will probably be just at its apotheosis when I leave for New York. The poison—I knuckled under and put some on the roses—seems effective. They're covered with buds but I don't yet know if the thrips have been conquered.

In the center beds a lot has come along, in particular the gladioli, which I think were not even in bud at the beginning of August. The ones in the front bed are not only blooming but probably at their height right now and all four beds are filled. I have a total of probably forty or fifty bulbs of a variety called "Zigeunerbaron"; it's a quite remarkable plum color with strange pink shadings down the middle, and as it ages it goes to a dark, silvery lilac. It's about the color of a bruise, quite unlike any gladiolus you normally see, and it's particularly effective with the very dark maroon Centaureas (*C. cyanus,* seedling variety) and all of the assorted annual asters which are intense candy pink and a beautiful true violet as well as strong purple. All of that is backed at the western edge of the garden by the hot (color) bed with all of the screaming yellows and oranges: calendulas, tithonias, montbretias, etc., and the last of the yellow asiatic lilies which you see distantly behind this pink and purple event in the front.

It's stunning, though you do have to view it through the weeds because at this point I am no longer really trying to maintain the garden for this year but to cut back and prune and mulch and organize and start to get ready to go away to live with Bill. I'm very much looking at the garden now with the eyes of someone who is going to change it substantially, smarten it up and make it more suitable for being here only two months of the year; but still I don't know what all is going to be entailed there.

Leslie

P.S. I have to tell you your always enthralling diagrams and lists are also intimidating. There's nothing comparable here, but I'm enclosing a guide to the white garden, just to give an idea. Your midsummer visit made me acutely aware of a gap—the peaks of gorgeousness in this garden are definitely spring, *early* summer and fall. Now that I'm going to be a midsummer visitor myself—well, that's exaggerated, but you know what I mean—I'll have to concentrate on altering what have become very familiar rhythms.

White Garden

1. *Arrhenatherum elatius (bulbosum)*
2. *Thymus praecox* subsp. *articus*
3. *T. pseudolanuginosus*
4. *T. citriodorus*
5. *Dianthus arenarius*
6. *Allium tuberosum*
7. *Satureja montana*
8. *Dahlia × cultorum* "White Spider"
9. *Ocimum basilicum* "Minimum"

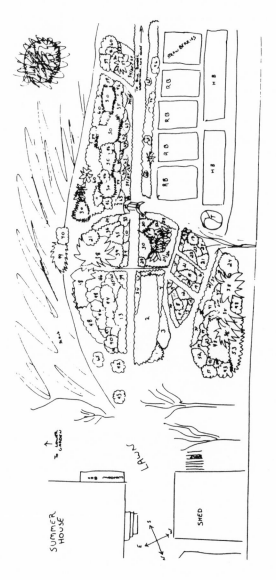

Detail of middle garden and border, upper
garden, looking

10. *Silene maritima* "Robin White Breast"
11. *Gladiolus hortanus* "White Friendship"
12. *Gypsophila paniculata*
13. *Portulaca grandiflora* "Swan Lake"
14. *Salvia argentea*
15. *Artemisia dranunculus* var. *sativa*
16. *Levisticum officinale*
17. *Thuja occidentalis* "douglasii pyramidalis"
18. *Rosa rugosa* "Blanc Double de Coubert"
19. *Salvia officialis*
20. *Allium schoenoprasum*
21. *Dahlia* × *cultorum* "Waterlily" (white selection from mixture)
22. *Phlox carolina* "Miss Lingard"
23. *Iris sibirica* unnamed gift, small white flowers with bit of yellow
24. *Phlox decussata* (*paniculata*) "White Admiral"
25. *Eschscholzia californicum* "Milky White"
26. *Petroselinum crispum* "Giant Italian"
27. Hybrid Tea Rose "White Lightnin'"
28. Climbing rose "New Dawn"
29. *Clematis maximowicziana* (*C. paniculata*)
30. *Artemesia ludoviciana* var. *albula* "Silver King"
31. *Nicotiana sylvestris*
32. *Lilium candidum* (*L. regale*) "Black Dragon"
33. *Angelica archangelica*
34. *Lobularia maritima* "Carpet of Snow" and "Snow Crystals"
35. *Echinacea purpurea* "White Swan"
36. *Monarda didyma* "Snow Maiden"
37. *Scabiosa caucasica* "Miss Willmott"
38. *Heracleum villosum*
39. *Dianthus chinensis* (*heddewigii*) "Black and White Minstrels"
40. Floribunda Rose "Iceberg"
41. *Achillea ptarmica* "The Pearl"
42. White peony "Elsa Sass"
43. *Hydrangea paniculata* "grandiflora"
44. *Lavatera trimestris* "Mont Blanc"

45. *Dicentra spectabilis* var. *alba* followed by Oriental hybrid lily "Casa Blanca"
46. *Delphinium elatum* "Galahad"
47. *Cimicifuga racemosa*
48. *Crambe cordifolia*
49. *Digitalis purpurea* "Alba"
50. White peony "Florence Nicholls"
51. Ground Cover Rose (company definition) "Alba Meidiland" (™)
52. Antique Shrub rose "Duchesse de something or other" that I cannot find for the life of me
53. *Macleaya cordata*
54. *Anemone japonica* (*A.* × *hybrida*) "Honorine Jobert"
55. *Lychnis coronaria* "Alba"
56. Climbing Rose "White Dawn"
57. *Yucca filamentosa*
58. *Chrysanthemum parthenium*
59. *Cleome spinosa* "Helen Campbell"
60. *Cosmos bipinnatus* "Purity"
61. *Verbascum*—wild, probably *thapsus*
62. *Papaver somniferum* "White Cloud"
63. *Gaura lindheimeri*
64. *Matthiola bicornis*
65. *Syringa vulgaris* "Miss Ellen Willmott"

P/W This border does double duty, starting out in spring as a wash of shirley poppies, followed after the poppies finish (in early August) by cosmos, gaura, alyssum, and matthiola transplanted from across the path. Self-sown *Nicotiana affinis* is also allowed to grow here.

RB: Raised beds devoted to cutting flowers and vegetables

HB: Hot color beds

T: Teepee for growing bean vines or climbing tomatoes such as currant types

H: is the giant hackamatack, *Larix laricina*

Eccleston Square, London

14 October 1991

Leslie,

I really am a lazy old bugger, I've never ever written to thank you for looking after us in the summer; it was really terrific, especially getting a pair of Maine lobsters each! Also whilst I am getting duties off my chest, thanks for the vegetable photographs; they were a very welcome addition to the *Vegetables* book, which now only lacks black carrots and some *Uluco*, another of those South American tubers. Martyn goes to Mexico tomorrow – he may get them – or I may get them in New Zealand in December when I go. Some of your potato pictures are in Frankfurt at the Book Fair at this very moment printed up for dummy spreads to sell the book to overseas publishers. They look wonderful.

18 October

Finally the mushroom season has got going over here – very late this year; normally the best time is the end of September and the first week of October. Interest in fungal things is growing apace. On Tuesday I did a radio broadcast from Burnham Beeches relating fungus to the whole wood ecology. On Wednesday I went with the TV South cook from Sussex looking for mushrooms – he of course was only interested in the edibles. On Saturday I am off to the New Forest to take a group out on a

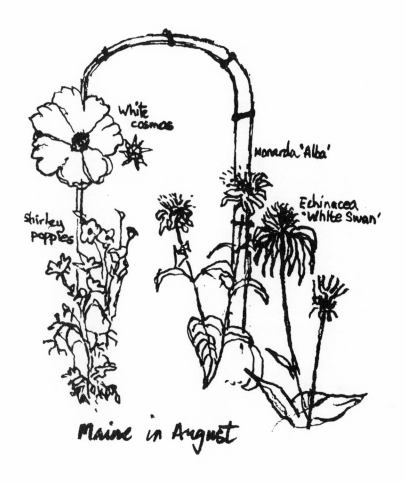

White
cosmos

Monarda 'Alba'

Echinacea
'White Swan'

Shirley
poppies

Maine in August

general foray helping them to identify and learn about all that we can find. Doing this much in one week has helped me to define my position. I am an amateur and all my books and my work are aimed at me. In other words, I go out and learn about a subject and then try and present it in a book, without patronizing other amateurs like me, who are in search of knowledge. In a sense I suppose I am a sort of bridge of communication between the academics with their complex language and ideas, and the keen but not academic naturalist or gardener.

As soon as I said that something was bound to give me my comeuppance. We have just been told we cannot put our garden waste in the giant bins that our local council have put on each corner of the garden. Years ago we used to burn our rubbish, especially the fallen leaves, but like good little citizens we have been trying to get greener and greener – indeed the council wrote to us and said that we must not burn! The vast majority of the leaves we chop up and compost down but of course there are many things like old stumps and roots that it is impossible for us to deal with. I suppose I will now have to take the whole matter up with the council and try to get a city decision on it – it's all mad, the street sweeper puts all his leaves in the big bins anyway.

This reminds me of another problem I had one summer. One of the more select ladies who live round the square rang me up and said, 'A young man and a young woman are making love in the bushes opposite my house, isn't it dreadful, the children might see or anything!' I said I would see what I could do about it. Fifteen minutes later (I judged this to be time enough even for the best of us) I went out to have a look, and duly found the young couple sitting quite respectfully on one of the benches smoking their post-coital cigarettes – leaving me with only one choice: say nothing. Is gardening a sex substitute? For the Greeks it was all about Zeus casting his seed upon mother earth. Perhaps it is simply that working close to the earth, with its fertility and the ever-present life and death of the seasons, gives you a more natural attitude to procreation as a fundamental fact.

Since seeing your garden in August I have been pondering the reasons for the difference of approach between our (English) and your (American) garden. My conclusions are not exactly momentous but here goes. English gardens always have straight edges, that is, they are formed within a rectangle or possibly a triangle; this affects the shape of everything; even if the gardener fights the geometry by having, say, two round lawns, there will still have to be beds around the lawns which back up to the rectangular edge. This shaping of the garden comes from the ancient use of the land and the way it is divided up into lots. Even when someone like a farmer builds a garden in the middle of a large area, they first divide it up into squares or rectangles. You only have to think about the way the grand houses had their lovely walled gardens to see the proof of that.

Your gardens, on the other hand, are often hacked out of woodland and have the appearance of a woodland clearing, and as the gardener gets more energy or has more time he hacks out another area of wilderness and turns it into a garden. The result is a shape that is never bounded by straight lines. So your yard/garden ranges from cultivated flowers to vegetables to wild flowers to totally wild woodland. It makes for a completely different feel from our rather geometrically formal approach.

This year snails have overtaken us. Next year I plan a concerted attack. One: discover where they overwinter and tread on them (they hide on flat, hard, hidden surfaces essential for them to stick to whilst they form the lid that covers the shell opening). Two: in the spring put down aluminium sulphate powder (it kills them off at a touch by stopping them making the mucilaginous slime essential to their movement; it does no harm to animals or birds, and has the added advantage of acidifying the soil – very good for camellias and hydrangeas, especially if you want blue flowers on the latter).

20 October 1991

Drunks in the garden again last night, one whisky bottle, one gin bottle, one vermouth bottle and many beer cans. They moved benches into the greenhouse – to sleep? – but did no damage apart from throwing-up on the path.

Love to you both,

Roger

Pleasant Valley, New York

October 30, 1991

Dear Roger,

The quinces are in the applesauce, the pumpkins carved, huge windrows of leaves—Bill rakes more daily—are piled in the new garden. Took the train to the city last week and got a second dose of leaf-peeping (got the first driving to Maine three weeks ago, rolling on for hours and hours through the oblivious autumn gorgeousness while on the radio the Judge Thomas hearings sleazed their way into history).

Last week was perfect, the sky forget-me-not blue, the Hudson the same, with a slate overlay. Between the tracks and the river a frieze of scrub flashed by, nothing but a blurred wash of bright yellow, bronze, green and brown with the occasional spark of magenta or crimson. Across the river, the hills were tapestried with second-flush colors: burgundy and brown-gold, ashes-of-rust . . . *is* there such a color? I remember my mother being very fond of something called "ashes of roses," pink with a silvery tinge to it, and this was the same, but dark orange.

And why tapestry? Why is that the autumn color cliché? Why don't we say "It's like Seurat!" or "Gee, Impressionism come to life," or something along those lines? At the height, heaven knows, it's bright enough, yet even the sumptuous reds of sumac and swamp maples don't remind us of paint. It must be that when we think "tapestry" we are in the museum looking at old cloth, its vegetable dyes deep in the wool, shining out of the silk, part of the natural fabric. Of course, this may be on my mind because I just *saw* some gorgeous tapestries—in a show called "circa 1492" at the National Gallery in Washington. I was down to take part in a seminar: "Good as Gold, Foods the Americas Gave the World." The usual litany, more or less: potatoes, corn, squash, beans, tomatoes, chocolate, peppers, a nod or two to amaranth, quinoa, manioc. (I'm attaching the list sent to participants.) It's really remarkable how airily we say "the Americas" when so much came from Central and South America, so little from the North. (Wild rice, maple syrup, pecans and hickories, assorted helianthus . . .)

It's also remarkable how unwilling some people are to admit that scientists may not be able to fix everything. This was a pretty sedate gathering, not much in the way of Columbus-bashing or railing at the gastronomic, nutritional and social evils wrought by factory farming, but when we got to the preservation of genetic diversity . . . Well!

After a bit of public hot-and-heavy, I spoke with one of the science camp, trying to get him to admit that gene banks and academic grow-out projects, even if they were much more extensive and better funded than they are now, could never save all the species that currently exist, never mind duplicate the wide range of random conditions that ensure continuing mutation. His response was "Oh, well, you're probably thinking of it as a gardener . . ." *Just* a gardener was richly implied in his patronizing tone. This led me to reflect on the contribution "just gardeners" have always made and, by extension, the precarious position of amateurs in our time. I wanted to shake my fist in his face and say Gregor Mendel was an amateur and so was Thomas Jefferson and so are the farmers and gardeners who are right now growing, saving, and passing on thousands of cultivated varieties that would otherwise be lost.

Our "heirloom seed" movement is still in its infancy, but it's growing all the time. No official support, of course, but private funding organizations are starting to take notice; both Kent Whealy, who started the Seed Savers Exchange, and Gary Nabham, of Native Seeds/Search, have won "genius" grants from the MacArthur Foundation and the recognition those grants bring will probably be as important as the money. On the other hand, I'm afraid recognition is a mixed and not entirely durable blessing. I've dealt with several editors who said of old-fashioned seed-saving, "We've done that story," as though there were only one. The last piece I wrote about genetic preservation and the contribution of amateurs thereto was mercilessly dumbed down (readers were deemed incapable of understanding anything about the difference between "hybrid" and "open pollinated" except that a difference exists). And slick merchandizers are already jumping on the bandwagon now that "Green" is hot in the marketplace. So I guess it won't be long before the pros take over.

Maybe it's romantic of me, and maybe I'm inspired by your happy example, but I have the sense that amateurs are better respected in Britain, that people there still see the Sunday painter and gentleman scholar as both admirable and capable. Here, on the other hand, we are obsessed with certified expertise. It's unlikely, for instance, that you'd have gotten to design the Loudon square unless you had a degree (or two) in landscape architecture. No matter how many societies you founded, how splendid your own gardens, how many books—actually, I take that back; the books would probably legitimize you. In the U.S., to write a book is to *be* an expert, Q.E.D., even if all you do in the book is prove that you don't know damn-all about the subject in question.

Cranky thoughts, and yet a minute ago I was thinking about how much I love forays, where intellectual democracy appears to be alive and well. The world of mycology seems unusually welcoming of dedicated amateurs, open-mindedly ready to accept people who don't have formal training. At the Rindge Foray, my first, I was amazed to see multidegreed professors mingling with, actually paying attention to, the whole complement of amateurs. Everybody from experts like Bill, who's been at it for years, to the rankest beginner regarded as capable of valuable contributions.

Of course, at forays every pair of eyes and hands does help. When you've got three hundred people combing the territory nothing but mushrooms on their minds, even somebody who doesn't know a *gomphidius* from a *gomphus* may trip over something interesting purely by accident. But there's more to it than forays. Look at Bill's pal Peter Katsaros, an internationally known authority (admittedly, on slime molds) who has no academic credentials in the field at all. Maybe mycology is still comparatively open because there's so much that remains unknown about fungi, because so many fungi are themselves as yet "undiscovered." And maybe, come to think of it, it's because there's very little money to be made. I once asked Dick Homola (from the University of Maine, Orono), the only mycology professor I know, how many professional mycologists there are in this country. He allowed as how there were probably no more than a hundred or so, even counting the ones (it's the majority, I believe) who work for various industries. But all the same it never ceases to amaze me how many of the big names are people like Rod Tulloss. I mean, the guy is an engineer for the telephone company, yet he's also Mr. Amanita, the fellow to whom everyone turns when there is a question about the genus.

And, of course, there is Roger Phillips, Le Phillips himself!

But I digress. One thing that seems quite distinctively American to me is our use in gardens of unorthodox outbuildings and dependencies. For example we have not only Lo's big, serious barn and my not-so-serious plastic quonset hut greenhouse, we also have a storage shed (mine) and a chicken-house converted to a potting shed (hers); also an old outhouse, converted to a toolshed, a new outhouse (the one you call the compost loo), and an outdoor shower all of them at Lo's. There's a root cellar, too, come to think of it, since the floor in the rock-walled basement of the old farmhouse is dirt. I use it to store dahlia bulbs, potatoes, beets, carrots, and bulbs for forcing, as well as wine and cheese.

Creative re-use of the buildings and the building of the loo are all Lo's doing. She has been getting maximum mileage out of everything for decades, was partial to simple solutions long years before such tendencies became politically correct. The old New England adage "Use it up, wear it out, make it do or do without" was just about invented to describe her, yet

The Outhouse
-beshingled-

hers is not by any means a conventional frugality. I really think she finds waste aesthetically displeasing and is attracted to low-tech solutions because their simplicity is elegant in the long run.

The loo is a case in point, built after some years' consideration to take pressure off the bathroom, which is heavily used in high summer when we have a lot of visitors. Its resemblance to a tower folly (it has absolutely the best view of the upper garden anywhere on the property) is somewhat accidental, not so much a reaching for grandeur as a taking advantage of the way the barn is set. As you probably remember, entrance to the throne room is through Lois's studio on the main floor. Since we didn't go into mechanics when you were here, I'll explain that each of the two seats is at the top of a sealed, vented chute that leads to a holding tank (fifty-gallon oil drum) a full story below. The drums are mounted on jacks that are supposed to make it easy for Lo and me to move them without help; in practice the full ones are so heavy we usually get aid. But having to ask for additional muscle is the only obnoxious part. As long as each user is careful to "flush" with enough peat moss to absorb all free liquid, the place doesn't smell, and each drum sits for about nine months before being emptied. By the time we turn out the contents the stuff is practically soil, but we give it a second composting, layered with garden waste and earth, just to be on the safe side.

Then, being very conservative types, we forbear to use it on the annual vegetables. We do use it on everything else: fruit trees, berries, and all the ornamentals. "I'll give it a shot of our special mixture" is Lois's standard solution to any and all plant problems.

I think one reason it works so well is that we try not to pee in it any more than necessary. There's an old coffee can for urine, so we can use that at once before the nutrients leech away. Since urine is non-toxic when first expelled, all you have to do is dilute it with water so it doesn't burn the plants. Theoretically you could pour it right around the spinach, but what we mostly do is use it to spruce up the lawn: it greens up anaemic spots like some kind of miracle drug.

I don't need to tell you we've run into our share of skeptics, but not many the year of Lo's grand design. 1987, I think it was. She started just out of curiosity dumping her regular morning whizz in a straight line across the lower yard. Then she made a huge cross, then a many-rayed star, bright emerald against the grass green and clearly visible to even the most dull-sighted. Big success, though I don't think we actually *converted* anybody.

I'll close here for now, but there's *lots* more to come soon. Papa comes to visit tomorrow and I have to do everything right now but . . .
Love,

Leslie

Foods Originating in the Americas
(North, Central, and South America and the Caribbean)

Cacti:

Cactus pear (prickly pear)—*Opuntia spp.*
Nopales (cactus pads)—*Opuntia spp.*

Fruits:

Atemoya—*Annona* hybrid
Avocado (alligator pear)—*Persea spp.*
Berries: Blueberries, highbush—*Vaccinium corymbosum*
　　　　　　　　lowbush—*Vaccinium augustifolium*
　　　Cranberry—*Vaccinium macrocarpum*
　　　Huckleberry—*Gaylussacia baccata*
　　　Juneberry (service berry)—*Amelanchier spp.*
　　　Raspberry, American varieties (red)—*Rubus strigosus*
　　　　　　　　(black)—*Rubus occidentalis*
　　　Strawberry—*Fragaria* hybrid (*F. virginiana*) and *F. chiloensis*
Cassabanana—*Sicana odorifera*
Ceriman (monstera)—*Monstera deliciosa*
Cherimoya—*Annona cherimola*

Cherries: Chokecherry (Amerian wild cherry)—*Prunus virginiana*
Pin cherry (wild red cherry)—*Prunus pennsylvanica*
Rum cherry (sweet black cherry)—*Prunus serotina*
Custard apple—*Annona reticulata*
Feijoa (pineapple guava)—*Feijoa sellowiana*
Grape, scuppernong—*Vitis rotundifolia*
Granadillas: giant—*Passiflora ligularis*
             sweet—*Passiflora quadrangularis*
Guanabana (soursop)—*Annona muricata*
Guava—*Psidium guajava*
Mamey—*Mammea americana*
Mamey sapote—*Pouteria sapota*
Naranjilla—*Solanum quitoense*
Papaya—*Carica papaya*
Passion fruit—*Passiflora edulis*
Pawpaw—*Asimina triloba*
Pepino (melon pear)—*Solanum muricatum*
Persimmon, American—*Diospyros virginiana*
Pineapple—*Ananas comosus*
Plums: American—*Prunus americana*
      beach—*Prunus maritima*
Sapodilla—*Achras sapota*
Sugar apple (sweetsop)—*Annona squamosa*
Tamarillo (tree tomato)—*Cyphomandra betacea*
White sapote—*Casimiroa edulis*

Grains and Grasses:

Amaranth—*Amaranthus*
Corn, popcorn (maize)—*Zea mays*
Quinoa—*Chenopodium quinoa*
Wild rice—*Zizania aquatica*

Legumes:

Beans: Snap, string, green, yellow wax, navy, kidney, etc.—*Phaseolus vulgaris*
    Lima (butter)—*Phaseolus limensis*
    Scarlet runner—*Phaseolus coccineus*
    Tepary (Texas)—*Phaseolus acutifolius*
Peanut—*Arachis hypogea*

Nuts:

Black walnut—*Juglans nigra*
Brazil nut—*Bertholletia excelsa*
Butternut—*Juglans cinerea*
Cashew—*Anacardium occidentale*
Hickory nut—*Carya spp.*
Pecan—*Carya illinoensis*

Poultry:

Turkey—*Meleagris gallopavo*

Roots and Tubers:

Arrowroot—*Maranta arundinacea*
Groundnut—*Apios americana*
Jerusalem artichoke (sunchoke)—*Helianthus tuberosus*
Jicama—*Pachyrhizus erosus*
Malanga (yautia)—*Xanthosoma spp.*
Oca—*Oxalis crenata*

Potato—*Solanum tuberosum*
Sweet potatoes: North American—*Ipomoea batatas*
Boniato—*Ipomoea batatas*
Yuca (tapioca, cassava, manioc)—*Manihot esculenta*

Seeds:

Pumpkin seeds—*Cururbita pepo*
Sunflower seeds—*Helianthus spp.*

Spices, Flavorings, Extracts:

Allspice—*Pimenta officinalis*
Capsicums (chili peppers)—*Capsicum annuum* and *Capsicum frutescens*
Cayenne—*Capsicum annuum*
Paprika—*Capsicum tetragonum*
Cassareep, basis of Worcestershire sauce, extracted from Yucca—*Manihot esculenta*
Chocolate, cocoa—*Theobroma cacao*
Maple syrup, sugar—*Acer saccharum*
Sarsaparilla extract—*Smilax spp.*
Sassafras extract—*Sassafras varifolium*
Spicebush berry—*Linder benzoin*
Vanilla—*Vanilla planifolia*

Vegetables:

Capsicums (sweet and bell peppers, pimento)—*Capsicum annuum*
Chayote—*Sechium edule*
Gherkin (Jamaica cucumber)—*Cucumis anguria*

Pokeweed—*Phytolacca americana*
Pumpkins—*Cucurbita pepo*
Ramp (wild leek)—*Allium tricoccum*
Squashes: Winter (Hubbard, buttercup, crookneck, butternut, kabocha,
      etc.)—*Curcurbita maxima*
      Summer (yellow crookneck, zucchini, spaghetti squash, etc.)—
      Cucurbita pepo
      Calabaza—*Cucurbita moschata*
Tomatillo—*Physalis ixocarpa*
Tomato—*Lycopersicon esculentum*

Food-Related Substances:

Annatto (food dye)—*Bixa orellana*
Beers made from corn, potatoes
Chicle latex (chewing gum) from sapodilla tree
Pulque (fermented maguey)—*Agave salmiana*
Quinine for tonic water—*Cinchona officinalis*
Tequila, distilled from pulque—*Agave tequilana*
Wines made from fruits

Eccleston Square,
London

18 November 1991

Leslie,

American autumn colour features in so many ads that we over here think it goes on all year over there. Our leaf change is minor compared with yours, yellows from the sycamores and browns from the oaks – reds are virtually nonexistent except for the occasional import – nevertheless they are much enjoyed.

Harking back to your loo (I suppose it may seem an excessive interest), a week or so ago there was an article about Abby Rockefeller, followed by a TV programme about her non-flush lavatory. She wants to potty train the world. Her system is much like yours except more expensive, more so-phisticated and more mechanized. She allows two years to compost down but then she does use the result to grow what look like superb vegetables. The TV programme highlighted the dispute that the compost was not clean of the possible virus and bacterial infections that it could carry. It seems the State of California did tests to see what the virus situation was. The trouble was that they didn't actually test for the harmful viruses but some other kind of testing which came up negative, and they advised against the lavatories. Now I gather new tests have been done specifically looking for harmful virus and bacterial contamination and the results prove that the compost rates just the same as normal soil. Typical of the powers that be attempting to refute development with false information – will they never listen? Perhaps you, Lo and Abby should all get together and pool resources (information that is). I thought we were eating toma-toes grown in it when we visited – they were really good anyhow.

I was fascinated to find you growing in your garden what I thought was giant hogweed *Heracleum mantegazzianum*, a plant we all try desperately to get rid of in England. You corrected me in no uncertain manner telling me it was really the giant cow parsnip and that everybody loves it. My only excuse is that by the time I took a peek at it it was in horrible condition, more or less totally gone over. To you it's a star of the white garden in spring when it blooms. You went into raptures about the great big tropical leaves, these immense toothed things, and were desperately trying to raise enough plants for gifts to keep your admiring neighbours happy. Let me explain my horror. Our giant hogweed has become a pernicious weed in England. It escaped from Kew or Oxford Botanic Garden years ago and is spreading madly along rivers and down roads, probably on car tyres or something. The real problem is that it's got this dangerous toxin that af-fects the skin (is the world photopathetic?). It bleaches the pigment out of the skin. The danger is if children cut a piece of stem and make a pea-shooter out of it, when they put it to their lips it will damage the pigment of their lips and then they'll get sunburned and get terrible blisters. Now I am home again and have found the time to look up your plant I find that it is by no means poisonous or dangerous. In fact the young stems can be cooked and eaten, although the books tend to warn against eating it in case a wrong identification is made (very sensible). All the same if you can propagate a few maybe you should try boiling it up!

Thinking about weeds, my big fear in tramping about the woods of North America is the dreaded poison ivy. I have seen a sufferer covered in the dreadful boils and sores caused by this plant. It is unknown in Britain, and I hope it is never imported or allowed to escape from some specialist collection to become the scourge of our highways and byways.

When we visited you in the summer, the children went round to those neighbours of yours – sort of down the lane and then turn left – and they had a very nice climbing frame in the garden that came from a Maine company called the Cedar Works. After leaving you we drove up to see them, and they really had a terrific display of first-class climbing frames. We discussed shipping with them, and they came up with a price of just under $2,000 for a really good big unit with about twelve accessories, rings, ropeladders, slippery poles, boat swings, baby swings and more. Back in England we got costings on comparable equipment; the price ran out at about £5,000, four times as much, and the equipment was neither as interesting nor as aesthetically pleasing. What's gone wrong in our poor country?

All this reminds me of the last time we did major work on the children's area. This story will give you some idea of what it's like to run a garden democratically. About six years ago we completely reorganized the play area. It was on a patch of the lawn under a weeping ash and a false acacia where nothing would grow, not even grass; if there were just a few drops of rain, it turned into a mud bath. I decided that it was time we had a more organized play area with a bed of bark mulch for the little devil darlings to fall on. At the same time we were in the process of relaying an adjacent patio. The plan was to lay the patio over the top of what was there, which apart from the main surface of loosely laid crazy paving included two different brick and cement floors (two sheds that were long gone). It took about three man-days a week just to keep the weeds down! We concreted over the whole lot and laid bricks in a series of patterns like a very simple mosaic. The area for the children was dug up and the edges finished off with bricks, it was then filled with grunged up bark to a depth of about eight inches. All this work had been discussed by the democratically elected garden committee, plans had been submitted and budgets drawn up and approved. This was when the trouble started.

A couple who had just moved into the square had been canvassing for the local Conservative party and thus had made contact with a great many of the residents. They came to the conclusion, for God knows what reason, that rather than trying to improve the garden the garden committee were trying to ruin it. An expression bandied about in reference to the patio was 'helicopter landing pad'. Using their contacts in the square they persuaded seven or eight people to write to the garden committee chairman to

protest. She was very upset and felt very insecure about it, leaving me no
other option than to ring around some of the residents that use the garden
and ask them to write to the chairman expressing their views. In a few
days she received more than forty letters, all supporting the new work we
were doing. Fine, the committee were happy. Next we had a letter threat-
ening the committee with an injunction for acting illegally! So we had to
go to a solicitor, at considerable expense, to get an opinion as to the legal
position. He examined the minutes of the committee and found that it had
been properly elected, and that all the work had been properly discussed
and agreed, all being minuted in an accurate and detailed form. The next
move was to report us to our local council for transgressing planning reg-
ulations. The planning department telephoned me and asked to come and
have a look. The man who came said: 'This is a private garden and as such
a structure has to be over five feet tall before planning needs to be applied

for.' This however did not seem to satisfy our opponents because a few weeks later I was again contacted by the council rescinding the statement of their officer and saying that the garden was not in fact private but a public garden and that planning consent would therefore be needed. A very contentious statement, as we do not allow public access; legal precedents in the past have referred to these London squares as built strictly as private gardens for the sole use of the residents surrounding them. We were advised, in the event correctly, to ignore the council's contradictory request. Of course one of the side effects was that our local councillors were for a while suspicious of the garden committee, the smear stuck for a bit. Now happily they have had numerous chances of visiting the garden and seeing the work that has been done and the way that it is run. Currently our relationship is very good and the council is very supportive. We have not heard a squeak out of our persecutors for some years now. This will give you a picture of what is involved in running a garden in a city, all the sleep that is lost not over droughts, floods and frosts but over the machinations of the very people whom you are working to help – moan – moan – moan. I hope I am not putting my head back in the lion's mouth by ordering the new Maine play equipment.

Our new book on perennials is just being launched and Martyn and I are being taken for lunch to L'Escargot in Soho, a restaurant that is irresistible not just for the food but for the wonderful Elena Savloni who is a superb *maître d'*. Never a face is forgotten – she knows every artist and writer personally and makes everyone so welcome. Keep up the good work on your compost.

Love,

Roger

Pleasant Valley, New York

Dear Roger,

Having left off with the outhouse I shall commence at once with the outdoor shower—a triumph of low tech efficiency if ever there was one. (Unlike the Clivus Multrum—Abby Rockefeller's loo, which is unlikely to catch on big not just because it takes quite a while for the fruit fly situation to sort itself out but because it's bloody *huge* and yet designed to go in the house. Well actually the throne itself is regulation but the underlying apparatus . . . after all ours is in the barn.) Anyway, the shower: water supply is a garden hose hooked up to a faucet on the back porch. Lois's son Eli made the heater part out of an old fifty-gallon copper water tank and a pane of glass left over from my little house. (When I put in the back window and skylight I got a deal on some huge (four by five and a half feet) thermopane windows. Several single-thickness pieces came along as part of the package. Very useful.)

Eli built a triangular box, painted the inside black and mounted the black-painted tank at the back. The glass went on as the front panel and the whole thing was mounted on the south-facing edge of the chicken house roof. (No chickens for the last thirty years or so.) It's an ideal spot: the curve of the yard, the big apple tree, and the old outhouse with its vines all screen the west side. On the east there's a dense, ancient lilac. With only a short length of fence the shower area—a simple wooden platform—was made completely private.

It didn't work too well the first year. You could use it only a few hours a day: from 10 to 11:30 a.m. or so and again at about 4:30. The rest of the time you'd have scalded to death. So the next year Eli rigged up a cold tap and now it's perfection, in regular use from mid-June until late September. The bugs are occasionally a problem—have I mentioned the black flies, deer flies and mosquitoes without which no tale of gardening in Maine is even remotely authentic? But other than that all we do is try to remember to use properly biodegradable soap.

As far as I'm concerned the niftiest thing is pure duration. The water's so hot that at midday in midsummer you can take about a forty-five-minute shower just standing there under the warm water looking out over the ravine at the ferns and birches and wild cherries, mosses and spruce trees. The blackberries aren't bothered—if anything, they're encouraged—so in fruiting time you can pick and eat berries while bathing.

Occasionally, you can bat watch, too. Just this last summer I was out there quite late in the season, already early September but still warm. I reached up to adjust the temperature and there was a little face looking down at me from under a loose shingle right below the hot tap. I think the water coming down the pipe must have warmed things up overmuch and forced him to move down, because when I went back later to admire him again he was back well up under the shingle and much harder to see.

Concerning the cow parsnip: I didn't realize I was so defensive but I *am* extremely proud of it. Its tropical gorgeousness won't seem like any big deal to you, but I have a lot of trouble with wide-leaved plants because the garden is so droughty, so I'm always delighted when I get something to balance all that spiky gray lace. Furthermore I feel very parental because it was a seed-starting success of no mean proportions. I first got interested by reading about it in the J. L. Hudson catalog, where it was listed as "*Heracleum villosum,* reaching ten feet in height with fragrant, Queen-Anne's-lace-like umbels four feet across." Clearly worth a try, though they did say the seed had to be stratified. So stratify I did, starting in, I think, January. I planted the seed in moist soil, then froze the pot for six weeks, as per instructions. Then, still following orders, I put said pot where the temperature was approximately 75 degrees. Nothing happened. I tended it all through the early spring, watering sparingly but keeping my eye on it so it never dried out . . . all the boresome usual. When the big spring crunch came in May I began to neglect it and eventually the pot was set aside in the front hall (under the shelf of jam jars) and forgotten.

It was rediscovered the following January, in my approximately once-a-decade thorough house cleaning, and in my more regular house cleaning style set aside to be dealt with later. Then in March when it was time to round up all pots, there it was. So I watered it. Eureka! or not eureka, I guess, but whoopee or something. Sprouts in any event. Which I planted out where they did nothing much but made handsome mounds about three feet around. They wintered over, got bigger, but did not bloom. Finally, in the third summer, giant umbels as promised, albeit only on two of six or seven plants. No fragrance.

Aphids, though. You would not believe how attractive the green seed heads are to aphids. They don't bother the plants or the flowers in bloom, but the seed heads get so covered they're black with the little bastards and unspeakably disgusting if you get close enough to see what's up. This is a great pity as the structure remains dandy even when completely gone by and dried up. It's a mystery, too. Aphids have never been a problem here except on fava beans—even the roses aren't usually bothered. This summer, 1991, it became clear that the cow parsnips die after flowering. Neither of the plants that had bloomed came back. All the others did, but they all *bloomed,* damn 'em, and since I'd lost the little bit of seed that had formed (aphids!) I was afraid I'd lose the lot. But then it turned out that several of the little plants that I thought in spring were self-sown anemones were actually them and *then* I went up to my land on the mountain above the Rockland bog and there was a whole slew of 'em merrily growing in the ditch beside the road. Smaller, less spectacular, but definitely the article. If there's a moral to this tale I'm not sure I want to know it.

The tale of the children's area is—well I was going to say "simply beyond belief" but of course it's all too believable. It also reminds me to tell you how my little house came to its present location.

Originally an old garage, the building had been moved to the hillside across from Lois's house about forty years ago. There it languished, the scrub growing up around it, until I came along and bought it. Well and good, but I still had to get it to its future home; we had figured out that it ought to be tucked into the slope on the other side of the road about 1200 feet to the northeast. Got estimates from moving companies that pick up houses with cranes and put them on flatbed trucks. Horrendous. Got estimate from a good friend, a lobster fisherman and part time carpenter, who is good at improvised solutions. Much more reasonable. He would jack up the building, which was resting on concrete blocks, set it down on raw spruce skids and then drag it across and down the road. This being winter, it would slide along handily when pulled by his bulldozer, his father's tractor, and the four-wheel drive truck driven by his father's assistant.

I prepared to call around to the planning board, power company and various other interested parties. "Bad idea," said my friend. "Expensive. A hassle. Fuck the permits." (The correct pronunciation is per-*mits*, accent on the second syllable, and I must tell you this phrase is the Rural New England National Anthem; you shouldn't think our case is unusual.)

The building (eighteen by twenty feet, clapboard, big windows, one and a half stories) was jacked onto the skids without incident. A path was cleared through the nascent forest of poplars and alders. The movers showed up on the appointed day and maneuvered the building down to the brink of the road. Where it sat, at a 45 degree angle, for approximately an hour while they went off God knows where to have lunch and I sat over at Lois's and had apoplexy. (They had forbidden me to come anywhere near the action.)

After lunch, they sent the luckless assistant to stand on the steep, snow-covered roof with a wooden pole in case he had to push up the power lines so they could squeak under them. You think I am making this up. I am not making this up. I was beside myself but that just made two of me as there was nobody else around. The building grunted onto the somewhat icy blacktop, which it pretty much filled both lanes of, and sailed smoothly along without incident for about seventy feet. Then the tractor threw a rod.

It took more than two hours to fix the tractor, during which time I stood at one end of the building and the assistant stood at the other and we waved along the mercifully few passing cars—there was just barely room to squeeze through on one side. All calamity, including the serendipitous advent of any members of the planning board, was miraculously avoided. By the time the house made it across the road it was almost dark, so they didn't bring it to the site until the next day. Then they put it down about 10 degrees off of the angle I had in mind. Wouldn't pick it up and move it, either, although I begged.

Then my friend and I built an addition (ten by twenty-eight feet), at the north end of the building. No permission needed, the house, being on posts, is a movable structure. In fact that was the original idea; neither Lois nor I thought I'd stay when I came. We always figured someday I'd buy my own land and emulate the turtle; the little house is my version of a trailer.

Oh well, Irony Time. The house is staying and I'm going, only not really. I'm seeing this move as First Page of Next Chapter. Everything is different now that I've fallen for the entire domestic package: partner, child, dog and cat, a large rather falling-down house (*two* bathrooms, *no* outhouse) in the suburbs. I'm still a little stunned to realize I've bought the whole nine yards. But I'll be in Maine every summer, expect the garden to gain in structure what it loses in detail as I plant more shrubbery, rearrange trees, finally plant my lilac hedge.

Of course, how could it be otherwise? Just as I finally learn how to make the Maine garden less labor intensive, just as the years of soil-building finally begin to pay off, just as I finally start to understand the needs of that land and landscape, I get to start all over in New York. The new property is smaller, only a bit over an acre all told, but everything that isn't house is garden, pretty much, and all of the garden is either ancient and grown over but extremely promising (the grounds of the house) or totally prospective and a tough row to hoe (the quarter-acre strip across the road that will be our vegetable garden but requires considerable work first as it used to be a railroad bed. You insert your shovel, or try to, and the ground fights back.)

Bill is an enormous asset. He's a hard worker, loves to garden, and is remarkably generous about saying "but this is really your specialty, dear, just tell me what you want to do and I'll help you." The downside of this is that he's not so much a hard worker as an addicted one. He'll do what I want if I can figure out what I want, but he won't stand still. He's not very good at just waiting a minute while I see how it should go, and if I don't express specific wishes he simply swashbuckles in there and does what feels right to him, regardless.

As you know, I'm more the slow type, and I'm especially eager to go through a full year here just noticing, before I start what will indeed be a major renovation. The last several owners of the house have done nothing, but there was a real gardener here at one time. According to the neighbors' stories, she was Beatrice (Wells) Allen, the last of the Wells (the road is Wells drive). Her family owned the place from the late 1800s through its whole career as a railroad station (did I mention that it used to be a railroad station?) until about 1980, when the old lady, long since too frail to do any gardening, could no longer keep up the place and had to sell.

Judging from the shrubbery, she was at her most vigorous in the 1940s and 50s, when, as far as I can tell, she bought specimens with mad abandon and then sprinkled them around the yard wherever she saw a space. Jeepers. But I want to try to find her (she's in a nursing home "somewhere upstate") and find out what I can *before* I start the considerable editing that will be required. Bill understands this, at least in theory, and fortunately he can practice on the vegetable garden when the urge to toil is too strong to resist.

I do already have all sorts of plans, but intend to leave them on paper until I know more. First order of business will be to return to Maine in March and build a (very small) addition on the little house so Bill's daughter Celia will have a room of her own. That loft-like open space was fine when I was by myself. In fact, I loved it, a box of light in a garden.

But now it's time for goodbye to all that—and to you. I'll write more about the new place next time.

Love,

Leslie

Eccleston Square, London

Dear Leslie,

Tomorrow off to New Zealand, for publicity tour for *Perennials*. I have got the most ghastly schedule – pre-breakfast radio then a breakfast including a talk, then on and on and on. But all very exciting. In between I will try to photograph the whole NZ flora for the up and coming books!

Chagrin! England, the country that pioneered health insurance for all and come to that education for all, has finally given up the struggle. Two days ago I was talking to a man who has business in Spain, Germany and England. Under the new European Community laws that come into action in 1992 you cannot have profits in all three countries at once, you have to declare your profit in one or the other. Vipin (that's his name) has discussed it with his accountant and been advised that the best of those three countries to declare profit in – from a tax point of view – is Britain. I am sure that Thatcher would be proud to hear him say it, but I am disgusted, what it means is that we pay less tax and thus have fewer services than anywhere in Europe. All the marvellous work done over the last hundred years, that made us the envy of the world (especially of America) in health care and education – especially for the poor and disadvantaged – has been undermined so that the better off can take home more pay. I am making a considerable saving under our new laws and I hate it. I would be happy to pay more national and local taxes (we used to call them rates), to help the poor sods who ain't got nothin'.

In my latest copy of *The Rose*, the magazine of the rose society, there are two articles about blue roses. Apparently the American company, Jackson and Perkins, are working on altering the genetic structure so that a rose can be grown to any specification including the introduction of animal and even human genes into the strain. This will no doubt mean that we can have a blue rose that smells of lavender that can dance around the garden to the music of an orchestra formed of yet other freaks.

Thirty years ago I saw a film that Jean Paul Sartre had something to do with, about producing hybrid animals – sheep as nimble as goats yet three times as large, pigs crossed with cows to give them an enormous size and other horrors, but after all this time I see no evidence of these monsters in mass production. Let's hope we will be excused having climbing roses with delphinium flowers and delphiniums with rose-scented flowers!

Two key dates in the garden: 1 November the first flower came out on a camellia – *sasanqua* 'Hugh Evans', a small red single, followed very quickly by *sasanqua* 'Narumi Gata', a lovely small cup-shaped white single flower with pink on the outside of the petals. We will now have camellias in flower until the end of next April except if we got a really bad cold spell in which case they will take a couple of weeks off. The second key date is 21 November the first touch of frost on the lawns, just enough to start to kill off the nasturtiums. It's now 1 December and the first lovely scented flowers have appeared on the *Viburnum × bodnantense*.

I will try to write on my antipodean route.

Here is a sketch and plant list for the hellebore bed which is starting to stir – I usually get a few flowers by Christmas.

Lots of love to you both,

Roger

BED 14
The Winter Bed

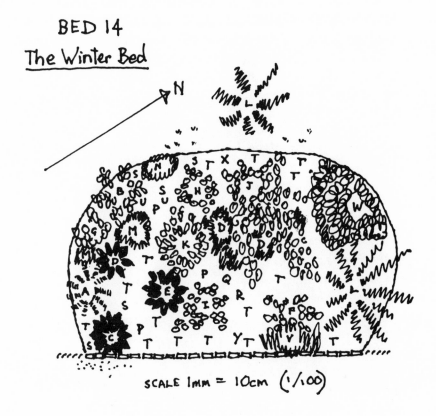

SCALE 1MM = 10CM (¹⁄₁₀₀)

Bed 14: The Winter Bed

Shrubs

A = *Acacia baileyana*
B = *Betula jacquemontii*, the Himalayan birch
C = *Camellia* 'Contessa Lavinia Maggi'
D = *Camellia* 'Cornish Spring'

E = *Camellia* 'Grace Bunton'

F = *Hamamelis* × *intermedia* 'Arnold Promise'

G = *Hamamelis* × *intermedia* 'Jelena'

H = *Prunus glandulosa sinensis*

I = *Prunus mume Benichidori*

J = *Syringa vulgaris*

K = *Viburnum opulus Sterile*

L = *Viburnum plicatum Mariesii*

Perennials

M = *Artemisia absinthinum* 'Lambrook Silver'

N = *Calamintha grandiflora*

O = *Digitalis lutea*

P = *Helleborus corsicus*

Q = *Helleborus foetidus*

R = *Helleborus foetidus* 'Western Fisk'

S = *Helleborus niger*

T = *Helleborus orientalis*, many forms

U = *Iris florentina*

V = *Iris germanica*

W = *Symphytum* 'Hidcote Pink', comfrey

X = *Symphytum* × *uplandicum, Variegatum,* the variegated comfrey

Y = *Viola odorata*

There are also annual Opium Poppies, Wild Larkspur, Godetia and clumps of Carex pendula, *that self-seed and come up in any open patches.*

Pleasant Valley, New York

December 16, 1991

What can I say, Roger? Oh, to be in England, where the flowers bloom all year! Nasturtium-killing frost came to New York in late September, it feels like eons ago. So far we've had precious little snow but the growing season is definitely over for at least a couple of months. *Our* key dates have been October 26, when Bill went out to the swamp behind the garden and shot (with bow and arrow) a large deer that will provide our winter meat; November 25, when I finally got the last of 22 big clumps of peonies out from under the overgrown lilacs and into safekeeping behind the vegetables; and December 4, when we discovered froggie hiding in the Christmas cactus.

I'm not much of a houseplant fan so all we have are a few odds and ends: A "Red Planet" fibrous begonia that has refused to die for so long it's become part of the family, a bucket of pink cannas that were still going strong when I packed up the Maine garden for the winter, a potful of *Asarina scandens* that moved indoors without complaint when winter arrived, and (point of story) the good sized *Schlumbergera × buckleyi* that old Mrs. Katsaros, Peter's mom, gave Bill as a housewarming gift.

Pace houseplants, one good thing to be said for epicacti is they don't need much attention, and not much attention is just what we've bestowed on Mrs. K's present. But then that day I was peering at it—rather balefully, only one or two buds and here comes Christmas so maybe in spite of the floppy joints it's actually *Rhipsalis gartneri* and won't do anything till Easter—when I saw a tiny frog crouched down near the base of the plant. It blinked, bubbled out its throat, and turned its head ever so slightly. I stared. Called the family. We stared. It bubbled its throat. End of interaction. Succeeding days have been just the same. He's cute, but he ain't lively.

Evidently, he's been with us since September, minding his (or her, it's impossible to tell) own business and we've never heard a peep out of him. So although he's probably a *Hyla versicolor,* the Common Gray Tree Frog, he *might* be *H. chrysoscelis,* Cope's Gray Treefrog. According to the Audubon Field Guide, the two species can only be told apart by their songs and their chromosome counts. Whatever he is, he's about the size of a quarter (4.5 cm) and either a sort of mottled pewter or a bright, rather bluish green depending on what he's been sitting on.

The book says "they live high in trees and descend only at night, usually just to chorus and to breed." Poor froggie, precious little of either *he's* enjoying. Bill had frogs in his greenhouse over on Verbank Road, and he says the beastlet will do fine until spring (when we'll let him go) with no help from us, but I think we'd better feed him. I gave him a couple of moth larvae—from a box of crackers that had become infested in the back reaches of the pantry closet—and they were very warmly engulfed.

Spring seems far away. There's not much we can do right now but prune a bit and plan a lot. For starters we have fenced the vegetable gardens, a pair of fifty-foot squares in the center of the lot across the roadway. Right now it's just wire mesh to keep out rabbits, dogs, and the less enterprising deer, but there's white picket to come. Everything in the neighborhood—or, more accurately, everything attractive—is mid-late Queen Anne or Mansard, white with black or green shutters and trim, so there isn't a lot of leeway in the design department. A real change from Maine: if it ain't regular, it ain't right. Even Bill, whose tastes incline to the picturesque, agrees.

He's at work building a new arbor to replace the falling down one. The new version will be slightly larger, even closer to the Eastern edge of the property, and quite a bit taller, all with an eye toward privacy enhancement. Our neighbor's drive is right on *her* side of the line, and there's no cover other than the lilacs. In time, there will be tall evergreens (uninspired but necessary; that way also lies a loud highway).

Meanwhile, grapes should help to do the job; this seems to be an ideal climate for them in spite of the summer heat (and the Japanese beetles). Last year the present incumbents made a huge thicket even though there are only two vines: a Concord and a seedless white that's probably Interlaken. Unpruned since Eden, they both have long, gnarley trunks and multiple arms. And both, contrary to all received wisdom, last year bore enormous crops that were mostly enjoyed by the birds. My guess is that they were planted in the fifties.

No knowing when the bittersweet came, but the evil stuff sure is well established, hideously robust, *everywhere*. It's woven in all of the flower beds, sprouting forth among the raspberries, waving in tall plumes high above the 50 foot juniper next to the carriage house. Bill gets periodic fits of bittersweet removal mania, but I just try to yank up a bit whenever I'm near one, on the "no flies in China" theory. "No" is not to be, of course, bittersweet is the kudzu of the North. Or the sort-of-North. By the time you get to New England, it's not nearly as much of a problem.

Same, alas, with the poison ivy, a scourge scarcely known in Maine that's more or less endemic here. I'm still not used to it. At Thanksgiving I almost picked several branches of the lovely ivory berries to decorate the house, was saved only by vine-recognition at the very last minute. Mercifully, there are zillions of hairy little rootlets that grow all over the trunks of older specimens, and this unmistakable feature provides a most welcome warning.

The sneezeweed, completely unknown in Maine, is quite pretty and

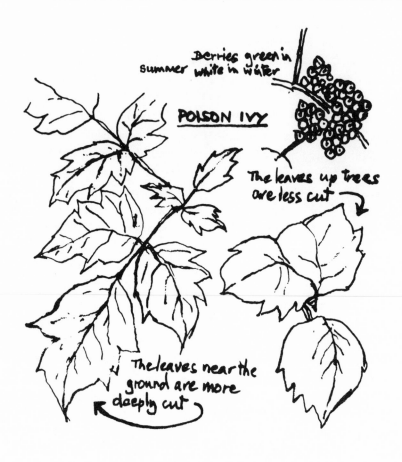

Berries green in summer white in winter

POISON IVY

The leaves up trees are less cut

The leaves near the ground are more deeply cut

easy to pluck up, unlike the ladies' bedstraw, which is quite pretty and not so easy to pluck up. The roots are right at the surface, but matty, and you never get them all. There's onion grass, too. Lots of onion grass. I see in *Wild Food* that all the wild alliums are edible. Where have I gotten this dim memory that there is a poisonous one, or a poisonous look/smell-alike? Our lawns and gardens are full of the stuff. Again, nothing like it in Maine.

I never dreamed the look, feel, smell, light of the place would be so foreign when so much is familiar. The difference between an evergreen-dominated treescape (Maine's sobriquet is "The Pine Tree State") and this domain of oak and maple, locust and sycamore is enough to make being in New York like being in a far-off country, even though I haven't so much as left my home climate zone. New Zealand seems almost unimaginable, and Christmas in New Zealand an adventure indeed.

We had the tree-trimming party just last night, having gotten the guest of honor at the last minute, the day before yesterday. Bill and Celia went out in a rainstorm to their friend John Forman's place, where there's a forest of overgrown Christmas trees that were somehow or other left unharvested until long past saleability. B. climbed a very large fir, cut off the top twenty feet or so, and brought the top twelve of that home. We further reduced it to seven and a half feet and in it came, without breaking anything *mirabile dictu*.

Celia had two of her friends over and we had a quartet of Bill's dear old pals: Gil and Margaret Nyhoff and Sue Hart and her partner, Jim Flynn. Like N.Y. itself, all was the same yet different. I made the gingerbread disks with blackstrap molasses this year—an accident that yielded gorgeous color (very dark and glistening) but did little for taste (bitter and dull). So the ornaments were strictly for show.

But having them icing painted by the children was a definite plus, as were the kids themselves—talk about a great time with the mistletoe! Jim, who is an architect, has the same precision of technique as my friend Chris. And a new ritual is in the making now that Celia is part of my life.

Last year when I was first getting to know her I gave her a Christmas ornament—just because it was pretty. This year, I got her some tiny brass French horns, a salute to her growing skill on that difficult instrument. Next year who knows, but there will be something. She's nine now, so by the time she's ready to set up housekeeping she'll have a nice little collection to hang on her own tree, pretty mementoes of Christmases past to help make a new place home.

I've certainly brought enough baggage here with that same end in mind; my grandmother's rocker for the living room, sage from Maine for hedging what we've taken to calling the garden of unknown roses. It seems to be working. The black hollyhocks look as good against the walls of this big white house as they did against the weathered gray ones of the little cottage. Turnabout being fair play, I plan to bring several clumps of New York's overabundant *tradescantia* to Maine, expect them to look right at home in the blue border.

Now I feel as well as understand the impulse to lilacs that moved the pioneers, now know that it was more than simply wanting to have lilacs when they got there. You take fuller possession of new ground when you grow old plants in it, prove to your heart that you too can thrive on unfamiliar soil.

I reread your letter and think of those less fortunate—almost everybody—and What Is To Be Done! And then I too think gardening is more fun and then I feel guilty and *then* I think: Well, wait a minute. The big problems: poverty, wars, the whole caboodle, all boil down in the end to one basic question: who gets to eat good food, breathe clean air and smell a few flowers in peace? And the answer is going to be "nobody," if we don't get our ecological act together.

So we might as well start in the garden, where the few home truths that have widest application are (are they ever!) ever-present: only the energy of the sun is limitless; balance is essential; human intervention is both inevitable and okay. The human hand, eye, mind and heart are also part of the garden, as natural as spruce trees, as lions and tigers, as swamp mud and weeds.

If I understand your travel plans correctly, Christmas will be history by the time you read this. But we'll have been thinking of you on the day, and again at midnight on the 31st when we plan to follow what I

believe is an old Viennese custom. As the clock strikes 12, we will all hold hands and jump off the couch as far as we can—away from the troubles of the past and into the New Year.
Until then,

Best Love
Leslie

Eccleston Square,
London

Dear Leslie,

The trip to the Antipodes was mind boggling: thousands of plants so different from our northern things, it's like being lost in a vast ocean of plants without a chart.

I started out in Auckland by visiting a man with a native plant nursery, called Graeme Platt. After about half an hour poking about in the nursery he proposed taking me out into the last area of native rainforest left in the Auckland district. I was dressed for mid-summer, just shorts and T-shirt, everyone having told me how dreadfully hot it would be. Wrong, I was absolutely frozen. As soon as we got to the rainforest it started chucking it down and in two minutes I was a crawling sponge.

One of the things I had planned to shoot in New Zealand was a group of wild tree ferns for the forthcoming *Annuals* book. Back in England I had done quite a bit of research to make sure that I would be able to find a good site. Wrong again. They were everywhere, virtually pushing up between the paving stones, covering old railway embankments and battling their way back towards the greens of a recently opened golf course. Apart from the rain and the cold it was very dull and dark which made photography incredibly difficult; I had to hand-hold at one eighth of a second at f3.5 (the only way to do that is to lean the camera against a tree or a log).

Apart from the stunning ferns, tree and giant ground (or should they be called shrub) ferns, the most remarkable thing was the giant kauri trees. The trunks are totally round and perfectly straight for about the first fifty feet without a single branch, then they continue up to a good two hundred and fifty feet and, like everything else down there, they are evergreen. They must be like a dream come true to a logger because the diameter of the trunk is something like sixteen feet, all of it excellent wood, for although they live to as much as 3000 years, they get very little heart rot. Graeme has been studying the way they grow all his life and has, in the last ten years or so, been able to start a breeding programme.

Firstly, he selects the best specimens in the forest, then he collects the seeds suspended from a helicopter! Getting seedlings started is not a problem but getting them to grow well has been the sticking point. Graeme's solution is not to dig holes and plant them in the soil but to put them down on top of the soil and spread out the roots and then cover them with rotted forest leaf mould. Of course you have to keep them very wet. It works like a dream; his three-year-old plants were putting on about three feet of growth a year. As far as I could see this growth was due to the mycorhizal symbiosis of the fungi that were rotting down the leaf litter. Even if mycorhizal fungi were not the mystery ingredient it must have been leaf-rotting fungi breaking down the leaf litter that supplied them with their nutrients.

After drying out there was a little reception in the hotel in Auckland, the address of which mystified me – 'Private Bag'. Is it a reference to their clients? We drank delicious local Chardonnay, but, and this is what I was knocked out by, we ate Kumara chips; to us in England they would be 'crisps'. Anyway, they were made from sweet potatoes, the big round yellowish type with yellow flesh. In New Zealand they call them golden Kumara. It was my gastronomic treat of the whole trip.

Many radio shows later (New Zealanders are very passionate about radio) I went to see Sam McGredy, the great rose breeder, the fourth Sam McGredy in line from the Irish rose breeders of Portadown. Twenty years ago Sam moved to New Zealand and has found the climate perfect for roses. 'I feel sorry for my old friends back in Europe spending money on greenhouses and then having to pay to heat them as well,' he said. Sam was terrific company, a great bear of a man with bristling grey hair and the strength and energy to carry the world's rose production on his back. He had kept back, to show me, the flowers on his latest crop of seedlings, fifty thousand bred from seven thousand crosses, this meant I could see them in all their glory. After I left all the flowers were to be cut and chucked out and about sixty per cent of the plants would be discarded also. Eventually he hopes that about four from this massive programme would come into cultivation. His passion of the moment? Sam believes that the Hybrid Tea is the way to go. He feels breeders have neglected them in recent years – thus few excellent Hybrid Tea roses have been bred and the public have started buying Floribundas and Old Roses. Sam is trying to develop some new striped Hybrid Tea varieties for the future.

Down to the South Island, more radio, etc. but on my last day I got the chance to go up in the high alpine mountain area with a local expert plantsman, Derek Rooney. We went up from sea level to about eight thousand feet, the snow line. The mountains are incredibly young in geological terms. Mount Cook is getting taller at the rate of about a quarter of an inch a year. Being so young, the higher areas have no soil at all: the slopes consist almost entirely of scree. We left Derek's Land-Rover and climbed up steep cliffs for an hour or two, finding the most extraordinary plants, me photographing desperately as we went until I sat down to look at a flower and the camera tipped out of my bag and started on a thousand-foot journey to the bottom of the scree and total destruction.

A New Zealand fact. There are only two native mammals, both bats!

Now Australia. Cars and trucks have bars on the front here, called roo bars. At night kangaroos leap into the road and then stand still in the lights. I am sure the bars are the same as Americans sometimes have to protect themselves against leaping deer. The only wild kangaroo I saw was a dead one on the roadside when I drove from Sydney to Canberra to see the Australian National Botanic Gardens. The long drive was well worth it, about two hundred acres of native plants set in a completely natural eucalyptus forest setting. I wandered around totally out of my depth amongst plants and forms absolutely new to me. I was conscious enough to shoot about twenty rolls of film though.

Christmas Day this year we spent on the beach of Mornington Peninsula, just south of Melbourne; it was a blissful 80 degrees, we had a small barbecued turkey (cold) which we tore to bits with our fingers. Phoebe went fishing – her new-found passion. That day she caught nothing but two days later we got up at dawn and had another try and she caught a Japanese blow fish. I didn't know what it was and we would have eaten it and probably died the instant death that the Japanese go in for every year, if we had not boasted of our catch to a local in the hotel who was able to put a name to it and warn us off it. On Boxing Day I went to see the cricket – the first day of a five-day Test match, Australia v. India, at the MCG (Melbourne Cricket Ground). Australia has a terrific tall lanky bowler called Reed who tore through the Indian batsmen. No doubt I have lost you. The last time I took an American to see cricket he could not believe how one game could last five days.

After Melbourne we flew to Perth. I was very excited to get amongst the wild flowers but January is really too late in the season, early September would be better. Never mind. I found more than I could take in. I drove north about a hundred miles up into the bush. It is astounding; miles and miles of shrubby woods consisting mainly of banksias with the occasional bright yellow grevillea poking out above them. I managed to get the car stuck up a dirt road and was just contemplating survival without water in near desert conditions – could I eat the giant fat lizards that were all over the place when a truck pulled up, the driver jumped out with a heavy-duty chain and pulled me out, 'G'day,' he said. 'You could have been here for days. I am the only fella ever uses this track.'

Back in England everything seems very small and old-fashioned. As a nation we have totally failed to invest in our future. I feel that it is most depressing: unless something radical happens we will become a very minor museum with our only asset our tourism. Oh well, maybe that will be better than the brash world motivated only by more money that I have seen so much of on this trip. Singapore for instance looked as if it handled as much shipping, or more, than all the ports in Britain put together.

Fujita, the people who got me to plan that garden square, are holding fire on the laying out of the Loudon garden. I suppose even the Japanese fear recession. What a shame. It was a real chance to do something with historical significance.

The first camellias are bursting into bloom – it's going to be a bumper crop. There are about twice as many buds as ever before!

Love,

Roger

P.S. Yes, I would love some morning glory seeds. I am desperate for good ones this year. Do you still have them?

February 1992–September 1993

Leslie spent 1992 adjusting to a bifurcated life, building the garden in New York while refining the one in Maine. In March, Bill went to Maine with her and they built a room on to the cottage for Celia, whose attachment to Maine was further cemented by two long summer visits. Winter brought increasing work for *House and Garden*, but spring of '93 saw that sixty-year-old publication fold. Leslie then became the food and garden director for *First*, a mass-circulation women's magazine sold in supermarkets. The position demanded much more time than her previous writing work, and required her to commute regularly to bleak offices in New Jersey, a two-hour drive from Pleasant Valley. The summer of 1993 was spent "in Maine, but at the desk," with garden work largely confined to evenings, weekends, and Bill.

Roger has spent a tremendous amount of time on television projects as well as non-stop work on the series of garden plant books he does with Martyn Rix. *Vegetables* was published in October 1993; currently they are working on a volume of conservatory plants for publication in about a year's time. He has also been working on an illustrated guide to garden history with Nicky Foy, a project that has caused almost non-stop travel.

Cushing, Maine

October 19, 1993

Dear Roger,

I'm on a flying trip to Maine, closing down the house, tidying up the garden. Feeling elegiac about the end of summer and feeling fed up with the telephone. Completely apart from the expense, there's something about our current mode of long-distance communication, something so ... I find myself wanting to say so impersonal. Quite a paradox, no? Our voices should make the medium more intimate, not less, yet ... Anyway, I've missed your letters and figure if I'm going to get any I'll have to write some myself. The big news is that I've planned major work on both house and garden, dormer and lawn respectively, all of it to be done over the winter while I'm not here—which is going to be interesting you bet. Endless discussions with workmen have replaced the usual weeding and mouse-proofing as end-of-season occupations. Still, I think it's worth a try; my few experiences of having work done while living in the house have convinced me it's much better to be as far away as possible during the actual event. That way the workers will have complete freedom to work and I will be spared daily agonizings and sawdust in the stew.

PLAN ONE, THE HOUSE: Neighbor Bob Matus, carpenter extraordinaire, will build a dormer while repairing the south roof. The thing is leaking like a bandit and must be replaced, so now's the time to add on if I'm ever going to. Lois's son Eli and daughter-in-law Robin are both architects and while they were here in September they made a dandy little model as well as many suggestions. Our goal is to get maximum light and space with minimum aesthetic damage—no easy task, as it turns out, given that the house is so ideally cottagey just as it stands, a moss covered, silver-weathered square with a very steeply pitched roof. Here's what; dormers are ugly and large dormers are uglier.

Nevertheless, by stepping the thing well back from the edge, using multipaned windows and weathered-looking roofing I hope to build something that looks as though it's been around here for years. Same deal with

PLAN TWO, THE GARDEN: in which neighbor Bill Long (an experienced landscaper who usually works for rich people with large estates) will bring bulldozers and megafill and do an earth sculpture/recontour of the back slope between the house and the lower garden. People have been falling down that steep hill for years; it's really treacherous after rain and even dew is enough to create a serious hazard. Many versions of grass-covered steps were considered and discarded as too grand before we decided to try and do the whole thing with terracing. One step at the top is essential, but other than that I'm hoping we can slice into the slope decisively enough to eliminate the need for any hardscape. Bill is skeptical but willing to try and he promises walkable grass by early May. We shall see.

It's costing immense sums, of course, but if it works out as planned no one will be able to tell that anything has been done at all. The price of tasteful alteration, I suppose. Regrettably, the immense sums are being provided by the loathsome job in New Jersey so I'm going to have to go back soon—probably the day after tomorrow, in fact, and before I go I've got to get the bulbs in. Not many this year but I do intend a good show of white tulips and a few (only fifty) *T. clusiana chrysantha* for the poppy walk. These little dots of color coming up through the poppy greenery will, I hope, be a cheery reminder that something other than chickweed is getting going in mid-garden in early spring.

And you? I expect the square is still blooming rosily and that it's too

early for bulb planting but I do long to hear from you and hope you will write soon!
Love,

Leslie

P.S. This seems to be a splendid apple year. All the wild ones that fringe the lower garden are loaded with fruit and the quality of the local orchards' offerings is very high. I depend primarily on the latter for dessert fruit, pies and the like, since our own is what might be called the dark side of organic. We don't spray at all and scarcely prune, so our apples are all buggy, misshapen and small. Still, the deer love them; they smell good rotting; and I usually manage to find a few good bits to season whatever apple item I'm making from purchased fruit.

Applesauce, for instance, is based on the sweet yet sharp McIntosh that's practically the state apple (amazing the difference between freshly harvested, well-grown northern macs and the insipid cardboard specimens that pass for them in the supermarket) but I always throw in a few chunks of fruit from the tree that for want of a better name Lois and I call The Best Green. It's actually yellowish once ripe, with a bit of a red blush. The flavor is sharp on the edge of sour but very spicy as well—it doesn't taste like any other I've ever eaten except maybe a little like golden russet. Now there's an apple! Hard to get, alas, although things seem to be improving in the heirloom apple department. When I went to the big greenmarket in Union Square (New York City) last October there were not one, not two but three different orchards all selling dozens of varieties: Newtown Pippins and Jonathans and Northern Spies (my fave for pies), and Rhode Island Greenings and Winesaps (I like a couple of these quartered inside a roast chicken and then baste it with Calvados) and Baldwins, Empires, Cortlands . . . as I write it comes to me New York really is the great apple state. We're too far north here for the late varieties, which are the tastiest as far as I can tell.

What's the situation over there? Jane Grigson's *Fruit Book*, my favorite on these matters, has a wonderful apple chapter in which she complains about the low quality and boring sameness of English commercial apples . . . it sounds like absolutely the same story as here, only the names being different. Copyright is '82 so perhaps things have improved . . .

Roast Chicken with Apples and Calvados

For a 4-pound roasting chicken to serve 4 to 6 you need:

6 medium-sized flavorful tart apples such as Spitzenbergs or Northern Spies, peeled, quartered and cored

2 large cloves of garlic, cut into thin, flat slices

flour for dusting

1 to 2 tablespoons of soft butter for bird, another for the sauce

2 large onions, cut in thick rings

a handful of parsley, several sprigs of thyme

½ cup Calvados

Remove the extra fat from the chicken and render enough to coat a heavy, shallow, nonreactive roasting pan. (Add butter if there isn't enough fat.) Put the pan over medium heat, add 8 of the apple quarters and cook, turning occasionally, until they are slightly softened and starting to brown. Let 'em cool.

While this is going on, loosen the chicken skin and insert garlic slices between skin and flesh wherever possible. Heat the oven to 450°F. Stuff the chicken with the cooked apples. Pat the skin dry with paper towels, then dust it lightly with flour. Rub the butter over the bird, sprinkle generously with salt and pepper.

In the unwashed pan, make a bed of the onion slices. Put apples on top and strew with the parsley and thyme. Put the chicken on the bed and pour ⅓ cup Calvados around (not over) it.

Cook for 15 minutes, then lower the heat to 375°F and cook 1 hour and 20 minutes longer, or until juices run clear when the thick part of the thigh is pricked with a fork. Baste two or three times with the pan juices during the first 40 minutes of cooking.

Remove chicken to a serving platter, discard parsley and thyme and carefully lift out onions and apples. Place these around bird. Degrease pan juices (which I do by pouring them into one of those gravy separators) and set aside. Pour a generous $1/2$ cup water into the pan and simmer, stirring and scraping, to get up all the browned bits. Combine pan gravy with degreased chicken juices and gently swirl in a heaping tablespoon of butter. Place in sauceboat.

Warm remaining Calvados, pour over bird and light. (This is not strictly showing off; the flames burn away the raw spirit taste and add a nice flavor to the chicken skin.)

Eccleston Square,
London

15 November 1993

Dear Leslie,

Lovely to get a letter from you after so long. Telephone calls are daft, expensive, always inconvenient and you never really say what you rang for in the first place. YES, YES, YES (as Fats Waller used to say), let's get down to writing again.

There have been loads of occasions when I have been wandering round the garden and thought, 'I will write and tell Leslie about that.'

FACT. Years ago I put a bunch of Nirenes in a very shady area, dotted Autumn crocus amongst them and then filled the whole thing out with *Liriope muscaria*. RESULT: years of nothing much, but this year, eureka! They have all flowered really well and all at the same time. I imagine that this is the result of our eight-year drought coming to an end. Yes, England is back to her old ways; plenty of rain, plenty of dull days, plenty of wonderful growth on all the plants.

Before I get started on my projects for next year a thought on the things you are doing; good idea to stop people falling down into the lower garden – the last thing you need is to get sued (we over here live in terror of sue-happy Americans). I vote for grass steps, hard landscaping will take away from your country cottage in the big woods, and that lovely wild garden that just runs away into the back country. As for the dormer window – done well, it will fit in, I am sure.

Two big projects are on the go. Stephen and Kim Mai, my Irish mates, have bought the ruins of Penn Castle near Cork and I have to go over to talk gardens to them.

The other is that my publishers (they used to be Pan Books but now I come under the banner of the parent company, Macmillan) have decided that it's time they got into electronic publishing; CD-ROM and all that. I love the idea. It means I can really use my pent-up experience in TV to let rip – you, though will have to wait two or three years to see the results. This kind of work takes for ever and costs an arm and a leg.

More on these two projects later as things get under way.

You know I told you about my TV thing *The Quest for the Rose?* It is all but done – one more session in the voice recording studio will tie up all the loose ends. I can hardly speak my voice is so hoarse from about seven hundred attempts to get the commentary right.

You ask about apples and special varieties over here. Well, we suffer from a surfeit of dull supermarket rubbish – perfect looking, but not worth eating. Not possible for me to set up the Square as an apple or-chard, but yes, I can get great apples. My friend Jocelyn put me on to it. The Royal Horticultural Society at Wisley have an experimental old fruit trial and they sell off the fruit week by week as it ripens (cheap too). Not only did I get some superb apples this year, I got loads of Quinces. Jocelyn has Spanish in-laws and they got her interested in Membrillo (Quince sweeties). Wonderful! Amy and I go potty for them.

More next time – over to you,

Love,

Roger

Cushing, Maine

January 5, 1994

New Year Greetings from icy Maine, where I'm staying with our pals the Magees and where it's cold and cold and cold again. The frost is especially deep this year, ground frozen solid five feet down instead of the usual three. At this rate, it'll probably be July before the place thaws completely. Fortunately, it's also totally snowy, which ought to keep the cold safely in; we have the worst problems (frost heave and rot) in open winters, and whatever the faults of this one, it isn't that.

I'm up to confer about construction details—happy to report the new dormer promises to be splendid. Lots of light upstairs at last and (until the cherries leaf out) wonderful views of the upper garden. Regrettably, it looks like the whole world will also have wonderful views of us. I fear a future containing curtains, my least favorite thing. The answer might be simple shades in some kind of light-admitting fabric, possibly old lace tablecloths from my large supply of damaged antiques but maybe plain oatmeal-colored linen if good taste for some reason prevails. As at the moment the thing is without roof or windows (or me) it isn't a problem that must be solved right away.

Right away is clearing up really a lot of tindery debris, because The Grand Pruning has taken place. The eyesore dead hackamatack, all 40 feet of it, is down. My old friend Sam did the deed with his chainsaw in about 2 minutes. Before this, of course, were 20 minutes of dire warnings—among other things the stupid tree was leaning in the wrong direction and there was quite a stiff wind. I was highly concerned about the greenhouse until he started asking how fond I was of the arbor vitae!

In the event he used the wind and put the thing down smack in the middle of the garden. I think the edge of at least one raised bed is terminally lunched but I am rid of a major problem and happily relieved. And I didn't have to ask anyone's permission to do it.

Love.

Leslie

Eccleston Square,
London

Dear Leslie,

Happy New Year!

Before I start on about the plants let me tell you the mad thing that happened on Christmas morning: The telephone rang at 8:50 and the old lady who lives next door, Mrs. James, came on the line: 'Mr Phillips,' she said, 'something very frightening has happened to me in the garden this morning as I was walking my little dogs. We were attacked by a ferocious peacock.' My immediate thought was how magical and what a treat for the children on Christmas morning. Duty bound I went down to the garden (having first donned a pair of trousers). Grave disappointment – the menacing bird turned out to be a Canada goose! It picked a dangerous day to risk life and the oven!

Now garden talk. People always feel that winter is an easy time in the garden but, here anyway, that's rubbish; we always have loads of work to do in the winter. We have twenty-nine large forest trees, mainly London Planes. As well as large trees we have eighty-five smaller trees and millions of shrubs. This gives us a terrific leaf fall which takes us until mid January to clear – thank goodness for the shredder. I have been putting more work in on my ecological ham cooking oven this year. So I bought myself a twenty-pound ham – nothing is done by half measures – and then tried to figure out how to cook it to perfection. It worked out OK last time, but I did wake up in the middle of the night wondering if I had poisoned the whole family. So this time I have gone into it in greater depth, even using a meat thermometer. Mrs. Beeton, in my 1906 edition, says '. . . for boiling a very large ham six hours . . .' As usual dear Mrs B was a bit cursory on the details so I consulted my friend Elizabeth Luard, who wrote a great book on peasant cooking, *European Peasant Cookery*. She did a bit of digging for me and told me that her father-in-law, who uses a hay box every week, said the technique is to heat things up first and then put them in for a long slow cook. But no one had any idea how long (except me – I knew that five days was too long). In the end I decided that I would just go for it.

This is how it went: I boiled the ham for an hour and a bit, whipped it out, skinned it, chucked on some bread crumbs and then wrapped it in brown paper followed by cling film, then into the leaf heap. The temperature was over 60 degrees centigrade (140 Fahrenheit). Twenty-four hours later it was ready to serve. At the same time I put in a jug of mulled wine, plus a jug of what looked like mulled wine but was in fact mulled grape juice, for the kids.

Recipe: One bottle good rich Spanish wine, one cinnamon stick, one ¼ teaspoon cinnamon powder, one whole orange chopped up in chunks, six whole cloves stuck in the peel of the orange, one cup of water, two heaped dessertspoons of sugar.

The next day I organized a boules party in the garden – only us, the kids and two or three friends. The game was going well or quite well (I was on the losing side), when I snuck off to the leaf mould heap with the children and produced a complete hot meal in seconds. We all needed it as the day was cold, dull and damp and our hands were freezing from handling the metal boules. It all went down great, unless everyone was just being polite. Anyway, the ham was cooked and the wine and juice were steaming hot – a bit of a miracle!

Nicky and I are very keen on organic food. The way I rationalize it is this: for 10,000 years the human race lived and thrived on organic food but for the last fifty years food has been more and more chemically produced – my fear is that if we carry on like this for another hundred years or so, we will begin to see the genetic effects of all these nitrates, weed and pest killers and, worst of all, the growth hormones, antibiotics and the sprays used to ripen fruit. Enough of me blathering on.

Nicky, who is much more worried about chemicals than me (and especially the effect on our children), thinks we should go into full scale organic production on our balcony. At the moment I am growing lamb's lettuce, lettuce and a large crop of Rocket (Roquette). Whatever you call it it's fantastic in winter; it keeps on and on growing. I've got about twenty plants and by just cutting the lower leaves I have a constant supply. Apart from lettuces, I have got two wild flowers – Three Cornered Leek (*Allium triquetrum*) which grows wild in southern Britain and has thin onion-flavoured leaves. I use it for stir-fry. The other one is an obnoxious garden weed called Hairy Bittercress (*Cardamine hirsuta*); we use it in salads – the flavour is rather hot like watercress to which it is related. This is where you come in. Next spring I want to grow enough tomatoes to keep us going through the late summer. I grew four plants last year and they did well. Seven or eight plants should see me through. I need your advice as to varieties for salad tomatoes; flavour is the top priority, after that I like some interesting colours for decorating salads. Can you send me half a dozen seeds of some of your favourites and we can see how they do for us?

I have gathered up a few bits and pieces to press and give you a chance to see what is on the go in January: loads of different Hellebores, Witch Hazel (this is an American variety 'Arnold Promise'), *Callicarpa bodinieri* is still a mass of purple berries, *Viburnum bodnantense,* great scent, *Rhododendron dauricum* one of the only Rhodos I can grow in my neutral soil, also a few petals of my first camellia 'Berenice Brody'.

This winter is again very mild. I take my frost values from looking at the nasturtium plants — when they shrivel up and die I know there has actually been a ground frost of about two degrees. This year it has only just happened and the ones in the tall pots on the patio are still alive! Love, wishes to Bill

Roger

Pleasant Valley,
New York

January 26, 1994

Dear Roger,

Thank you for your nice New Year's letter, as usual it fills me with awe to contemplate London weather. Boules! The boules would sink about 3 feet through the snow if you tried to play here. It will be months before I can even plant *my* hellebore, a fine (potentially) large, green-flowered *H. corsicus* purchased last fall at Carey Arboretum. Twice a year they have a 2-day sale where civilians like me can buy divisions of their choice plants. It's always an obscene crush and you must go earlier than the advertised opening or you won't get anything interesting. But did I immediately plant this hard won prize? I did not. As usual, desire preceded planning and there was no appropriate spot. The plant has made it through the winter so far in a pot indoors, leggy and pale but still livin' so with any luck it will survive until spring. Bill and I are planning to build a small woodland area in the southeast corner of the yard here—a "woodland" about 1,400 feet square—and the hellebore will go there along with anything and everything else that wants a bit of shade, which right now we have not got.

It's just at the beginning stages right now (see drawing), but the idea is to eventually have a little glade that will 1. add interest to the otherwise boringly rectangular back yard and 2. block out the sight and sound of a major highway that's only a block away and sounds nearer, especially

in the wintertime. A very narrow path will wind through, but other than
that it'll be solid and about 40 feet deep. I'm looking forward to choosing
the plants but already see I'm not going to get to choose many. (Had big
plans for the lilac walk that approaches the wood from the north side and
it turns out I get to buy about 3 more kinds. Rats! I want fifty, at least.)

Also want to be in London next New Year so I can attend the party . . .
though I must say it sounds as though you left the ham in there a helluva
long time. Did you make any sandwiches combining the leftovers with
the rocket on the balcony? That's one of my favorite combinations, especially with aioli.

The seeds are in Maine at the moment—I have to go up soon and will
send you the requested tomates as soon as I get there.

Meanwhile, Bill sends love. I send that and the recipe for my favorite
easy aioli/skordalia hybrid—just in case you don't already have a favorite
aioli and assuming raw English eggs are not forbidden. (We're having a
big salmonella *furore* here, largely because of some scary food poisonings.
I believe all of 'em were caused by restaurants, where large quantitites of
raw eggs get mixed together and then get to sit around, but the net result
has been total panic and you can't call for raw eggs in print anymore—
very inconvenient and I think a bit silly unless you're a vulnerable type
(elderly, AIDS, babies) and if you are I should think you'd know it and
act accordingly when reading recipes.)

xxxx Leslie

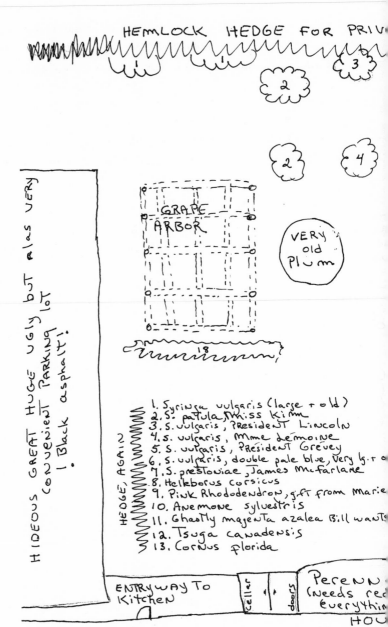

HEMLOCK HEDGE FOR PRIV

3

2

2

4

GRAPE ARBOR

VERY old Plum

HIDEOUS GREAT HUGE UGLY but alas VERY convenient parking lot ! Black asphalt !

'8

HEDGE, AGAIN

1. Syringa vulgaris (large + old)
2. S. patula, Miss Kim
3. S. vulgaris, President Lincoln
4. S. vulgaris, Mme Lemoine
5. S. vulgaris, President Grévey
6. S. vulgaris, double pale blue, Very lg. + o
7. S. prestoviae, James McFarlane
8. Helleborus corsicus
9. Pink Rhododendron, gift from Marie
10. Anemone sylvestris
11. Ghastly magenta azalea Bill wants
12. Tsuga canadensis
13. Cornus florida

ENTRYWAY TO Kitchen

cellar   doors

Perenn
(needs red
everythin
HOU

QUIET GOES AROUND EAST AND SOUTH ↓

6   8   9   10   11   12

17

7   13   13

14

16

15   12

17

"FOREST" AREA →

APPLE
OF
CONTENTION
(I want to
cut it down;
Bill doesn't)

BACK
YARD
N.Y.

14. Vaccinium corymbosum, Patriot
15. peach azalea I want to keep
16. Clethra alnifolia
17. thuja occidentalis nigra
18. aristolochia durior (on ancient trellis, falling down)

To the rose
AND HERB GARDEN
↓

ed
ong with
e

Semi-Aioli, Semi-Legit

For a generous 2 cups:

6 cloves garlic

1 teaspoon salt

1 small floury potato, boiled and
  mashed (about $^1/_2$ cup)

3 very fresh egg yolks (preferably
from a local farmer with a small
operation rather than from a giant
egg factory)

$1^1/_2$ cups nice fruity olive oil

unstrained juice of 1 large lemon

Mash the garlic with the salt until it is pureed. Combine thoroughly with
potato and egg yolks. Add the oil in the usual manner, first drop by drop,
then in a very thin, sturdy stream. It'll be thick; thin with a few drops
of water from time to time if necessary. Beat in lemon juice, then 2 or 3
tablespoons tepid water. I think I learned about the water from the Alice
B. Toklas cookbook. Neat trick.

Cushing, Maine

February 1, 1994

Hello from the Magees' again.

I seem to be spending half my life up here—using the excuse of checking on my various projects but the truth is I think I'm just homesick for Maine. Right now the place is at its coldest. A bit of the snow is gone but what's left is glazed over solid with ice. There's a thick skin of ice on the trees, on the twigs, on steps and railings and gutters and sills. Everything sparkles in the . . . I was going to say thin sunlight but it isn't. Already there's a faint smell of spring and the light is getting stronger and brighter every day.

Time to get the seedlings going. I've cut way down on the flowers but with vegetables what choice is there? After asparagus, all is annual when you live in Maine, so I've got Francey the faithful seed starter up to her ears in eggplants, assorted herbs and about 40,000 tomatoes. Especially excited about Green Zebra, a round tomato with green stripes on a yellow ground that should be gorgeous if it works out. It's bound to be prettier than my old favorite Evergreen, which was one of its parents, but I'm not sure it'll be as sweet. Can't plant both; there won't be room if I'm going to have at least two of everything on a list that appears to be dominated by open-pollinated oldies, probably because the catalogs make them sound so appealing. Who could resist something supposedly saved for posterity by a Native American gardener active in the 1930s? It's called Djeena Lee's Golden Girl and will be my yellow slicer for this year. I'm also planning on Riesentraube, both delicious and unspeakably prolific if we are to believe the catalog. There will be Green Grape—tastiest cherry tomato going—and Sugar cherry, supposedly an improved currant type with more tender skin. White Wonder is on the list, in the hopes it will be tastier than the hardy but rather bland White Beauty. Yellow Bell, La Rossa paste . . . when it comes to tomatoes I'm just a girl who can't say no.

There will be two, four or six plants of each, depending, but a nice comfortable dozen of the Brandywines. Don't know where I'll find the space but there's no way to do with fewer and get enough fruit to put up. As I believe I've mentioned before these are the totally top tomatoes— fruit like sweet wine and more complex. You taste a wonderful tomato at first bite and then you have another wonderful tomato in the aftertaste. And you feel you deserve it because they're so damned hard to grow.

With that caveat, here are the seeds. Maybe you'll be lucky and there'll be a record heat wave and it will be warm and sunny in London for 80 days (from setting out). I do think it would help if you rigged up something to protect them from wind. That balcony of yours is bound to be drafty and Brandywines wind stress even more easily than tomatoes in general. I'd send along something earlier, more cold-tolerant or otherwise better suited to British weather if I thought it were worth it, but where you have such limited space you might as well go for broke and devote it to something that's worth having when (if) you get it. I've yet to find an "early" tomato that came out any better than what you can buy in the store, so why—except for the pesticide question—bother?

Well, on second thought, better safe than sorry. Also find enclosed some Oregon Spring, not splendid but not bad and much more of a sure thing if the weather stays as tomato-repellent as your letter suggests it's been. Finally, I've put in some Yellow Currant, super-prolific cherry tomatoes that are very tiny, very decorative and very tasty—albeit a bit tough in the skin.

Maybe your splendid compost will help them all overcome London fog; compost seems to be good for just about everything under the sun, so why not things that aren't under the sun enough? Our compost supply is chronically short, as a result of which I am obscenely jealous of your heap of leaves. It's all conifers here, needles useless except for mulching strawberries. When I think of all that humus quietly borning in the square it just makes me want to gnash my teeth—though where on this property we'd find room for a couple dozen sycamores and a gazillion shrubs I cannot readily imagine.

Finding *anything* on this property is a bit of a job at the moment, as I learned when I went out to make a response to your lovely flower pressing. I brought it up with me to answer from here so you could see what was going on in Maine and it certainly does make the differences clear. There's nothing green here that's not evergreen. White and gray are our dominant colors, earth and sky alike, with a minor in blacks above and browns below.

Until you look closely, when the red-purple of bramble and rose stems and the gold lace of empty mallow seedpods become apparent to the eye—and available to the artist board. Gathering up enough to send has been an interesting exercise, not least because as I slogged around snipping needly bits it occurred to me that one of the things that makes Maine so wonderful is this background of unchanging bones. The same spruces, pines and firs define the world in deep summer; they're black then against blue skies instead of green on gray, but shape and volume are consistent. It's a great comfort to live in this structure, serene and steady from snow to summer to snow again. I'm big for rocks, too, come to think of it.
Love

Leslie

Eccleston Square,
London

9 February 1994

Dear Leslie,

Things are really looking good at the moment, the winter has been very mild; *Prunus mume*, the Japanese apricot, is in full blast giving off a cloud of wonderful scent.

My TV thing *The Quest for the Rose* is on at the moment, so people keep ringing up and telling me odd stories — the most interesting so far came up after the second programme, which was mainly on Josephine Bonaparte and her rose garden. I had a letter telling me that a servant of Napoleon took roses from St Helena to New Zealand, and that they can still be seen growing in a churchyard in Karoa (where is it?). They are now gigantic!

I mentioned my new major project for this year. I was summoned to Cork in Ireland by my friends Kim Mai and Stephen Pearce. They have bought the ruins of William Penn's castle, in a little village near the sea called Shanagarry, and are rebuilding it as an arts centre and restaurant. Where I come in is designing the garden! There is an inner courtyard, an outer courtyard, a field with a stream and more. Kim Mai wants the inner courtyard to contain a herb garden with special reference to the herbs used in aromatherapy. We thought that we must relate William Penn into the whole thing so I have been chasing up the herbs that were known in 1670. I consulted a lovely little book *The Tradescant Collection* originally published in 1656. It is a fact that nearly every herb known to aroma-

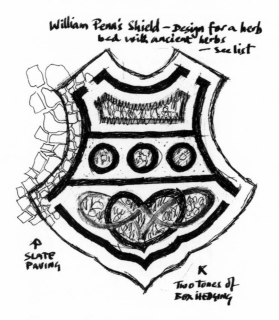

William Penn's Shield – Design for a herb
bed with ancient herbs
– see list

↑
SLATE
PAVING

K
Two tones of
Box Hedging

therapy was also known to the early Quakers. We have agreed to have a sunken herb garden planted in the form of Penn's family shield in the middle of the inner courtyard and the rest of the courtyard will be paved walkways over gravel set with Versailles boxes planted with orange and lemon trees; again, as far as I can obtain them, they will be the types known in the seventeenth century. Of course this will mean building an orangery to keep the plants warm in winter, but think what a wonderful ancillary room this will make to the restaurant; drinks in the orangery, think of the scent – it will be all the rage in Shanagarry.

Stephen is passionate about water works, as per Granada. My solution to this need is to build a folly near the stream and hide a water tank in it, pump the water from the stream up fourteen feet into the tank, and then use the height gained to carry water all over the garden in a series of mini-aqueducts using the elevation to make little waterfalls. Also there will be ponds, tanks and eventually rills so that wherever you go there is the sound of running water. The cost of all this is another thing, but Steve says that Ireland is full of people who can do building of any sort, and most of them out of work to boot! The plans are just about finished and I expect I will go over and talk them through with Kim Mai and Steve (when you abbreviate Stephen does it loose the ph and gain a v?).

steps to top

Ivy

Gothic Folly to hold water tank for aqueducts

Plan and Plant List for the Sunken Herb Garden in the Inner Courtyard at Penn Castle Near Cork in Southern Ireland

Those plants associated with Aroma Therapy that were available in 1670 have one star ★; those marked with two stars ★★ are those that would be suitable for the herb bed or the pots.

Plant list:

★★ Bergamot
★★ Black Pepper (as an annual)
★★ Chamomile
★★ Camphor (annual)
★★ Carrot Seed (annual)
★★ Clary Sage
★ Cypress
★ Frankincense
★★ Geranium (but only from European plants)
★★ Ginger (annual)
★★ Grapefruit
★★ Jasmine (1548) grow in a pot
★★ Juniper grow in a pot
★★ Lavender
★★ Lemon grow in a pot
★★ Linden Blossom planted by the car park
★★ Marjoram (use Wild Marjoram)
★ Myrrh
★★ Orange grow in a pot
★ Palma Rosa
★★ Parchouli (annual)
★★ Peppermint
★ Pine (Scots Pine on the Island)

★★ Rose (Rosa Mundi & The Apothecaries Rose) in a pot?
★★ Rosemary
★★ Tagetes
★★ Tea Tree (Camellia – grow in a pot)

The edging. I think, that to do the rather elaborate parterre based on Penn's shield, we would need two colours of miniature box.

★★ *Buxus suffriticosa* .... 400 plants
★★ *Buxus suffriticosa* Light green var ...... 200 plants

Later . . .

At this time of year everything starts to change, buds are breaking, bulbs are shooting and optimism is in the air. Busy, busy time – we have let rip on bed preparation, cleaning up and then, most important, mulching and feeding the youngsters. The azaleas, for instance, get a deep mulch of our fresh-made, not broken-down leaf-mould, which serves about a hundred purposes: keeps in moisture, keeps out the annual weeds, gets the bed warmer for the perennials to come through and it also breaks down to a fine tilth. By about April it's a perfect surface for starting annual seeds. The irises get a feed of blood, fish and bone (everything is as organic as we can make it); this fertilizer gives them a burst now and also something to keep them going for the rest of the year. I have irises all madly planted in the same bed as azaleas. There's a trick to it – the way I make it work is to have a wall through the middle of the bed with dry (for irises) on one side and wet leaf-mould (for azaleas) on the other. The roses are getting a good covering of cow manure – I buy it in bulk, about three years' supply, five hundred sacks in one go, so by the time it goes out it is really well rotted down.
Love,

Roger

P.S. I enclose tubers of *Tropeaolum tuberosum* 'Ken Aslet', the summer flowering cultivar of the climbing nasturtium. Remember it hates frost — get them going indoors in a 6″ pot, as with a normal annual, but above all dig up the plant and take all the new tubers inside before the first hard frosts in the autumn. They will survive a quick overnight four or five degrees once or twice but then you've had it. They need loads of water: put them in the shade and let them run up a shrub for five or six feet to find the light. They should come into flower by the end of June and keep going until October at least.

RP

Cushing,
Maine

once more chez Magee

February 20, 1994

Dear Roger,

Ice on the river, booming and cracking as the tide goes out. We had a brief driver rain that melted off a lot of snow, but I failed to get over to the garden to do the last bit of cleaning up.

It doesn't really matter; the place is utterly barren with or without snow cover and I should be able to get a good look at what's wanted whenever the chance presents itself.

"Arrange more architectural elements" is likely to be the answer; I'm really sick of all this flatland. The horrible origins of carpet bedding are all too clear when you look at a flat garden and start trying to have an idea. It's even flatter than usual at the moment because this winter's bitter winds have finally done in the black pipe-metal arch. It was on the flimsy side by itself but did make quite a statement when covered with autumn clematis. On one side: the main garden, full of vegetables and brightly colored flowers, on the other: whiteness entire, broken only with green and gray and the purple blossoms of thyme. No question that the arch must be replaced, this time with something sturdier. An interesting job, since I don't want to kill the clematis and don't want its companion climbing rose ("New Dawn," which is extremely thorny) to kill me.

Arch replacement is as far as I've gotten but it's not nearly far enough—one arch and one lonely arbor vitae do not a structure make.

Suggestions will be warmly welcomed—especially if they're inexpensive. Hardscape costs like the dickens and I'll have to replace a serious ($$$) amount of soil if I want big trees to thrive.

Knowing what these things tend to run to (in time as well as money) I was awed by your description of the project in Ireland for your friends. To have that tantalizing bit about William Penn to hang it on and what sounds like a most generous budget. Waterworks! An orangery! Did I ever tell you I always dreamed of building something along those lines? Nothing as simple as a warm room used to winter over what is for all its larger scale a bunch of potted plants. Uh uh; I want to dig a deep foundation-like cellar and surround it with a dead-air space so the soil doesn't freeze. Then over that—way over that, like forty feet—I want to build a roof of sliding panels (insulated glass, of course) that can be retracted in summer. Indoor trees is what I crave. Big Trees. Major trees. Mango trees.

Meanwhile I may make a stab at something distantly similar to the Penn aspect. A local historic house has become museum property and the curator in charge of the place is thinking about recreating the gardens that grew there in the forties, when the last of the founding family were in residence. It's interesting for two main reasons. The first is its proximity in time; there are living sources to consult and at least some of what was planted may still be available in more or less the same form. Additionally, I'm intrigued because there was so little "gardening" done. The sister planted a small flower bed with common bright things: zinnias, marigolds, dahlias. The brother had a truck garden with equally common vegetables: corn, cucumbers, snap beans, peas.

No recherché plants in rare combinations, no formal borders or borderie. In other words it's history not horticulture and for some reason that's peculiarly attractive. There may be a problem, however, in that I would not be alone in this endeavor. There have been warnings about determined club women and other interested parties, people unlikely to be content with a garden that isn't stylish, people to whom authenticity is of little or no interest. There's an unhappy example of their zeal, a pretty little garden blooming full of glaring anachronisms—bunchy hybrid marigolds and the like—on another museum property. So I fear the worst.

Three days later: It's still very cold and raw, my plans to spend contemplative time in the garden have changed to a reality that mostly involves hanging out at Magees and having lunch.

To celebrate the garden, I brought up lots of what's left from last summer's harvest. Canned brandywines, dried mushrooms, frozen squash soup, potatoes from the root cellar. Potatoes turned out to be the biggest hit. No surprise to me as I never get tired of them. Yesterday we had three different kinds: "Rote Erstling," "Augsberg Gold" and "Purple Cowhorn." According to Monika an erstling is a first-born child, so I guess these are red first-borns and in fact they are very early. Pretty too, the red from the skin bleeds over into the flesh a little. Augsberg gold is just that—real buttery. The purple cowhorn is, well, odd. Right between a boiler and a baker, pale fleshed with dark blue streaks and blotches. Tastier than it looks and an excellent keeper but not as crescent shaped as I thought it would be. One of those things only the gardener notices. We had them steamed plain, with cashew chutney, and they were a big hit.

After the potatoes, the last of the brandywines, served royally as a separate course. It's always a wrench to part with them—I don't think I'll ever put up enough, don't think I'll ever *have* enough. There was a roast chicken with wild mushrooms, to continue the "summer preserved" theme, and for dessert I made the Magees my guinea pigs and worked on the recipe test for the column: chocolate truffles for Valentine's day.

White Truffles for Valentine's Day

For about 3 dozen:

12 ounces best quality white
chocolate, coarsely chopped
2 tablespoons butter
¼ cup heavy cream
1 tablespoon orange liqueur such as
triple sec

2 tablespoons seedless raspberry
puree (about 1 cup fruit)
sifted confectioners' sugar for
coating

(Thaw and drain raspberries before pureeing if using frozen fruit.) Melt chocolate with butter over *very low* heat or in a double boiler over barely simmering water. Remove from heat and stir in cream in a thin stream— don't worry about curdling. Cover tightly and refrigerate until cool but not cold. Beat mixture until it resembles very thick whipped cream, then fold in liqueur and fruit. Drop mixture on waxed paper in walnut-sized lumps and chill until firm. Roll into balls, roll each in sifted confectioners sugar and chill again. Keep refrigerated, tightly covered, for up to 3 days.

Eccleston Square,
London

5 March 1994

Dear Leslie,

Many thanks for your presssed flowers that arrived a bit bashed up after weeks in the post – the spruce was minus all its needles! Can I refer to bits of spruce as pressed flowers? You have no flowers out at all, so I suppose I must refer to them as pressed leaves. First thoughts on the arbour/structure on the cheap that you are planning: how about a hardy evergreen that will grow tall and can be tied/trained to make an arch; what about Common Hemlock *Tsuga canadensis?* Or does Holly do well for you – variegated even?

The weather varies overnight from cold and snow to wet and mild, changing so quickly that I don't know what to wear. For the plants it must be worse – they throw out fresh buds then they are destroyed by frost; but this does not stop our toughies from the Antipodes. We have an Australian family living in the Square and after being here for years they have got homesick for the plants from the outback. Jim, Julie and their two sons Ben and Mike have now taken over a bed and planted loads of really odd Australian plants, most of them incredibly tender. The bed they have taken up is on a slight incline facing south and rather dry, so we hope that they have a hot dry area that the frost will run off in the winter. The red and white Coreas that they planted seem to have never stopped flowering. I am keeping a record of the plants they put in so that I can see how these reportedly very tender things make out in our city climate. The nrst efforts were mainly shrubs but they have just got hold of a number of perennials from a wonderful nurseryman called Brian Hilley. He grows all his own stuff in a run-down group of greenhouses in Wallington just south of London. I love these nursery men who battle on against the forces of the big garden centre regime, growing and propagating the plants they love, ignoring profit and popularity, while the big boys bring everything down to the common denominator of easy to produce, keep and sell – buy it in, mark it up, sell it on. But is this gardening? NO! To my mind gardening ought to be a personal thing, a care of plants, a search for knowledge – here I go off on one of my moans again.

My workload has just about quadrupled. CD-ROM has arrived! Macmillan are very keen to make a start in the world of electronic publishing, so am I. It's a very exciting medium. Publishers have realized that the people to create the discs are the authors, which means a real opportunity for me to bring together all my visual plant thoughts. What has gone on in the first few years is loads of games and silly discs showing off all the funny things that can be done – rubbish, in other words. I hope we are going to be able to do informative CDs – things people will turn to when they have gardening problems to solve, and return to again and again. My son Sam is a wizz kid with the technicalities of programming – so all of a sudden we are working together. Not only that – it works out well! So far we have thought of 200 different ways that the disc can be accessed for information on the 2,000 plants that we are going to feature. That makes 200,000 boxes that have to be filled with text, maybe one million words. Wow!
Love,

Roger et al.

In Maine

[at Magees' natch]

March 17, 1994

I should have known. There's no getting it right when you're trying to plan around Maine weather. Bill and I have come up to work a bit on the ravine/proposed pond garden—chose the time at least partly because I had this fantasy that a mid-March trip would mean we'd get here between the snow and the mud. What happened is we've gotten them both. Deep snow when we arrived two days ago has segued seamlessly into shallow-snow-with-mud. There's been absolutely none of that nice bit when the ground is still frozen but there's no snow so it's easy to work and you don't have to worry about compacting the soil. Instead it's wet and slushy and soft a foot down, with a bit of tired and dirty icing on top.

Syrup season, in other words, when the maple sap runs in the trees and those of us inclined to such things tap it to boil down for home-made syrup. There aren't as many taps around as I've seen in other years, but there are buckets hanging from some trees—especially in Thomaston—and they're the handsome old-fashioned ones you hardly see any more.

This property is maple-poor but there are a few trees across the road. We did a test, then put spiles, the hollow spikes that carry sap from tree to bucket, into two of the most promising. The idea is to bring a few gallons of sweetwater (aka maple sap) back to New York, add it to the general boiling, and thus ensure a taste of Maine for the entire year's pancakes. Admittedly, a romantic notion. Since it takes forty gallons of sap to make one of syrup the amount we'll get from those two trees is literally a drop in the bucket, and though different trees do have different flavors it's unlikely we'd *taste* anything significantly different. But I'm hoping the Maine sap will have a homeopathic effect and help keep me from getting homesick.

Aside from moments taken out for things like tapping (and more time than I wish on the phone to the everlasting office) we've been spending all day each day clearing and burning. It has been at least forty years since anyone paid any attention to the ravine, so the whole thing is grown up to alders—it isn't just the little pond area—and with Bill the demon worker here we're really whacking them trees.

Getting permission for open burning of what is called "slash" is easy at this very wet time of year—you just go to Fales' general store and ask Johnny, who's with the fire department—but getting the damn stuff to catch fire is no easy task. Everything is unutterably soggy and of course most of the wood to be burned is green. Fortunately the dead hackamatack has proved to be admirable kindling. We've managed to get major blazes by layering bits of it here and there in the pile, along with plenteous newspapers and some old rotten roofing boards. (Very handy to have to roof parts and the dormer is progressing well although there's still a great mothering hole in the house where the windows will be as a result of which it's none too cozy in there.)

No semblance of ordinary domestic life. We're still completely in the house guest mode and I've now spent so much time at the Magees' I'm beginning to feel related. They may be beginning to feel the same way but I've tried to make our presence painless by doing a lot of the cooking. Only the simplest sort, of course, in view of our work schedule, but when the simple thing is steamed lobster nobody complains. It's so much better right here at the source, freshly caught, yet somehow it has remained a special occasion food, one of those things you tend to eat only when there is a celebration.

They're all still in their winter hard shells, less sweet than summer lobsters but far meatier. We had a big feed the other night featuring lobsters from Sam's. (Quite the adventure procuring them as Sam's extremely steep wharf road faces south and is thus well advanced toward terminal mud.) I overbought, rather, and was thus able to make my very favorite "other" lobster recipe:

Campfire Lobster

For 2 servings:

2 cooked lobsters, each about 1¹/₂ pounds

6 tablespoons butter (3 ounces) at room temperature

a small handful dried mushrooms such as boletus edulus, crushed to fine crumbs—about 2 tablespoons crumbs

1 tablespoon cognac

1 to 2 tablespoons minced fresh dill (amount depends on the strength of the herb; sometimes it's bland in winter)

heavy-duty foil

Split the undershells of the lobsters and pry them partially apart. Remove the inedible stomach sac, saving the tomalley (liver) and any coral in a small bowl. Loosen the tail meat, remove sand vein, and split meat in half for easier eating. Return tail to shell. Cream butter until soft, then work in mushrooms, cognac, dill and reserved tomalley. Stuff body cavities with this mixture.

W rap each lobster securely in a double layer of foil, double folding the seam, which should be on the belly side. Place in a bed of medium hot but not rip-roaring coals (or 450 degree oven), seam side up, and cook until heated through, about 15 to 20 minutes. Serve in the foil, with plenty of napkins. Enough butter sauce will flow out to season the claw meat.

I wouldn't normally have made a campfire at this time of year, but burning all that slash meant B. and I were well supplied, ideally positioned for a winter picnic.

The day we ate the lobster we also had some pineapple—it tastes great grilled over coals—and some blackberry jam tarts that set off a fit of nostalgia. The jam is Celia's favorite flavor and each year I make it from berries picked in the very area we're clearing now. I'm hoping the canes will grow back and give the same good fruit, but this time among ferns and shrubs instead of these Burn and begone, Damned alders!
Love,
Leslie

P.S. from Pleasant Valley. The nasturtium tubers arrived safely but they looked so shrivelly I decided to pot them up right away for fear there'd be nothing left if I waited until later in spring. No sign of any growth yet, which is probably just as well . . .

Eccleston Square, London

written on 10 March, posted 29 March 1994

Dear Leslie,

Today is a big day. I am entering camellia blooms into the Royal Horticultural Society Early Camellia Show — the Early means that it is the show for indoor camellias and, of course, mine are all outdoors. The reason I have to do it this way is that mine flower so early that by the time the outdoor show comes around in mid-April they have all passed their best. Wish me luck — I shall be up against the Duke and Duchess of Devonshire, who grow loads in their greenhouses at Chatsworth. I HAVE NO CHANCE!

I am entering: 'Yours Truly', 'Adolphe Auduseon', 'Lady Clare', a deep red one with lovely golden stamens called 'Dr Burnside', 'Melody Lane' and 'Dear Jenny' in the 'any 6 Japonica' section and also single blooms in the single, semi-double and the Peony-form subsections.

Many thanks for the tomato seeds — all in their trays now. Brandywine sounds great, apart from the eighty to ninety days from setting out to ripening: your seeds looked pretty dried up, I'll eat my hat if they germinate. I have also just planted seeds for rhubarb chard which came leaping up one inch high in two days in my little propagator.

I have decided to work a bit more on the garden layout. The Cubitt construction is protected by a preservation order as the whole square is listed as an historic building. I like his simple symmetrical layout but I also love things to have a more human — some would say more childish — scale. All this preamble means is that I have plans to put more little paths through the middle of the large shrubby beds. Many beds already have them, as I started on this work in 1987, but three big ones are still to be done; I think of it as working to augment Cubitt by making a sort of counterpoint to his grand and dramatic straight paths. When these three are done it will be possible to walk all around the garden by taking little secret winding paths.

The whole family have arm ache today, as yesterday we all went for our pre-China trip jabs; Hepatitis A and typhoid. We have been madly researching the ancient gardens of China and also the gardens of Japan — the whole schedule is quite mad: garden after garden, sometimes as many as three in a day. If I ever get time I will send you a card or cards. The Chinese gardens sound a bit neglected but this should be fun; the Japanese gardens on the other hand sound as if they will be swarming with camera-flashing Japanese tourists. For me to try and take photographs that will show up the structure may well be impossible.

You have incidentally solved a mystery for me: when in Maine everybody has always talked about the wonderful Maine lobsters but I have found them to be soft shelled and half empty, the flesh rather watery too; being a well mannered guest I have refrained from complaining. In Europe we tend to eat our lobsters with hard shells and very fleshy. I suppose the truth of the matter is that I have only eaten them in the winter.

By the way what the heck is a truck garden?
Love,

Roger

P.S. I got second prize!
The Duke and Duchess won!

Brick path using 2 colours red & yellow

Cushing, Maine

Congratulations, Oh King (or is it Prince?) of Camellias. What a thrill to finish in the money against all those glass-house types and right after the duke. Well! Consider me thoroughly impressed. On the other hand, I'm an impressionable type and still somewhat daunted by the very idea of outdoor camellias in early March. I returned to Maine two weeks ago and it was still absolutely freezing. Still is, in fact. I keep tooling around in my thin spring jacket pretending it's in the forties and I keep shivering, because it isn't.

The new dormer is absolutely gorgeous. Glorious light upstairs at last is the real payoff and all that additional floor-space (already eaten up by a larger desk and bookcase) is not bad either. And it looks like I will get to enjoy it at length because—BIG NEWS!! I have quit my job at *First* and will if all goes well become in June the senior editor for food and home at *Yankee* magazine. It's smaller (circulation about 700,000), but still a national presence. Much nicer, much classier and generally a vast improvement—not least of which is that I will be working out of my home office. No more commuting to New Jersey. If I'd just beat the duke with my camellias I couldn't feel prouder or happier.

The garden is still mostly mud city, relieved by a few scilla and a few hundred bunches of badly-eaten tulip greenery. I don't know if it was rabbits or woodchucks or both, but something has been feasting for quite a while. Small-animal repellent (Repel, it's called) has been liberally sprayed and that and/or my presence seems to have halted the depreda-

tions, but I don't have high expectations in the blaze of blossom department. Not sure about the *T. chrysantha* among the poppy plants either.
The little tulips are doing fine but the poppy plants are mighty scant for
the first time in a decade. Don't know if they were smothered last fall by
the lushness of the late white border or if maybe the very hard winter and
late spring have kept them from germinating. Guess I'll reseed if things
don't improve, but there's still a little time before it's time to worry.

Gardening right now mostly consists of driving up to Camden and
transplanting things in the greenhouse. The baby seedlings (roughly 2000
plants if you count the leeks and onions) are all doing very well considering what a brutal winter it's been. All, that is, expect the ten or twelve
salmon-colored delphiniums on which I decided to take a flyer. The
seedlings have only one or two rather anemic true leaves and I seriously
doubt they'll do anything. This may in fact be a mercy; I'm not sure a
salmon-colored delphinium would be any too attractive. Looked at in
black and white a delphinium has little to recommend it. It's that blue,
the blue that saves them and without it . . . On the other hand, I've been
lusting after the yellow one (zlalil) for years and I don't think merely out
of a vulgar hunger for novelty.
Love,

Leslie

Eccleston Square,
London

29 April 1994

Dear Leslie,

Back after twenty-five days of eastern promise, the square garden has hardly changed, I gather, and it shows – the spring has been cold, damp and wet. I have missed nothing. Seeing the gardens of China and Japan has been a great experience. In China a principal design element is that private gardens are seen as scroll paintings – each garden is surrounded by a high white wall (the background paper of the scroll). As you walk around you only see one part of the wall at a time as it is broken up by buildings, tiny rooms and paths. This slow exposure of the whole represents the unwinding of the scroll to view it. Against this pure white ground the garden itself is laid out: compositions of rocks, plants and structures, sometimes more complicated with a small stream and bridge perhaps overhung with a magnolia tree. As you walk around, the pictures constantly change.

There are five main components to a Chinese garden; rocks, water, structures and buildings, plants and tranquillity. I was struck by the very sparing use of plants. The tendency is to have one very fine example of the main flowering trees and shrubs, thus: one wisteria, one magnolia, one almond, one 'Lady Banks' rose, a camellia (or perhaps two), a planting of lotus in the pond. In the case of conifers often more than one; azaleas also would be used in larger groups. The rocks are all water-shaped pieces of limestone from the bottom of Lake Ti tending to be stood on end to make upright shapes. They are then turned and positioned to allow any resemblance to animals to be stressed, especially those animals that stand as symbols for the years, so you will see lion rocks, dragon rocks, monkey rocks, tiger rocks, elephant rocks, bear rocks, et cetera.

I found the gardens of Japan very different although they are historically based on the Chinese. The Japanese use rocks but not the amazing limestone sculpture rocks of China. In Japan rocks are used much more in the naturalistic way that we use them in Britain. They resemble mountains and valley gorges and cliffs rather than beasts. But the real difference is in the preponderance of Zen gardens constructed only for contemplation, raked gravel in place of grass or water allowing the key elements to be isolated again. There is often a white wall behind, but it is subtly different – it really just stops the mind wondering about what might be beyond. The landscapes are then created with a very few plants, often just one superb cherry tree for instance, or a small group of shaped evergreen shrubs, possibly a camellia or a conifer, an arrangement of rocks as at Rioanji or a small lake with a tiny island, or even an arrangement of rocks and pebbles that represent a stream or a waterfall.

Another great difference is the attitude of the visitors. Modern Chinese greatly enjoy the gardens, usually though as recreational areas. They run, leave behind litter and shout and laugh just as children do in a playground; the tranquillity that the garden builders attempted is lost among millions of visitors. A Zen Buddhist garden, on the other hand, even when there are crowds of visitors has an air of respect and tranquillity, of study and thought; talking is in subdued tones, children do not run about, everybody takes off their shoes if they venture into the buildings, dropping litter is unknown!

I wrote a series of postcards to you during my journey, then failed to send them. After about three failures, I decided to bring the whole lot home and send them to you *en masse*. That way they won't get lost.

Open day for the National Garden Scheme is on 1 May this year;

everything is looking at its best although about two to three weeks behind. I am now going to have to spend a couple of days labelling things – my principle is to put labels on things that are at their best at the moment, either because of the new foliage or because they are in flower. I have got a new system to try out using metal labels, with a pot of acid to etch out the names, making them permanent I hope. The only thing is how to apply it – it comes with no pen or whatever – hope I don't rot my fingers off in the process.

Here's a recipe from Nicky for her favourite kind of cake, the one she always makes for our garden open days. It's plain but quite rich and we all love it.

Madeira Cake

8 oz butter (preferably organic) or margarine	16 oz self-raising, white, organic flour
8 oz light brown, raw cane sugar	2 tablespoons organic milk
4 large, organic eggs	

Cream the butter and sugar. Add the eggs and beat vigorously. Sieve in the flour and mix thoroughly, adding the milk to get a soft, dropping consistency. Grease and flour a cake tin (7–8 inches in diameter) and fill with the mixture. Place a piece of greaseproof paper across the top of the tin to prevent the cake from browning too much on the top and place in a preheated oven (150°C). Cook for one hour, then check how it's doing by placing a skewer into the middle of the cake. It will probably need about half an hour more to reach perfection. Remove from the oven and allow to cool for 10 minutes before turning out onto a cake wire.

SERVING SUGGESTIONS: For the teetotaller, consume with Earl Grey or China tea; for the non-teetotaller, eat accompanied by a sweet, dessert wine such as muscat.

It feels like the first day of summer weather here; having had a very late and delayed spring the early things like the camellias and tulips are still at full blast and the later things like *Prunus Shirofugen* and the ceanothus are roaring along; to date: 'Pugit Blue' deep purply blue; 'Burtonienis' clear blue and millions of flowers; 'Trewithen Blue' – we have a smashing big plant. They are all superb and under the trees we have a mass of wild bluebells – heaven. People/books often refer to the scent of ceanothus but I find it very difficult to detect – are they lying or am I losing my sense of smell?

Your Brandywine tomatoes have come up – I was sure they were too old and dry-looking but no, virtually every seed has germinated. Now all I need is about ninety days of hot sun and I shall have fruit the way you do.

I have decided to follow you down the annuals trail. I have cleared an area about fifteen feet square and ordered loads of seeds – when I plant them out I shall send you a little map. The inspiration for the choice of seeds came from a book by Mrs Loudon published in about 1845 illustrating so many wonderful things that are extremely rare and difficult to get hold of. The best source thing I have come across is a catalogue called Chiltern seeds. I have now finished with it (the catalogue) so I am sending it on to you. I am a bit late getting started so I expect the bed won't be at its best until about mid-August.

Nicky and I have been together twenty-five years so we are having a bumper 3 July party. So far the guest list runs to about 400 – you and Bill are way up there. It will be a massive barbecue lunch with loads of wine – this will mean getting about ten separate barbecue fires going, and the guests will have to cook their own. I hope you can make it.
Love,

Roger

Pleasant Valley, New York

May 3, 1994

Dear Roger,

Pardon me if this letter ends up sounding swoony, I'm awash in the difference 400 miles can make. When I left—two days ago—things in Maine were still at the start stage. Down here the joint is blooming. Tulips in full stride, dogwood—why doesn't this elegant little tree have a prettier common name?—everywhere. Bleeding hearts in the shrubbery, starry columbines . . . and we have been having the most splendid morelling: absolute bushels and the biggest haul from under a dead elm in the tick-infested bramble thicket/swamp behind our land. Clusters, no less, of *M. esculenta*—big clusters. Plus the lilacs are gorgeous and the viburnum in the yard that I can't identify and keep forgetting to photograph so you can identify is perfuming everything. Especially in the evenings, which have been just faintly breezy and a little cool, the whole green yard is suffused with marvelous fragrance: as strong as lilies—stronger—yet not at all heavy or overpowering.

An inspiring spring, in short. Which has moved me in the direction of roses. I've planted a whole slew . . . well, a little hedge . . . of old and shrub roses. They're at the back of the herb patch, where my tiny collection was already ensconced. Morden Blush, Golden Wings, Gloire de Guilan, Mary Rose, Conrad F. Mayer, Jens Munk, and Tuscany. Not in that order (see bed plan). They've been chosen with an eye to foliage, which, if the Japanese beetles don't eat it all, should act as a background for the hybrid teas planted between them and the herbs. Since there are edibles in the bed and since in any case I'd rather not there won't be any poison used on the roses, so this will be a real test of their ability to withstand pests when helped only by good culture.

Having already moaned and whined about the oxymoronic aspects of organic roses I will confine myself to saying it's even worse in NY than it is in Maine. More bugs and more kinds of 'em, more vicious fungi (you wouldn't believe the black spot) . . . I suppose it's the price to be paid for more of everything—more morels and chanterelles in the fungus department, more birds—there's a wren house at the top of the trellis Conrad's on and it has got two wren families in it and there are bluebirds . . .

Meanwhile, the beautiful little painted iris (*ruthenica?*) is blooming in Cushing, and I've got to get back soon if I want to put up this year's rhubarb.

So I'm off to Maine the day after tomorrow. More thence.

Love, Leslie

P.S.—Thanks for your call, it was lovely to have a phone chat after so long. I'm enclosing the trout with morels—wish I could send some of the asparagus B. was going on about (it really is delicious; did I ever tell you how he planted it before we closed on the house?).

Roger,

She's right, it's full blown spring. For some that means baseball but for me it's trout and morels. I dream of baiting my hook with one to catch the other . . . It was great to hear your voice; come next spring and bring a hot skillet.

Bill

1. Nameless red climber,
2. Nameless pink climber
3. R. Rugosa, Conrad Ferdinand Meyer (on fa Trelli
4. R. Rugosa, Jens Munk
5. R. Spinosissima cross (altaica/xanthina) HT Soeur Therese, Golden Wings
6. (D. Austin), Mary Rose
7. Damask, Gloire de Guilan
8. ? (shrub), Morden Blush
9. Hybrid Perpetual, Reine des Violettes
10. R. Gallica, Tuscany
11. Test roses from AARS (They're usual Hybrid Teas
12. Papaver Orientalis, Marie Louise

WEIRD JUNIPER

Greenhouse will go
inside dotted line —
probably in 1995

this is the SUNROOM - Neu

GARDEN, N.Y.

Hibiscus syriacus, Blue Bird
Artemísia absinthium

Allium schoenoprasum

A. dranunculus

myrrhis odorata

Satureja montana

Thymus praecox ss. articus

Origanum vulgare (ss. hirtum)

T. x citriodorus 'aureus'

T. Herba-barona 'nutmeg'

T. x citriodorus 'argenteus'

T. vulgaris

    ✳ = self-sown larkspur + digitalis
    ⫽ = Annul Herbs: parsley, basils
            coriander, dwarf dill,
            Chervil

GIANT MAGNOLIA

WEIRD JUNIPER

...hen if I ever get rich

Trout with Morels

Sauce:

1 oz. unsalted butter

6 oz. morels, sliced crosswise at $^1/_2$
    inch intervals, about $3^1/_2$ cups
    prepared

2 sprigs fresh lemon thyme, each
    about 2 inches long—this is
    optional, but it IS nice

1 large clove garlic, minced fine

$^1/_4$ cup diced green pepper

$^1/_2$ teaspoon salt

a generous pinch of caraway seeds

1 cup heavy cream

Plus:

2 trout, about 8 oz. each

2 small branches lovage (optional)

flour to dust trout

$^1/_2$ oz. unsalted butter

1 tablespoon olive oil

1 tablespoon cognac

Start with the sauce: Melt the butter in a wide, heavy skillet. When it foams, add the morels and thyme. Cook over medium heat, shaking frequently, until morels have shed their juice and are just starting to brown, about 8 minutes.

Remove the thyme, lower the heat and add the garlic, green pepper, salt and caraway. Simmer for about 5 minutes more, then add the cream and turn off the heat.

Rinse and dry the trout. Stuff with lovage if you've got it. Give 'em a good dredging in flour and set aside. Put the butter and oil in a non-stick skillet just big enough to hold the trout and place over medium-high heat. When the fat is *almost* smoking, slide in the trout. Fry fast—about 4 minutes a side.

As soon as the trout go in the pan, turn on the heat under the sauce. Let it bubble vigorously while the fish cooks; it should reduce by about half and just achieve a nice pouring consistency when the trout is ready.

When trout is cooked, pour cognac over and toss until spirit evaporates. Serve in the restaurant fashion—puddle of sauce on the plate, trout on top. You can garnish with violets if you feel like going whole hog.

Cushing, Maine

May 11, 1994

Dear Roger—

A treat to arrive and find your letter—thanks for all the orientalia. Sure makes one realize how different things are . . . and then again, maybe not. Design principles do vary—if nothing else we westerners seem to prefer living walls of dark green to flat white ones of stone—and the architecture of the buildings themselves is certainly nothing like ours. But when you look at the garden parts, well, who doesn't concentrate on the big five of water, rocks, structures, plants and tranquillity? Lenôtre I suppose you could say didn't care much about two and five, Capability Brown was a tad heedless about individual plants (no single magnificent magnolias for him) but what strikes me about these gardens, at least in the postcard pictures and your—very interesting, by the way—reports, is how much one big public garden resembles another. A Chinese or Japanese garden lover who came to the States on a tour like yours would see things like Dumbarton Oaks and Naumkeag and Longwood and Wave Hill and that splendid cactus assemblage in Berkeley that I can't remember the name of . . . all of them very beautiful and all (except, ironically, the cactus) very "western" in their use of lawns and shrubs and garden rooms, but all of them full as it sounds like yours were of fellow spectators, all of them built with buckets of money and maintained by fleets of help. Hardly our story. Did you get a chance to see any small, private places? Is there anything analogous to a cottage garden? There, I think, may be a big difference. From what I can remember of my reading the idea of mixing ornamental with edible, cutting flowers with those for display is completely unknown in the East.

Right now it's hard to focus on philosophy; what I really want to know is: How were the Chinese bugs? These little details seem to get lost in the grand overview, but when the details bite they do rather attract your attention. In other words, WHAT a year for black flies we seem to be having. All planting and weeding—and walking to the loo—takes place in a buzzing haze reminiscent of *The African Queen*. Maybe it's the winter's humongous snows or maybe I'm losing my resistance as punishment for spending so much time in New York. Oh well, I'm here now and happy to be so, grumbles notwithstanding. Have to take another trip to Pleasant Valley, then both of us will be in Maine for the last week in June and the entire month of July.

So we won't be able to come to London for the party, I regret to say. Congratulations early on your big anniversary. We shall be with you in spirit and will raise a glass in your honor.
Love,

Leslie

P.S. Good luck with the annual bed. It's hard to get old-fashioned flowers here as well—the preservational types have so far focused mostly on the vegetable garden. There are a few places that claim to specialize in old-fashioned or cottage garden flowers but they don't really have anything all that unusual and most of them, putting the accent on fashion, charge more than the general merchandise seed houses. I get most of my annual flower seed from Parks, Johnny's, J. L. Hudson, and Thompson and Morgan. The old-time New England firm of Comstock Ferre also has a few nice things. I'll send catalogs (or seed) if requested but I have a feeling you've got better access there than I have here.

Eccleston Square,
London

5 May 1994

Dear Leslie,

You will never believe this.

St George's Square up the road from us is under CAR PARK THREAT, 'mobilize the troops' time all over again, just when I thought it had all gone quiet. The problem is that developers see profit in car parks and are unremitting in their attempts to make money irrespective of the desires of the residents and the local and national government policies on reducing the traffic in inner cities.

This time it is the local Westminster Council themselves who are the owners. They have got a French car park construction company involved and discussions had obviously gone a long way down the line before we heard anything about it. They have prepared rather detailed plans and exhibited them in a school hall for consultation. The company have been led up the garden path and wasted a lot of money setting up an office in London staffing the week long exhibition, drawing plans and commissioning reports. I would have thought that seeing the reaction of the residents in Eccleston Square the councillors would have advised them to have a discussion with the residents groups first; but no, it is all as if our battle never happened. To play devil's advocate for a moment and put the councillors' position: they said when I wrote to them that they have received a lot of letters of complaint from people trying to find somewhere to park and that they were investigating car parks under gardens as a possibility, but if the mass of local residents were against it they would drop it. The problem with this is that there are large blocks of flats in the area owned by rather well-off people who use them in the week and thus have very little concern or involvement in the area — they will always vote for the easy life and pay to park their cars. The only thing we can do is show the councillors the depth of feeling of the permanent residents in the area against it. In other words we have to go on with the good fight and get the vote out. St George's Square are lucky in that there are one or two very concerned active people up there who have already joined battle, in particular Barbara Richards who is indefatigable. I have written to the hundred squares that are part of our group the Society for The Protection of London Squares and replies decrying this attack are beginning to pour in.

The opening of our Square last week was a great success; we had over 350 people and made over eight hundred pounds for our charities, in fact we beat our previous record take by about 50 pence. Loads of the ceanothus were in flower, all the lilacs, most of the camellias still had flowers, the *Iris germanica* were out — I can go on and on; anyway I think it is unfair to do two day openings every year. The residents have done their bit, so next year I think it must be just one opening day; roses time seems like the best bet.

Just had another forty-two visitors in the garden, this time from New Zealand on one of those garden tours.

I have been keeping watch on the roses to try and work out the best time to open the garden next year. Today we have about eighty different roses in flower but I think that by about 1 June we should have about a hundred. The tennis court is in full blast; all the netting is covered in climbing roses so that some people who come into the garden fail to see the court at all and just think of it as a gigantic rose arbour — those who play love the scent (I hope).

My TV career is in jeopardy. The *Quest for the Rose* has all finished now. I have had, and am still getting, loads of letters from all over the country. Everybody seems to like it, except the man who is in charge of doing the gardening and nature programmes at the BBC; he doesn't think much of me and he especially dislikes my red glasses (dare I say I have made him see red). Anyway, the end result is no future contract at all. Apart from this rather crucial criticism I have had an invitation from the Royal Horticultural Society to speak in November, quite an honour for me, plus Clair Martin, the man at the Huntington Garden in California, has invited me to come over and give a talk at their Rose Symposium in spring 1996. Not loved by the powers at home but maybe the pirated copies of the video creeping abroad are received with more enthusiasm

It is a shame because what Martyn and I felt was, that there is a real gap in serious plant TV and that looking at plants in their historical context would be a very worthwhile contribution. So much of TV just touches on the surface of the subject. Gardening, and especially the subject of garden plants, is full of fascinating tales and escapades, particularly the tales of the plant-hunters. Oh well, better to have tried and failed rather than never to have tried at all, as my beloved grandma Sally used to say.

I tried to have a go at identifying your scented viburnum (it was ages ago that you mentioned it), how about *Viburnum × caricephalum* a medium-sized shrub with great scent − flowers in spring; if it isn't this then maybe you should try planting one for its scent anyway.

I have made a list of the roses in flower in the garden in late May to remind me of the best week for flowering.

Roses in Flower on 22 May 1994

Going over:
Canary Bird
Frühlingsgold
Frühlingsmorgen

May Gold
Rosa ecae

Fully out:

Allen Chandler (Beryl's bed)
Bantry Bay
Cecile Brunner
Cupid
Danse des Sylphes
Danse du Feu
Ena Harkness
General Schablikine
Gertrude Jekyll
Gloire de Dijon
Golden Showers
Guinée
Handel
Hermosa
Joseph's Coat
Lady Hillingdon
Lavinia
Lawrence Johnson
Marguerite Hilling
Mme Grégoire Staechelin
Mutabilis
Nevada
Old Blush China
Ophelia
Penelope
Rêve d'Or
Royal Gold
School Girl
Surpassing Beauty
Sympathie
Winchester Cathedral
Zéphirine Drouhin

Half out:

Adam (Tea)
Alchemist
Aloha
Ardsover (Handkerchief Tree)
Autumn Sunlight
Charles Austin
Constance Spry
Emily Gray
Etoile de Holland
Fantin-Latour
Iceberg
Lilian Austin
Mary Rose (Hermosa)
Masquerade
Meg
Mme Alfred Carrier
Mme Edouard Herriot
Mme Isaac Périer
Morning Jewel
Mountbatten
Parkdirector Riggers
Paul's Lemon Pillar
Pink Bells
President de Seze
Tour de Malankoff
White Cocade

This sort of list is a bit boring but even more boring is trying to remember which was the best time for rose flowers six months later when the autumn leaves are falling. My rough and ready interpretation of my little bit of research is that by the end of May the species roses are finished, the climbers are in full swing and the bush roses and ramblers are just beginning.

Hoping for a letter soon.

Love,

Roger

Cushing,
Maine

June 10, 1994

Dear Roger,

Happy to hear the opening went so well, very sorry to hear the car park story. INFURIATING! It's not just the general again-ness but the bland ability to disregard *all* that has gone before. A lesson about the importance of eternal vigilance, I suppose. It sort of reminds me of the troubles we have with highways here. The current models get overcrowded and new ones are built, at great expense, with money that might better have gone to public transportation (which is at complete crisis in rural areas where it is impossible to go anywhere, even in the towns, without having a car). The new highways fix things for about 20 minutes, then there is yet more auto traffic, new overcrowding and a return to the same scenario. Each event brings protests from environmentalists and from those whose homes and businesses are affected, each event gets media attention, each event then promptly falls into some limbo of forgetfulness that enables the authorities to ignore its lessons completely.

No wonder we'd rather talk garden. I've been in this one for weeks but there's still buckets of stuff to do. All tidying has been set aside until the planting's done—weeding, mulching, fertilizing all will have to wait, there's just no time.

Lois got here a couple of days ago and, having only one lousy lilac to plant, promptly set about weeding, clearing and setting up our assorted recycling systems. Largely thanks to her, we have special bins for the glass, the aluminum, the newspapers and the cardboard. There is a place—long since overflowing—for paint rags. Used clothing is donated to (and purchased from) the annual church fair. When her iris need dividing they move to my house and I in turn need never discard so much as an extra pansy because somehow or other the woman will find a place. She's certainly the only person I've ever known who could say with a straight face, "I've always wanted a composting outhouse."

Since annual maintenance comes before use, The Changing of the Cans is first on our list of spring chores. As I think I may have mentioned before, each 50-gallon drum is permitted to age a year or so in situ but then we have to haul it out so the contents can be further composted before being used. It isn't smelly but it is heavy work so unless we can rope in a strong helper we have to do it together, a contrast in that most tasks around here are divided up and we each do our own assorted bits in comfortable solitude.

The house is a mess and I'm behind on about six deadlines but my list at the moment is almost entirely about planting. Seeds and seedlings alike are clamoring for attention and how to choose between being sure there will be beans and getting the tomatoes in? Among other things the whole nightshade-destined section of lower garden has gone to weed and must be reworked. I'm doing it one bed at a time to give myself courage, poor old peppers are still in their pots but the potatoes are now well up and I've just taken care of the tomatoes. The favored Brandywines take so damn long to produce they got topmost priority.

Planted them before even the beets, which says a lot (around here anyway). But the beets: *Albina vereduna,* "*Chioggia,*" "Golden" and "Early Wonder," since I do all the Lutz Winter Keepers in N.Y., will be next. Like the carrots, beets do great in the double-enriched, absolutely stone-free raised beds in the upper garden. The beds are also a one at a time proposition, but they go quickly because the soil is so loose.

Most of the pruning was done back last spring but I'm still clipping away at the apple tree that canopies my mom's ashes. I love the way it sweeps to the ground and makes a green shelter all summer but there's so much shade the lilies of the valley under it don't thrive or bloom and since they were her favorite flower I keep cutting back and trying to find a balance. Plan is to take a tiny bit at a time until it all works. B's clearing of last winter on the stream side opened things up considerably to the south and that should help quite a bit. Meanwhile the baby hostas are happy in the extreme and columbine is taking hold nicely. I've got a pretty double dark purple one from a friend and a new glaucous leafed anomaly—will I like brown flowers? Would *Moth* have liked brown flowers?—called *A. viridiflora* that looks gorgeous in the catalog and has grown well so far in the greenhouse. Final effect may be a bit sepulchral but I'm hoping it will come out more pre-Raphaelite, warmly dark and mysterious and vaguely medieval.

While I garden, Bill is building a wood-burning clay bread oven, twin to the one he built in New York. As before, he based it on the plan suggested by *The Bread Ovens of Quebec*. It's not a how-to book at all but between the pictures and the graphs it tells you everything you need to know. (Thank heavens anthropologists have to publish to get degrees.)

He's really got the technique down now. First you make a frame from bent saplings—a good use at last for the pestilential alders—then you cover it with bricks made from clay and straw. It's all very biblical, except that I have to report the bricks look a great deal like giant cowpats. Fortunately more clay gets smoothed over the outside until you have this very beautiful humongous dome that holds heat for hours and hours. The inside of the New York one came out very rough, so this time we covered the frame with an old sheet before adding the clay, hoping that'll smooth the interior surface.

We'll know once we burn out the frame, something that doesn't happen until the clay has dried thoroughly. It'll be weeks before oven-firing time but once it's here it's forever (unless it melts, to prevent which B will build an A-frame roof). Counting the major masonry base the thing weighs about three tons.

During oven building the alder frame got me thinking. Net result: Bill

has at my request built a beautiful cedar and alder arch to replace the black one that was destroyed. The bent wood makes a terrific lace work, sort of rustic wrought iron, a decided improvement over the old model. Bigger, too, as it needs to be; the clematis are eating all in their path. I figure that by the time the alder rots—probably in three or four years—the clematis will have built up its own woody structure to climb on.

But will the new rose climb on it too? I decided, as long as I was messing around in the area, to remove the two roses I had there. One, the "New Dawn," acted more like Dr. Van Fleet but didn't do much of anything anyway on account of mostly dying back every year. The other, a "White Dawn," grew pretty well, considering, but had an unhappy tendency to black spot and in any case appeared to be nearly expired after the rigors of last winter. Decided not to replace the "New Dawn" as doubt anything can coexist with the obscenely robust clematis on that side of the path. Replaced W.D. with "Mme. Plantier," recommended as unusually hardy and trainable as a climber. The white flowers look demure in their pictures and I hope will be at least moderately fragrant (opinion seems to be mixed on this score). The infant Mme. seems comparatively healthy but I expect it'll be years before there's much of an effect.

Right now *everything* is rather infant and not presenting much of an effect. The cold and wet of early spring has already been replaced by unseasonable warmth and drought. There has been much more fog than rain and even the evenings are shorts-warm, most unusual for June. Lilacs are blooming away undaunted and in fact rather extended, especially considering, but iris are moving into bloom and so is the rhubarb, although I keep cutting it back.

We've been eating it like mad and I'm still on my rhubarb and dried cherry kick. This year it's pie, made in my new version of old-fashioned crust—you cut the butter in little bits before you add it to the flour, so the dough never gets a chance to get pasty and tough.

Rhubarb and Dried Cherry Pie

Pastry for a double crust 9 inch pie:

Filling:
7 cups rhubarb, cut in 1½ inch dice
2⅓ cups sugar
¼ teaspoon salt
½ cup dried sour cherries
½ cup dried sweet cherries

2 tablespoons triple sec or other
  orange cordial
¼ cup flour
¼ cup (2 ounces) butter, cut in small
  pieces

Roll out bottom crust to fit into deep 9 inch pie pan, leaving a generous overlap. Chill.

Combine rhubarb, sugar, salt, dried cherries and triple sec.

Allow the mixture to sit for an hour or so, stirring occasionally.

Heat oven to 425. Roll out dough for top crust. Either plan to make lattice or use a 1 to 1½ inch cookie cutter to make several holes—stars, hearts, what have you—in the center area. Set aside.

Remove pan from refrigerator. Sprinkle about 1 tablespoon of the flour over the bottom crust. Spoon on a layer of filling, sprinkle with flour and dot with butter. Repeat until everything is used up. Apply the top crust and crimp edges securely. Place pan on foil-lined cookie sheet (to catch drips). Bake for 10 minutes, reduce heat to 400 and bake 30 to 40 minutes more, or until the crust is richly browned and filling is bubbling. Allow to cool slightly, then serve warm, preferably with a pitcher of heavy cream.

Eccleston Square,
London

17 June 1994

Dear Leslie,

About twenty-three years ago I made a little amateur film — in those days Nicky and I were deeply into pre-Raphaelite fashions — anyway that is not my reason for mentioning it. The point is that we showed the film to Phoebe and Amy and after seeing it we felt that we had to go back and have another look at the location we filmed in. Most of it was shot in a run-down garden in Bedfordshire called 'The Swiss', an incredible romantic garden with little Swiss-style summer-houses, a tiny chapel, a tree with a thatched roof for shelter around it, marble books displaying poems, gigantic rose arbours, miniature lakes and bridges — I could go on and on. Seeing the film again after all this time made me realize how influential this garden has been over my thinking.

The garden is designed as a series of little winding paths that give you new vistas at every turn. The whole garden never reveals itself to you and in fact when you see a view from the opposite direction it looks so different that you don't recognize it. The little paths and the secret areas I have developed in the middle of the shrubbery in Eccleston Square (I now realize) get their inspiration from 'The Swiss', although I have not the resources to build summer-houses and buy Italian pots and fonts to create the really romantic feel (I wouldn't even if I could)—inspiration rather than plagiarism, I hope.

The garden, of course, has a romantic story to go with it. Apparently in about 1820 Lord Ongley built it as a trysting place to meet his young mistress. The way I heard the story she died at the age of sixteen and is still to be found wandering through the paths and mooning over the bridges as she waits for the return of her long-dead lover. The garden itself is built quite a way from the house and is reached by a tunnel under the fields. Could it be that Lord Ongley's wife was old and infirm and could not manage to get down there and catch him red handed?

Our summer is not too dry so far only having to water about twice a week. I feel for you. Drought is something we really know about in England after the summers we have had for the last ten years — in fact this is the first time we haven't had a sprinkler ban for yonks.

My MP is a man called Peter Brooke; he is very interested in history and heritage subjects, so I have written to him about my latest plan. In 1851 there was an enormous exhibition of things British called 'The Great Exhibition' and in 1951 just after the war they repeated the idea calling it that time 'The Festival of Britain'. There is a plan afoot to have another major exhibition in 2001 and the government are looking for ideas and themes. My solution is: 'A Celebration of Garden Squares'. They are such an exceptional thing and although Paris, Rome and even New York have a few no one can come anywhere near the 420 recognized in London. All ours are gardens of one sort or another, whereas squares in other cities are often paved over with sculpture or fountains instead of living plants.

I thought that starting with the hundred squares in the SPOLS association we could organize clearing up, replanting, replacing broken railings, making sure that the legal problems were all sorted out, etc., etc., in time for a grand public opening right across London in 2001. One of the main points I would like to get across, perhaps at a planning forum, is Garden Squares as a solution to urban problems, a focus for residents, a village green in the city, solving problems of isolation, alienation, loneliness and even crime. The idea is particularly apt in that the vast majority of the squares we have today were built around the time of 'The Great Exhibition'.

I'll let you know how things work out.

Love,

Roger

Cushing,
Maine

Well, Roger dear, I don't know where the summer is going . . . To Hell in a basket is I suppose the short version. It's so endlessly damn hot and dry. Hotter than usual by a long shot, way up in the eighties and nineties and scarcely cooler at night, though June is classically a month in which dark-time sweaters are required and frost itself not unknown. I can barely bring myself to write about the dry part—June is supposed to be a month of frequent rain. Hah! There hasn't been so much as a drop for weeks. I heard on the radio the other day that Massachusetts got only ¾ inch of rain for the whole month of June and I doubt we did any better—probably it was worse. Mugginess is frequent, as is the prediction of showers and/or thundershowers and occasionally I can see it raining over Waldoboro to the south. But it does not rain here, or if it does it's like yesterday's performance, just enough to wash the leaves while the ground beneath never even gets damp.

Nothing is growing, nothing is germinating, nothing would be alive at all if I didn't spend all my gardening time watering. There's still huge tons of planting to do but no incentive to do it because I can't even water what's in the ground already. The well is dangerously low and it isn't even July yet. Once Bill comes up we'll reconnect the pumping system he put in last year to run water up from the stream to the lower garden and at least that will survive, but running a hose all day (and night) is hardly a substitute for a good soaking rain. The annuals look like they just left their pots in spite of having been in the ground for weeks. The perennials are all stunted. Delphiniums are just about to bloom, albeit somewhat sparsely, and I'm going to be very surprised if they get any taller than I and I'm only four feet ten. (They don't tower here, ever, but they do generally get to a respectable six or seven feet.) On the other hand, shortness may turn out to be a blessing in the blowing-over department and I'm just as happy the blossoms themselves are more spread out along the stalk. It's the same deal as the hyacinths: when they're doing it right the tightly-packed bloom stalk is too waddy and bunched-up to suit me.

That's one nice thing about perennials: you do usually get something, and if you have a cheerful temperament you can find something to enjoy about it. Vegetables, alas . . . Well. I'm sure glad I put the tomatoes in the lower garden, glad the whole joint is well mulched. And I'm glad the potatoes were planted early. But that about exhausts my joy at the moment—I'm really depressed and scared; this is the worst it's ever been.

And at the very worst time, too, since I've decided—wherever did I put my brains?—to have a major garden party to celebrate my new job at *Yankee*. About once a decade it occurs to me to have one of these big fandangos, probably because by then I've forgotten the pain of the previous occasion. I get thinking about how nice it would be it x met y and both of them got to admire the delphiniums and the next thing I know I've invited all these people and then of course I'm for it.

This time is likely to be a real humdinger since I somehow (briefly) thought it would be fun—and a fitting tribute to Tim, my new boss, who commissioned the original story—if I recreated The Salmon in the Bathtub. Of all the pieces I ever wrote for *Yankee*, the tale of how I poached two giant salmon in a bathtub (so I wouldn't have to cut them in half) has gotten the most and most enthusiastic response. It gets reprinted all the time and everybody at the magazine still speaks of it fondly, although it has been about fifteen years since it first appeared.

So brightgirl ordered up a bathtub and a pair of salmon, hired a band and bought two gross of sparklers—did I mention I'm planning to have this thing on the Fourth of July? Pray for me.
Love

Leslie

P.S. I think that the idea of the "Celebration of Squares" is terrific. Hope it happens!

Cushing, Maine

July 7, 1994

Dear Roger,

Whatabout if I ever mention anything about entertaining again you tie me like Ulysses to the mast until I'm myself again?

No, I'm kidding. It actually went very well mostly, especially cooking the salmon. I don't recommend it—in fact I strongly advise against it—but just in case you ever want to poach a very large fish here's what we did:

Prepare, prepare, prepare is nine-tenths of the whole deal. I did things like ordering really a lot of ice, locating the salmon and of course painting the outside as well as triple scrubbing the inside of the eponymous bathtub, a handsome old enameled iron job on ball and claw feet. Bill created a clay-lined fire pit at the edge of the garden and made a cage to encase the rocks so we could get them in and out of the fire easily. He also built a poaching rack out of an oak board and a bunch of cake-coolers. We assembled cheesecloth, lemons, bay leaves—all the standard poaching stuff—and 2 big rolls of heavy duty foil and a big sheet of plywood.

Bill made a major hardwood fire early in the day and we set the rocks in as soon as it got going. Then we went our separate ways, he to help get the garden tidy and the dance floor area mowed, I to the kitchen to cook my brains out (menu follows).

After several hours we met at the tub, me with the fish and he with the fire-resistant gloves. I stuffed the creatures with the lemons, onions, bayleaves and peppercorns and wrapped them up securely (securely is important for later) in cheesecloth. We pre-heated the tub with several kettlesful of hot water, drained it, inserted the rack, placed the fish thereon and poured in multi-gallon batch number two of hot water (having a lot of kettles is a good idea—I forgot to mention lots of kettles).

At this point the idea is to move fast, so the poaching liquid and tub will all stay hot and here naturally came our first Big Drama. The cage-lifters—aka the former black arch, now in pieces—fell apart just as we were lifting the rocks out of the fire. Backup lifters, a pair of wires, impossible to use in spite of efficacy at trial-lift time. So we scurried around like mad persons finding other arch pieces and did in fact manage to lift the cage though without a moment to spare as the second pair of lifters also broke. It was especially interesting because the cage was *also* falling apart. And hot? HOT! HOT! HOT!

Continuing the teamwork motif, B. lifted the rocks one by one, tossing them back and forth between the gloves to keep them from burning through. He dumped each rock as rapidly as possible on the tea towel that I had waiting, then I used said towel like a sling, holding the ends and conveying the rock over the side of the tub. It was lowered—lower, don't drop—to a position as close as possible to the fish. This was repeated about two dozen five-pound rocks' worth.

Great clouds of steam and hissing and bubbling. Whoopee. We were truckin', I'll tell you, trying to get those rocks in there fast and as soon as we did we whipped the tinfoil over the tub to tuck all the heat and steam in. Then for good measure we topped all with the layer of thick plywood.

After that, waiting and wondering. How long will be long enough and it's just like popovers. You can't peek, you just have to guess. We let them steam for about fifty minutes, then uncovered and let them cool in situ. They were done, as it turned out, to a turn.

Once they cooled we lifted them out—by the cheesecloth, which is why the wrapping must be so secure—and stored them on ice in the mas-

COLLECTED IN ECCLESTON SQUARE
JANUARY 17 1994

UNIDENTIFIED
COMFREY

LENTEN
ROSES
HELLEBORUS
ORIENTALIS

HAMAMELIS
ARNOLD
PROMISE

CALLYCARPA
BODINIERI

RHODODENDRON
DAURICUM

CORNELIAN
CHERRY
CORNUS
MAS

CAMELLIA
BERNICE BODDY

VIBURNUM
X BODNANTENSE
DAWN

Dried specimens of plants in flower on 17 January in
Eccleston Square.

Left: Leslie harvesting sugarsnaps. There are many modern varieties of snap pea but none are as tasty or high yielding as Calvin Lamborn's original Sugar Snap. That's a six-foot step ladder and the vines are still blooming (Bakaitis photo).

Below: Roger emerging from the bushes after searching for a lost cricket ball.

Above: The
Japanese Coral
Bark Maple *Acer
palmatum* 'Senkaki'
doing its autumn
thing in Eccleston
Square.

Right: Outside the
kitchen door.
Bill tends the fire in the
clay bread oven.
Capacity: 18 large
round loaves or, as
he puts it, "just big
enough for one
small woman."

Left: Maine, late summer in the blue border. Elusive combo captured at last—Globe Thistle, Plume Poppy and Joe Pye Weed bloom together, with our prize Hackamatack in the background.

Below: Lois painting the Minton border in late June. The lawn has already succumbed to drought, but Oenothera makes a strong, golden show punctuated by the last pink blossoms of digitalis, opium poppy and Asiatic lily "Parisienne."

Above: A great sight in spring in Eccleston Square: the bright red young leaves of *Pieris formosa*.

Right: Weigela florida 'Variegata' in full bloom in the Square.

Left: August in the upper garden, view south toward Lois's house. Pole bean trials shade the greenhouse; summer squash, leeks and *Zigeunerbaron* Gladioli grow in the raised beds (foreground).

Below: July looking south into the garden. Blooming Mother of Thyme billows violet full of bees, and self-sown allysum makes a honey-fragrant border beside the path through the white garden in Cushing.

Above: The creamy bark of Himalayan Birch, *Betula utilis* var. *jacquemontii* against the pure white flowers of *Viburnum plicatum* 'Mariesii' in the Square.

Below: The most successful path edging—it works both in sun and shade—is *Geranium endressii* together with the cultivar 'Wargrave Pink'.

Above: Overview of the Cushing garden blooming in late August; the Saint George River gleams in the upper right-hand corner.

Right: The Square just as the London Planes are starting to get their leaves at the beginning of May.

sive packing box they came in. There was a lot of debate about where to put a box almost as big as the kitchen but in the end that's where we put it. I kept having visions of Mamselle happily feasting and figured security was paramount. (We call all the skunks Mamselle, which is the best name for a skunk in America.)

Not to bed until late in spite of best intentions, then up early to thick-afog and apprehension aplenty but by nine or ten it was shaping up gorgeous and indeed it had the grace to continue to not rain when not raining was for once what was wanted. Terrific party in spite of the fact that every blessed person I invited came. Terrific party even though the well went dry right before it was time to skin and glaze the salmon so I had to do it all out of doors and as a result scaled way back on the fancy trimming and assorted decor. Paper plates, too, in spite of the stack of waiting crockery. I just couldn't face forty people's worth of fishy dishes without running water.

Nobody seemed to mind. Everybody seemed to like everything, though there's no doubt in my mind that the gastronomic hit of the party was not the salmon or indeed any of the main attractions. The food that went faster than everything else was an almost-afterthought mango and cherry salsa confected at the last minute to go with the sliced ham I set out in case anybody was anti-fish.

They ate large quantities of everything, actually, including the star-shaped strawberry shortcakes, getting it all down shortly before the mosquitoes attacked in force. We had a ghastly half-hour or so, but routed them with the fireworks. Billowing showers of colored sparks and beautiful clouds of pale pink sparkler-smoke and after that dancing into the night. The party started at three p.m. and the last guest left around midnight, so I'm calling it a success.

Now if it would just rain.

A Menu for the Fourth of July

hot and spicy roast pecans
marinated feta with herbs and olive oil
chicken and wild mushroom crostini
crudités with cashew chutney

coleslaw with hot pepper peanut dressing
potato salad with roasted cumin and cream
poached salmon with dill sauce
sliced ham with mango and cherry salsa

strawberry shortcake

Mango and Cherry Salsa

For about 5 cups, 10 to 12 servings:

1 large vidalia or other sweet onion, minced fine, about 1 cup

1 pound firm black cherries, pitted and finely chopped, about 2 cups

2 large ripe mangoes, peeled, seeded and coarsely chopped, about 2 cups

$1/2$ to $3/4$ cup minced hot green chilies—a mixture of jalapeno and serrano is nice if those are available.

$1/2$ cup lime juice

1 teaspoon salt

1 cup minced coriander leaves

Combine everything but the coriander and let it sit for at least 30 minutes, up to several hours. Taste and adjust salt, lime and chilies; the sauce should be quite fiery. Add coriander just before serving.

Cucumber, Dill and Gin Sauce
for Cold Salmon

For about 3½ cups, 8 to 10 servings:

1 smallish, young cucumber (pick
   before seeds start to thicken)

½ cup finely chopped onion

1½ teaspoons salt

2 cups sour cream

½ cup minced fresh dill—thin
   feathery fronds only—or more to
   taste

3 tablespoons gin, or more to taste

pinch of sugar

Peel cucumber and shred on the large holes of the grater. Combine with onion and salt in a non-reactive bowl and allow to sit for about an hour—until vegetables are limp and have shed considerable juice. Drain very thoroughly, then taste—if there's still *lots* of salt, rinse and drain again (but remember that this will be the seasoning for the sauce).

Combine vegetables with remaining ingredients. Let sit at room temperature for 15 to 20 minutes, then taste and adjust seasonings.

Eccleston Square, London

Leslie, I have got another problem over London Squares. The Fujita company are trying to turn Craven Hill Gardens into a semi-Japanese garden. They started out with a sort of prison yard arrangement with a gravel walking area with nothing to look at – really the antithesis of a Japanese garden – they always have things to study: rocks, trees, moss, plants and not forgetting cherry trees for the cherry blossom time. The council have rejected the first submission and they have put it up again changing the gravel for grass – to no great advantage. Anyway I am un-happy. I suppose this sounds like whinging – compared to building car parks it is certainly a complaint of a much lower order. All I feel – and I feel it very strongly – is these are London Squares and although I want to see variety it should be in a context of appropriate gardening for our city. These squares are important to the local community and they should be interesting visually from both the inside and the outside so that even the passing visitor can get some benefit from them.

Glad your Fourth of July went off OK, wish I had been there. We had a wonderful day on our twenty-five years together party on the third, hot and sunny all day, loads of people that we hadn't seen for twenty years or more – we loved it. At the end the kids all lost patience with behaving themselves and started up a massive water fight soaking about a hundred of the remaining guests.

My son Sam is thirty today. He was born nine months after that awful day Kennedy was assassinated.

The weather has been hot, dry and very humid – apparently the hottest July this century. This means solid watering. The first plants to be hit were the hydrangeas – we have four of the more unusual types: *H. aspera*, *H. sargentiana*, *H. aspera var. macrophylla* and the oak-leafed thing *H. quercifolia*. Some of the leaves went brown before we caught up with them but they are now in full flower and, I think, magnificent. Midsummer is a difficult time to have much in flower in what is essentially a shrub garden. Hydrangeas fit the bill, but I keep struggling to find really interesting things, although at the moment *H. sargentiana* and *H. quercifolia* are my favourites, I am open to suggestions. Just a quick note because I am getting all worked up about our forthcoming holiday.
Love,

Roger

Cushing,
Maine

Rain for real at last—first rain in almost two months!—and as usual nothing halfway. I got up at five to close the windows (quite a struggle as the recent humidity has swollen all the wood) and it was pounding down so loud and hard I decided to just plain get up. Out belatedly to close the shed—in Bill's new raincoat, a marvel of water-repellence—and the door yard was running with rain, a solid quarter inch sheet of water coursing over the matted brown grass.

It was all done by six or so. Not much damage as far as I can see. The delphiniums were already pretty much shot. One eight-foot sunflower went down. Big Joe Pye weed and globe thistle plants now giant funnels, leaning over everything and hollow at the heart. Since this is simply an exaggeration of the problem they've been presenting for the last two weeks or so, all it means is that I'll finally have to get around to tying them up. Lilies, God love 'em, are unaffected though the daylilies are a tad on the bedraggled side at the mo'.

Of course every last tomato currently extant is going to crack, but that's a small price to pay for the possibility of some kind of crop by the end of the summer. It has been so hot and dry most blossoms have been dropping . . . or maybe, come to think of it, pollination is the problem. There have been a few bees here and there but this has definitely not been a bee year. I've never used those hormonal blossom set sprays but think this

might be one time when something like that would pay off. I know tomatoes are supposed to be self-fruitful but you'd never prove it by my observations. Usually the flowers among the foodstuffs bring all the bees I
could ever need, but this year they are (comparatively) conspicuous by
their absence.

Slim pickins in the bug department all around, actually, except for the
mosquitoes. First the June bugs, most accurately named insects in creation, never appeared. Then the flea beetles were, well, not missing exactly, but scanty (except on the potatoes). By now there's usually a grand
array of pests but . . . Not even much in the way of earwigs though the
season is young for them and I'm just now starting to have some dahlias
for them to eat which of course they are obligingly doing. Sometimes I
think earwigs are spontaneously generated by dahlia plants. I'm scrupu-
lous about removing old stems, curved bits of bark, all that sort of thing,
but those bastards can find hiding-places anywhere and do. The garden
magazines continue to publish articles about how they're harmless and
mostly eat decaying matter and won't really do any damage, and readers
keep writing in to yelp and complain that THEY DO TOO, dammit, and the articles march on all the same. Do they do this in England?
Some day I shall write a Restoration farce: *The Triumph of Expertise over
Experience*.

Fireflies ended early. They're about gone now and I'm wondering if
it's because there have been so few slugs. I read somewhere that fireflies
eat slugs and if that's it they're in big trouble because after the spring in-
festation there's been no way for *los slimos* to make it. Happily for us, the
monarchs have shown up to lay eggs on the milkweed right on schedule.
Our formerly enormous milkweed patch dwindleth yearly—maybe because of the string of droughts, maybe because simple succession means it
has used up the appropriate nutrients—but there is still enough of it to
perfume the entire property, especially at dusk, and any trip over to Lois's
is a heady pleasure.

We've been taking regular night walks. The full moon and clouds
have been obligingly picturesque and the traffic still does mercifully abate

to nothing once the sun goes down. I miss the daytime observation jaunts—no swallows this year, either, come to think of it—but it has been too blazing hot to do anything in broad day and both twilights are still mosquito-filled.

Bill is in town as I write. When he comes home we'll do the first baking in the new oven. Both very excited, I think he even more than I, which is only reasonable considering how hard he's worked on it. Covering the branch frame with a sheet to make a smoother interior has produced the most beautiful ribbing. It's even more cathedral-like than the one in N.Y. Now to see if it will bake as well. We used the same plans but this one looks much bigger inside to me, and the clay body itself is certainly different, Maine marine clay rather than the blue river type. The one fires as red as the other, however.

The 28th

Success!

I made four loaves of whole wheat, in pans; six big rounds of peasant-style sourdough (and two baguettes) on the hearth; a plum tart, a pork roast and a pan of potatoes. This filled the oven about three-fourths full. It's BIG!

Leslie

Eccleston Square, London

Dear Leslie,

We have just had a two-week holiday in Cornwall, staying in a little hamlet called Rinsey with a beautiful rocky cove that is totally covered by the tide twice every twenty-four hours, meaning it is perfectly clean. They all went swimming but I hate the water – too cold. I went off hunting edible seaweeds: the rocks are covered in a green seaweed called *Entromorpha intestinalis*. I collect it, dry it in the sun and then deep fry it – serve with a little sprinkled sugar and some Chinese vinegar, crunchy and exotic. In fact it is the very seaweed that smart Chinese restaurants serve in China Town. They have it specially imported from China! My favourite seaside edible for the summer is marsh samphire, sometimes called sea asparagus. This is to be found growing in vast quantities all over the salt marshes. I wash it, then dunk it in boiling water for about five minutes then serve v. hot with butter, just as you would asparagus. This goes down well even with cookery philistines. By the way, I have found it in the US on muddy inlets on both the east and west coasts.

Dulse and Cucumber Salad

Dulse Palmaria palmata is a lovely deep red seaweed that grows in the middle of the tidal area and can be collected from spring to autumn.

This recipe is inspired by the Japanese use of seaweeds.

Serves 4

80 g (3¹/₂ oz) dulse	3 tablespoons dark soy sauce
1 cucumber	1 teaspoon sugar
4 tablespoons vinegar	salt

Wash dulse and pat dry with a clean cloth, then cut into 4 cm (1¹/₂ in) lengths. Mix together the vinegar, soy sauce, sugar and salt. Combine the cucumber and dulse in a salad bowl and pour the vinegar dressing over it. Mix gently and serve.

I did manage to visit a couple of gardens; one, Trebah, is built in a steep valley with a great mass of mixed blue hydrangeas in the level part at the bottom, thousands of them. I turn blue myself with jealousy just looking at them. The other one I got to is the garden of Patrick Heron. I think he is the greatest living English painter. His garden is incredible. It is built in or on a tor – a mass of gigantic boulders. The planting was started by a wonderful man who was responsible for introducing and growing loads of New Zealand plants. He found that they did well in the very windy, very salty, but mild conditions of that part of Cornwall (Zennor). Patrick is an abstract painter but through his later paintings there is a feeling of light and wind and the forms that he develops also have a relationship to the great rocks that he lives amongst. He is to have a major retrospective exhibition at the Tate Gallery in a couple of years, nine rooms full!

A meaningless piece of information for you. England just smashed South Africa in the final cricket test match. Devon Malcolm (our fast bowler) took nine out of the ten wickets in the last innings – please jump up and down with your fists in the air to join me celebrating.

More things are hotting up on the talks about *Quest for the Rose*; I have now been invited to go to Bermuda next March to give a talk to the rose society there. I am very interested to visit as so many of the ancient Tea and China roses are still to be found in their gardens. Also I have been invited to Australia to go to their big rose meeting outside Sydney, in November next year – great, as it will get me down south for their spring just when everything starts to get depressing over here.

The tomatoes are ripe! Oregon Spring and Brandywine, we are going to sample them served rather plain so that we can enjoy (I presume) the flavour – just oil, olives, basil and mozzarella cheese – more later.

It's happening again like a recurring nightmare: yet another garden square is under threat of being dug up to make a car park. This is a lovely square in the Boltons area at the back of Chelsea, entirely surrounded by big mansion blocks and very quiet and serene. I have been helping the Garden Committee with some planting ideas. Suddenly out of the blue I get a letter from their agent telling me that there is another car park deal that the owners, Gunter estates, are trying to push through on the back of a planning appeal on the work they want to do on the building extension. We haven't had any time to gather thoughts and find out how the residents stand on the proposal, as it goes up for ministerial appeal within a week.

I have taken up having tennis lessons: Guy the coach keeps saying: 'Not like Long John Silver, you act as if you've got a parrot on your shoulder.' Oh well.
Love,

R.

P.S. The clay breadoven sounds wonderful; maybe you could even cook a giant salmon in it – on second thoughts it might ruin the bread.

Cushing,
Maine

August 30, 1994

Dear Roger,

Well I was only partly right—every *ripe* tomato cracked, but the green ones seem to be okay. All my tomatoes were early this year. I attribute it partly to the weather (even the nights are hot) and partly to the Stupice tomatoes, far and away the earliest genuinely tasty ones I've ever grown. Much better than Oregon Spring. They're a Czech variety, according to Southern Exposure Seed Exchange, source of most of this year's weirdo tomatoes. So far they're doing exactly what the catalog said they'd do, producing numerous clusters of six to eight juicy, flavorful, two-ounce fruits, most of them near the base of the plant. I hope the Czechoslovakian Black hot peppers (from the same source) also live up to their description as early, delicious, productive and ornamental, though it's a lot to ask for given that there's only one plant. Most of the pepper seedlings went to New York, where they were promptly eaten by a family of woodchucks that moved into the garden as soon as Bill and Celia left for Maine.

Not surprisingly, the peppers seem to be the most drought-stunted of all the greenhouse-started plants (except maybe the lavatera, alas) with eggplants a close second. Tomatoes by and large picked up and got moving once Bill's watering system came to the rescue but the peppers are scarcely larger than they were when I set them out six weeks ago, and at this point I don't have a lot of hope. The largest and best looking are those in the row of hot types at the bottom of the garden. Maybe being hot they don't care about heat. Maybe they appreciate partial shade (the apple trees hang over there a bit) and maybe it's just that water runs down hill.

The poppy walk is history and—how else would we know it's August—the poppy-free spot looks like unmitigated hell. Local nurseries have been offering very little in the way of suitable filler (they're having drought problems too) and some of the things I did plant, including a pair of soi-disant "swamp azaleas" (mountain laurel from the looks of 'em) are not pleasing. Petunias should come around eventually and so will the other annuals and I think the two late hydrangeas (*tarda*) will work out fine. (I'd love to have *quercifolia,* by the way, but I don't yet. Too big for the current scheme.) The unpleasing azaleas will have to be moved, probably down to the stream where things are marginally wetter. If they don't look better there it's off to the compost heap or, more likely, Lois's place somewhere.

I try to keep my mind off the white garden by looking at the lilies, all of which are shorter than usual but not otherwise diminished. Tigers in abundance will be splashier when I cut back the spent lovage and rip out the dead poppies in front of them but the yellow asiatics, the Hyperion and Stella d'Oro daylilies, the yellow tigers and assorted aurelians (a mixture for cutting) are all performing splendidly. So is a nameless peach daylily smack in the middle of the pink and yellow border. I swear the wretched thing gets oranger as well as bigger every year. It'll have to go somewhere else, but where? It's too delicate for the hot section, all wrong among the whites. The sad truth is peach-apricot is not a color that gets a lot of play here. I may get daring and put it among the blues, where there are a lot of "pink" asiatics that look rather peachy already. Unfortunately the whole blue border is getting crowded—I just stuck in a Cotinus where the rose of Sharon used to be—and taking things out would probably make more sense than putting things in. (I did take out one aconitum, albeit purely by accident. Discovered it totally smothered dead when I pushed back the mighty thistle.)

One positive, well, semi-positive side of the drought situation: wonderful blueberries. They're scarce and small, which is not so great, but the flavor is beyond compare, sharp and sweet at the same time, very intensely fruity and not at all wishy-washy the way blueberries so often tend to be. Lois and I went picking in Annie's field the other day and got a quart between us in about an hour. Ate 'em plain, though Lo was making major pie noises. As usual I told her I'd make the pie if she picked the berries and she has promised to do so.

It'll probably take her a while to get around to it. Eli, Robin and the world's most adorable baby have just arrived and Lo is on full granny alert. Me too. Emma is now just one—on the 24th of July—and walking. Love

2.
P.S. Made this cake while waiting for pie—ideal, you only need a few of each kind of berry to get a large effect.

Summer Cake
(Blueberry Peach Upside-Down Cake with Raspberry Cream)

butter for the pan

$1/2$ cup sugar

finely grated zest of 1 lemon

4 or 5 peaches (or nectarines), peeled and sliced $1/3$ inch wide, enough to thickly pave a 10-inch square pan

1 tablespoon flour

Batter:

2 cups all-purpose flour

$1/2$ cup sugar

2 teaspoons baking powder

$1/4$ teaspoon salt

$1/2$ cup (4 ounces) chilled butter

2 eggs

approximately $1/2$ cup milk

$1^1/4$ cups wild blueberries

Raspberry cream:

1 cup raspberries

2 tablespoons sugar

1 tablespoon triple sec or other orange cordial

1 cup heavy cream

Heat oven to 400°F. *Thickly* butter a 10×10×2-inch baking pan.

Combine the first ¹/₂ cup sugar with the lemon zest and sprinkle it over the butter. Layer on peaches, in closely spaced but not overlapping rows. Sprinkle on the tablespoon of flour.

In a wide mixing bowl, thoroughly combine the flour, second ¹/₂ cup sugar, baking powder and salt. Cut in the butter to make a mixture the texture of coarse meal.

Break eggs into a measuring cup and beat lightly. Add enough milk to make 1 cup total. Stir liquid into dry ingredients, mixing only enough to dampen. While there are still lumps of flour, stir in the blueberries. Carefully spoon batter over peaches and bake for 30 to 35 minutes, or until cake is risen and well browned and a toothpick inserted in the center comes out clean.

Cool on a wire rack for 2 or 3 minutes, then reverse cake onto a large plate. Make raspberry cream: Crush berries and mix with sugar and cordial. Whip cream to soft peaks and fold in berries. Serve warm cake in squares with a dollop of the cream on top.

Cushing,
Maine

September 10, 1994

Dear Roger,

We have been having the typical August right into this month, all sorts of people coming and going, performances and art openings in town and of course the stupid drought put a late twist in all things horticultural. That's over now, thank heavens. Finally at long last and rather too late the garden is splendid, full of good things to eat, all in bloom, refreshed and reinvigorated by a return to more normal rainfall. I assume (read hope) the same is by now true in England. Funny to think of you having similar weather in your so dissimilar locale. At least it brought you Brandywines. (And perhaps made you grateful for city water? You don't say anything about water rationing this time and it sounds as though the thirsty hydrangeas were able to get all they needed.) Bill's ingenious watering system proved to have one great systemic flaw: when it gets *really* dry, the stream that feeds the whole deal slows to a dismal trickle—no more water available until rains refill the swamp that feeds the stream.

Oh well, the worst is over now and we seem to be having a nice late fall. No sign yet of the slightest frost. Even and still it's starting to be clean up time. All the ranunculuses are spent, a big wind storm knocked down the tall cosmos, assorted blights and mildews are starting to creep into the squashes, tomatoes and beans. I want to keep things tidy so the autumn pleasures can shine. The big pink dahlia is blooming at last, New England asters—bright magenta and strong violet—are coming out among the oranges and yellows of the calendula bed. The roses have recovered nicely and I'm having quite a good show of late oriental lilies (Bill hates that heavy perfume so I guess it's just as well he isn't here).

Last major social event of the season was two weeks ago, when I had the annual meeting of the Penobscot Bay Lady Foodwriters' Association at a luncheon in the lower garden. We are a small, very exclusive group (others have tried to join but as we all talk all the time already it has been decided there's no airtime for anyone else). Our sort-of president is Nancy Jenkins, formerly and long-sufferingly of the *New York Times*, now teaching, consulting, and writing freelance. She's just done a book called *The Mediterranean Diet*. (I'll send you a copy. It's mouthwatering, much dandier than the title suggests.)

Nancy gets to be chief because she is the most unimpeachably Penobscot Bay, having been raised in Camden on the very banks thereof. Other members besides moi are Sandy Oliver and Susan Loomis. Sandy lives on an island out in the bay (Islesboro) and publishes *Food History News*, a quarterly newsletter full of research and advice for those who run the food aspects of living history museums. (Reminds me of your remarks about the possibilities for gardens on TV. So much more to food than pretty pictures and show and tell.) Susan is a cookbook author who moved to the area from Seattle, made friends with us all, then went off to spend two years in France researching a book about natural farming there. We are all extremely jealous. Activities of the society: eating, drinking wine, arguing about the meaning of everything connected to food, discussing (very objectively of course) everybody else in America who writes about the subject. We have a good time.

Of course making lunch for old pals like these does not admit of going out for cold cuts. Compensation for the pressure is you know they'll appreciate it if you do something special. It being very close to Nancy's birthday I made her cake the star of the lunch. It was a kind of culinary in-joke: Nancy hates cake, so without telling her I made a *trompe-l'œil* one. It looked incredibly like the real thing and she was fooled until it was set right in front of her. The basis was a tall loaf of peasant bread (from the famous oven), split into four layers, dampened with herbed olive oil and stuffed with sliced tomatoes, grilled eggplant, zucchini and peppers, roasted onions, lots of garlic, bits of oil-cured little black olives . . . every good Mediterranean thing. A sort of super-colossal *pan bagnat*. I let it rest under a weight all morning, then "frosted" the outside with a mixture of cream cheese, softened feta and ricotta salata, whirled in the processor with heavy cream until it was fluffy and spreadable. I tinted a little bit of it with tomato paste and wrote "happy birthday" with an icing tube. Decoration was very simple, lightly poached *Cantharellus cinnabarinus* to represent flowers, with basil leaves for leaves (Nancy, who needs new glasses, thought the mushrooms were tiny nasturtiums).

You will be wondering where in Maine I found the red chanterelles. The answer of course is that I found them in New York. With Bill and Celia both back at school I am in the pingpong mode and go down every other weekend to spend time with them. Only love would make me do it, the garden is at its highest beauty right now. Surrounding trees have gilded leaves, the sky is blue and clear. Last goldfinches are at the white Italian sunflowers, darting and singing. They're so tame they don't scatter until I'm within a foot or two of where they're feeding. The plants made hundreds of flowers and I thought there'd be plenty for everybody but I think I'd better go gather some seed before they eat it all.

Oh, I almost forgot to tell you. "Mme. Plantier" has grown like anything; the bush is almost as tall as I am and quite robust looking; I shall be sure to hill it up well for its first winter and with any luck there will be flowers next year. The funny thing is that after all this I may end up wanting to move it anyway. The white perennial sweet peas (*Lathyrus albus* "White Pearl") have done admirably what the rose was supposed to, namely twine into the clematis and bloom whitely when it wasn't. The vines, which are now three years old, began to bloom in early July, lovely long pannicles of waxy flowers, and they are *still blooming!* In fact they're loaded with buds, about twelve feet tall, healthy and green as can be. I'd take a picture but there appears to be no way—if you back off you can't see anything but white dots, get close and you've got a catalog illustration. Phoo.

This seems to be a problem with all my favorite vines. The purple bells (*Rhodochiton atrosanguineum*), canary creeper (*Tropaeolum peregrinum*), and scarlet cypress (*Ipomoea quamoclit*) did spectacularly this year—all are heat lovers that can take a fair amount of drought—but leaves and flowers are so delicate they only photograph well in close-up. I guess the moral is Be There.
Love

Leslie

P.S. You will be amused to know I was dead wrong about the bugs. No sooner had I written about their scarcity than they appeared in force. Never much in the way of beetles and the earwigs stayed at tolerable levels, but *caterpillars,* OMIGOD, and grasshoppers ditto. Doesn't pay to gloat.

P.P.S. I want you to try these chick peas, invented (ho ho, a likely story) for the lady foodie lunch. Not only are they delicious but they have no fat and may thus be pigged out upon guilt free.

Chickpeas with Lime and Roasted Cumin

For about 3 cups, 4 to 6 servings:

1 heaping cup (dry) chickpeas	1 teaspoon salt
2 tablespoons whole cumin seeds	3 to 4 tablespoons lime juice

Cover the chickpeas with cold water, leave overnight, drain, cover with fresh water and simmer until tender. Drain. (Canned could be used in a pinch, but they never have that lovely, nutty-floury taste and texture and where this is such a simple dish . . .)

Heat a small heavy skillet, dry, over medium heat. When the metal is hot, add the cumin and toast, shaking the pan constantly, for 20 to 35 seconds, or until the seeds are fragrant and very lightly browned. Do not let them scorch. Turn them out of the pan at once and allow to cool.

Combine chickpeas with a scant tablespoon of the cumin, the salt and the smaller amount of lime juice. Taste and adjust seasonings as suits you.

Eccleston Square, London

27 September 1994

Dear Leslie,

Do you remember me talking to you about my crazy Irish friend Stephen Pearce and his garden project? It's all going full steam ahead. I have just come back from a weekend over there. He has about twenty men working on the site. Anyway he and Kim Mai are really keen on the idea of an orangery, but apart from this I am trying to get a price on the plants for the main garden which we hope to buy this autumn and store for an early spring planting. It is very, very mild over there and we could plant as early as February but there is one snag — it rains all the time and the site becomes unworkable.

Do you grow the ordinary Passion Flower *Passiflora caerulea*? It's the only one we ever seem to grow outdoors in England, the others are really too tender, I have plants draped all over the tennis court netting and they are fruiting like mad. I met a terrific cookery woman in Ireland called Doreen Allen (she writes loads of books and runs a cookery school, have you heard of her?). She said that the ordinary garden passion flower is just as good to eat as the brown crinkly job in the shops; it's true! As I play tennis I pick them from the tennis court netting, they are wonderful, much more appetising than the shop things, bright orange outside with stunning scarlet seeds. You could add them to a fruit salad for a touch of the exotic, but I think they are best picked fresh and just sucked from the shell.

The azaleas bed is very dull at this time of year so I have planted masses of a tall aconite. They come bursting into bloom in August and are fabulous in September and October. I can't remember where I bought it and I have been unable to name it, but Martyn (Rix) came to my aid by pointing me at an entry in the book *Perennial Garden Plants* by Graham Thomas. He says that *Aconitum carmichaelii var. wilsonii* 'Kelmscott' is a six-foot-tall early autumn violet-blue plant – that must be what it is, such a wonderful thing to have in a garden for this time of year, also it self-propagates and after a few years you end up with loads of them.

Last night I got a letter from Westminster Council saying that we have won the 'Westminster in Bloom' Private Squares category first prize. Dancing in the streets will last all night.

I spent nearly all of yesterday in the car driving up to Norfolk, the roads not too fast, to visit the nursery of a man called Reads who specializes in tender plants and has a terrific collection of Citrus – oranges, lemons, tangerines and all the other relatives. The reason, of course, was to buy some plants for the conservatory in Cork. In the end I bought eleven different types covering the most ancient types still in cultivation, although actually pinning them down is extremely difficult; Reads felt that the bitter Seville orange is probably one of the oldest and certainly the *Citrus medica* is extremely old.

By the way, the rhubarb chard that I planted in the spring was not a great success, although we got a few meals off them, the plants were all rather small. I put three or four out in the garden and they are massive. I presume the reason that they do not do well in pots is that in the wild, Sea Beet, from which Chard is developed, grows on the coast just above the tide line and puts down roots about six inches max.

We have managed to resist the second car park threat, the residents got really well organized under Barbara Richards and others and sent a resounding no vote to the council who have now buried it, for good (ha ha).

The painter I mentioned, Patrick Heron, has just had an opening for the exhibition of his latest work – a series of very large paintings, about ten feet long by five feet high, at a place called the Campden Arts Centre.

It was a fantastic show, he calls them his garden paintings and gains his inspiration from his Cornish garden. They are really vigorous, lively and refreshing, they look like the paintings of a young man full of spirit and life with no holds barred using amazing colour combinations. If you had to guess his age and you knew nothing of his life, I am sure you would say these are paintings of a man who has just found himself – a man probably of about thirty-five. In fact he is well into his seventies. The only rotten thing about it was that he fell ill about half an hour before the exhibition and spent most of the evening in the loo!

It looks as if it is going to be a really good mushroom year – things like rare Phlegmaciums are popping up all over the place.

Love,

Roger

Cushing, Maine

Dear Roger,

My goodness what a lot of interesting news. First allow me to add loud huzzahs and of course I will dance all night in honor of your first prize. Do you get money for further beautification? a glorious trophy with gold leaf upon it? Does this mean they will listen more attentively to SPOLS? I doubt it. (How do they think the place can keep blooming if they insist on building a bunch of blooming parking lots under it?)

Not to . . . what do you call it? whinge—great word—it just drives me nuts that bureaucrats can be (are, perhaps almost by definition) so short-sighted.

And here you are not only having all this gorgeousness but even growing food—of a sort. Did you eat the massive rhubarb chard? It does occur to me that growing food in downtown London you might want to be a little careful of too much greenery. I have read that leafy things like chard and spinach can pick up a lot of lead from the soil . . . It's probably not enough to bother, just don't tell Nicky.

I'm as usual amazed and in awe of the climate that allows you outdoor passion fruit. Passiflora is a popular houseplant here (though not with me) but I've never heard of one fruiting indoors except in some kind of ritzy greenhouse. Do you have to have male and female plants or are they self-fertile?

Same question haunts me anent the citrus. I *think* they're all self-fertile and I am ferociously jealous of your Irish friends. Partly I envy them the rare fruit but even more I envy them the flowers. Seville oranges—the only kind to use in a large number of extremely interesting dishes including the true *canard à l'orange*—are very difficult to get here but you can occasionally buy them at fancy urban groceries. The flowers however, the flowers from which the perfume is distilled, those you must live with if you are to have the pleasure of them. Perhaps when Bill builds our greenhouse . . . It hasn't happened, but he has promised we will have one for the Pleasant Valley house, there to grow among other things a fig tree descended from the one his grandmother tended long ago in Pennsylvania. (Various family members have bearing trees grown from slips taken from the original, and we in turn will take a slip from one of them.)

Meanwhile I must comfort myself with apples—less abundant than last year and I think less tasty (probably the drought) and strawberries. Now that it is cool and damp the Tristars are bearing quite well—a handful a day—and for whatever reason the jays haven't discovered them yet. Catbirds are the primary predators as far as berries are concerned and they're all flown.

Big news from here is big, big rain. When they look back at this summer/fall it will have had above average rainfall because on Friday, September 23, it began to pour just at darktime and it rained all night and poured steady all day Saturday and spit a bit on Sunday and when the whole thing was done the midcoast area had received over 11.5 inches of rain, just shy of a quarter of the average annual total. Post frost, of course, and far too late to do this year's garden much good, but at least this way the trees, perennials and shrubs will go into the cold well fortified.

As luck (this summer's luck anyway) would have it, that was the weekend of Common Ground Fair, the yearly harvest festival sponsored by MOFGA, the Maine Organic Farmers and Gardeners Association. On Sunday, in spite of what we knew would be fearsome mud, we went. Lois wanted her friend Elizabeth, who's from Ireland, to see a bit of the countryside and anyway it wouldn't be summer's end without the fair, a fantasy mishmash of Renaissance Festival, Harvest Home and Late Hippie

Delight. The thing was started quite modestly, ten or twelve years ago. Its founders wanted a more agriculturally-focused alternative to modern country fairs, something kinder and gentler that would not have motorized rides, a midway, freak shows or girlie shows. Scarcely a country fair at all if you ask me. But almost immediately the idea took off. Nowadays tens of thousands attend. It's three days of jam-packed rural New Age. Visitors can go through an exhibition hall laden with quilts, canned goods and prize rutabagas, pick up a nice cup of herbal tea (no coffee is permitted), check out the healing crystals, be entertained by stilt walkers, strolling musicians and Morris Dancers, visit barnsfull of splendid animals—everything from Highland cattle to Angora rabbits and really a lot of weird looking chickens.

There are contests in things like wood-splitting and manure slinging (The Harry S. Truman Memorial Manure Pitch-Off) and of course there is tons to eat. The food, though wholesome (concessionaires must use whole wheat flour, no white sugar is allowed) is much better and more various than that at other fairs; you can get things like grilled eggplant sandwiches and homemade lamb sausage with organic tomato sauce. And there are always good crafts, interesting demonstrations and new things to try. This year I bought several bags of dried tomatillos from a farmer who used his wood-heated sauna for the drying process. *Delicious!*

Do you know tomatillos (*Physalis ixocarpa*)? You have to have them for Mexican green sauce. They're easy, practically weeds which alas is what they look like. Not an attractive plant but you only need one to have more fruit than you'll ever need. I've always frozen the excess, never thought of drying it but these little units are really tasty, very much like dried tomatoes but sharper, almost peppery. Best use so far: cut in dice and stir at the last minute into cooked rice. Serve with browned butter.

Browned butter has been figuring largely in my cuisine lately—you know how you get going on something and suddenly it's everywhere? I'm liking it very much with late summer vegetables: mature green beans, early potatoes, yellow crookneck squash. Now that I'm back in harness

(*Yankee* job is full time and quite demanding) I'm cooking again with an eye to how things will look when photographed. Right in the middle of canning eight million tomatoes I made myself a handsome stew of the above-mentioned vegetables, garnished with ricotta salata and a big handful of the fresh coriander which is flourishing in the autumn coolness. Recommended.

Autumn Vegetable Stew

For 2 main dish, 4 side dish servings:

2 tablespoons butter

1 large onion, diced

1 sprig lemon thyme, about 2 inches long

4 small boiling potatoes, yellow, purple or a combination, about 1 pound, cut in thick slices

4 small yellow crookneck squash, about ¾ pound, cut in thick slices

½ pound flat Italian green beans, cut in 2 inch lengths

½ cup heavy cream

½ cup minced coriander leaves, plus extra for garnish

salt to taste

4 ounces ricotta salata, cut in small dice or flat tablets

Melt butter in a heavy saucepan over medium heat and cook until it turns golden brown and smells nutlike. Add onion, turn heat to low and cook until translucent, about 15 minutes. Add potatoes and stir well. Pour in water to come just below potatoes and cover pan. Raise heat to medium and cook until potatoes are about half done, maybe 10 minutes. Uncover pan, add squash and cook 6 to 8 minutes more, stir occasionally. Add beans and give it a final ten minutes. All vegetables should be cooked through—*not* al dente—cook a few minutes more if necessary. There should be very little liquid in the pan at this point; boil it down if things are soupy. Stir in the cream and minced coriander and add salt to taste, remembering this will be garnished with salty cheese.

Arrange cheese around outside of small, heated plate, spoon stew in center, garnish with coriander and serve at once. A plate of perfectly plain sliced Brandywines goes well with this.

Soon it will be time to put mushrooms in everything, or so I hope. There were zillions after the big rain. I went out eagerly with my basket, only to discover that they were zillions of cortinarii. Lots of late amanita, paxillus, every inedible thing you can think of but except for some truly splendid *Agaricus Rodmanii* found on the way home from the fair—largest cap ten inches across—there has been nothing to eat. I'm headed for New York tomorrow but will once more into the woods and fields as soon as I get back here. Although it hasn't rained again since the deluge I still feel there should be a good crop of Bill's favorite *Armillaria Caligata*. It's a real late variety, and I'm praying for blewits in the garden. There were two small ones in the tomato patch a couple of weeks ago, so why not hundreds now that there has been rain?

Well yes, I know why, but please leave me my illusions.
Love

Leslie

P.S. Yes of course I know Doreen Allen (or more accurately I know her name). Among American foodies Ballymaloe is more or less synonymous with what's best about modern Irish cooking.

Eccleston Square, London

20 October 1994

Dear Leslie,

The mushroom season goes on apace; Nicky and I are off to Chewton Glen Hotel today for a two-day mushroom event. I hope the mushrooms down in the New Forest are as good as in other parts of the country. I went down to an old beech wood in Devon two days ago and made a mushroom meal on an open fire in the wood – two mushroom dishes. First Hedgehog Mushrooms: I diced an onion and softened it for about ten minutes in olive oil, then I slung in the mushrooms chopped in small pieces cooked them for a further eight minutes (open fires always seem to cook at just the right rate), then I heated some brandy in a big spoon and slung it on – flames about three feet high – topped the whole thing off with chopped parsley and served flaming hot. The other dish was made

Lots of
Cortinarius
speciosissimus
this year
V. DEADLY

with *Boletus badius*, Bay Boletus; it started with chopped garlic fried in olive oil with small shreds of bacon. After five minutes the bacon was quite crispy. I added the chopped mushroom, cooked that for a further ten minutes then added hunks of tomato swiftly followed by a pot of plain yogurt followed by a spoonful of paprika. Cook slowly for about three or four minutes more – really, really succulent.

More on mushrooms, not very momentous, but I have now collected and identified fifty different species in Eccleston Square garden:

Agaricus arvensis
Agaricus bisporus
Agaricus bitorquis
Agaricus campestris
Agaricus luteolus
Agaricus vaporarius
Agaricus xanthodermus
   poisonous
Calocybe carnea
Conocybe persincta
Conocybe pseudopilossella
Conocybe subovalis
Coprinus atramentarius
   dangerous with alcohol
Coprinus disseminatus
Coprinus micaceus
Coprinus plicatilis
Coriolus versicolor
Entoloma turci (?)
Hebeloma crustuliniforme
   poisonous
Hebeloma mesophaeum
Hygrophorus russocoriaceus
Hypholoma fasciculare
Lacrymaria velutina
Lepiota excoriata
Lepiota josserandii
   deadly poisonous

Lepiota leucothites
Lepiota rhacodes var. hortensis
Lepiota subincarnata (?)
Lepista nuda
Lyophyllum decastes
Marasmius oreades
Marasmius rotula
Melanoleuca adstringens
Melanoleuca melaleuca
Meripilus giganteus
Mycena avenacea
Mycena flavo-alba
Mycena leptocephala
Mycena setipes = swartzii
Panaeolus ater
Panaeolus subbalteatus
Paxillus involutus **poisonous**
Pluteus cervinus
Psathyrella candolleana
Psathyrella gracilis
Psathyrella hydrophila
Ramaria stricta
Stropharia cyanea
Tubaria furfuracea
Vascellum pratense
Volvarella speciosa

As mushroom season comes to an end it's 'back to basics'. In this case the basics are getting on with a great deal of cutting back of shrubs planted years ago, they now need major pruning — otherwise joggers won't be able to get round the paths.

But first I must go to the market to get chickpeas to try out that cumin and lime idea you sent me.

Love,

Roger

Cushing, Maine

Cushing adieu

November 6, 1994

Dear Roger,

I'm just packing up and preparing to shut down the house. This is the latest I've been able to stay in years and the truth is the weather is still so mild I'm tempted to remain. But the commute is getting to me—it's eight hours to Pleasant Valley—and I fear a hard frost will catch me unawares and bust every pipe in the house.

Furthermore, there are and have been no mushrooms. True to form for this year the rain of late September was an aberration and it has been totally dry ever since. I went out hunting in mid-October, right after I got back from New York, and there wasn't a thing. Zilch, unless you want to count a few wizened *Hebelomas*. Which I don't. No blewits, natch, nothing mushroomy in the garden at all but even in a good year this place is nothing like Eccleston. What a list! We mostly have huge fruitings of *Lepiota naucina* in the lawn and colonies of *Suillus grevillei* right where they should be, under the hackamatacks by the road.

The garden has had a sort of afterlife in the blue border. Starting in late September and going on until just a few days ago there was a second blooming of Globe thistles, *Salvia transylvanica,* and delphiniums. Hyssop stayed late and the spring-blooming annual *Phacelia,* a wonderful intensely blue variety called "Royal Admiral," managed to seed itself and flower once more. The plants were right under the *Rosa rubrifolia,* which was covered with bright orange-red hips. They were surrounded by black pansies, the glaucus foliage of a *thalictrum* and some rosettes of bluish columbine leaves. Final picture: color of unmatched autumnal intensity, far better than anything I've ever planned. These serendipitous gifts are why we garden, in the end.

And to feed ourselves, let's not forget that. Here are a few results of this year's vegetable tests:

Best pole beans were Garafal Oro, a roma type. The vines were slow to germinate, slow to climb and slow to bear, but once they got started they produced more beans, of better quality, than old-fashioned Roma, Trionpho Violetto, or Northeaster, the previous record holder. The Garafals were also more resistant to the mildrew and rust that always attack here in late summer (no sprays used).

Among tomatoes the Brandywines were as usual the champs for taste but I hardly got any. They dropped a lot of blossoms in the heat, then most of what fruit there was got eaten—I thought by Mamselle but just yesterday saw a porcupine suspiciously close to the patch. Very discouraging to see those bites out, I'll tell you. Fortunately the old-fashioned "Trappey's Finest," also a late potato-leaf beefsteak, was almost as good. "Green Zebra" not as sweet as "Evergreen," "White Wonder" far less tasty than "White Beauty" and mealy to boot. Djeena Lee's "Golden Girl" the hit of the summer—great big tomatoes, round and firm, first yellow then orange and loaded with flavor. I will send some seed.

Eggplants were essentially no show. Bad year. Peppers almost the same except for loads of jalapenos and a few very tasty anchos. The Manzano Rojo, sunk in a pot because I knew it would take at least a year to do anything, has loads of very pretty purple flowers and about three tiny fruit. I will take it to New York and put it in the sunroom and pray.

No experiments undertaken with potatoes and squash, unless you want to count trying to get any in a rainless season. Remarkably, "Summertime" crisphead lettuce actually germinated, though spottily, and even more remarkably made delicious heads.

I do hope you can get something edible going in the square. For all the

joy my flowers bring me in the end it's delicious that takes my heart—maybe because it's easiest to share.
Love

Leslie

Sent inside package marked

DO NOT OPEN TILL CHRISTMAS

It's just early November as I write, heavy frost in the mornings and leaves all fallen, start of the bleak time and not yet winter. But I am thinking forward thoughts. As you read this it should be festive Yuletide, your tree I hope up and all of you in holiday-happy moods. I would *so* much like to have you at our tree-decorating party that I decided to have you there in spirit—or more accurately, now I think of it, to have myself over there. Enclosed are some tree-ornament cookies made with Eccleston and its guardians in mind. Decorations are from the garden. (Don't eat the one with delphiniums on.) Merry Merry Merry Merry.

Leslie

Eccleston Square,
London

12 November 1994

Dear Leslie,

I have just been down to the houses of Parliament to meet up with Peter Brooke (MP), to talk over the scheme for 'Celebrating London Squares'. He is very enthusiastic, and it seems that there is going to be a fund of money available through an organization called the Millennium Committee. They will be funding some very major projects across the country, things like a new opera house for Cardiff, but there will also be funds available to tackle smaller more regional ideas like mine. I also talked to David Macmillan, my publisher. He is very, very keen and would like to become involved himself in the work.

We are bulbing the garden at the moment, loads of the small wild fritillary in the lawn. Ten years ago I put a few in and they are still going strong so I thought them well worth inceasing. The daffodils, or rather narcissus, tend to go blind after about four years so it is time to have another go at them too. I have bought only one kind this time, 'Ice Follies', pure white petals with a flat creamy cup. Arthur the gardener has his own sort of alpine gritty bed and I have got him a load of dwarf *Iris reticulata* to give a show early in the spring.

We went en masse to the Mayor of Westminster's parlour last night, that is Nicky, Phoebe, Amy, Derek Archer (chairman of our Garden Committee) and his wife Gladys, to receive the garden cup. After the for-

water from
overhead
aqueduct
splashes onto
rock 6' high.

water level flush
with edge
of pool to
give maximum
reflex

malities, loads of drinks and snacks. I got over enthusiastic and very much overdid the former – still suffering.

My latest thought for the Irish garden is a fountain *comme* mirror pool, the sketch will give you an idea of how it will work.

Do you go in for Guy Fawkes? Phoebe and Amy go potty about it, I think it's in the genes. My father always loved fires and fireworks, any time any place. We had a party in the garden for their friends; sausages and about a million pounds' worth of gunpowder. Result: lots of very excited children. Parents have got very paranoid about fireworks over the last ten years or so. When we had a go as children it was all much wilder, but much more dangerous I suppose. One year we had a party at St Christopher's, the boarding school I went to. In conjunction with a friend of mine we went around tripping people up and a girl in my class, Jane Unwin, fell over backwards and broke her wrist. Oh Yer, times was tough back then. Actually my parents went potty when they got the bill.

By the way my rocket has gone mad reseeding itself on the balcony, we now have really large plants and about five months to go before it bolts again, a dearth of lettuce at the moment though. Maybe someone will give me a heater for my little greenhouse for Christmas (not a hint to *you*), then I will be able to keep them going all through the winter − the lettuces not the hints.

At last we have a fountain in Eccleston Square, or almost in the Square. Some clowns were digging a hole to lay a cable TV network in the road just by the north-east corner of the Square when they hit the main waterpipe. The main, that is, in the sense of supplying all of south London. Anyway, the fountain ran for about two hours, and the jet went higher than the houses − that is about ninety feet in the air! By far the tallest fountain in the whole of London.

Best wishes, love,

Roger

Plant Lists and Bed Plans

Sources

Annual Flowers and Vegetables

Comstock, Ferre and Co.
263 Main Street, Wethersfield,
    CT 06109
203-571-6590

The Cooks Garden
P. O. Box 53528, Londonderry,
    VT 05148
802-824-3400
Especially for salad greens

J. L. Hudson, Seedsman
P. O. Box 1058, Redwood City,
    CA 94064
*Seeds for lots of very unusual
    things, from annuals to trees*

Johnny's Selected Seeds
Foss Hill Road, Albion, ME
    04910
207-437-4357

Nichols Garden Nursery
1190 North Pacific Highway,
    Albany, OR 97321-4580
503-928-9280
Especially for herbs

Park Seed
Cokesbury Road, Greenwood,
    SC 29647-0001
800-845-3369

Ronniger's Seed Potatoes
Star Route 55, Moyie Springs ID
    83845
(All business in writing, please)

Select Seeds–Antique Flowers
180 Stickney Road, Union, CT
    06076-4617
203-684-9310

Southern Exposure Seed
    Exchange
P.O. Box 170, Earlysville, VA
    22936
804-973-4703

The Tomato Seed Company
P. O. Box 1400, Tryon, NC 28782

Thompson and Morgan
P. O. Box 1308, Jackson, NJ
    08527-0308
908-363-2225

Horticultural Heritage

The Garden Conservancy
P. O. Box 219, Main Street, Cold
    Spring, NY 10516
914-265-2029

Native Seeds/SEARCH
2509 North Campbell, #325,
    Tucson, AZ 85719
520-327-9123

Seed Savers Exchange
3076 North Winn Road,
    Decorah, IA 52101
319-382-5990

Society for the Protection of
    London Squares
15-A Eccleston Square, London
    SW1, England

Perennials, Bulbs, Fruit

Dutch Gardens
P. O. Box 200, Adelphia, NJ
    07710-0200
908-780-2713
Bulbs

Edible Landscaping
P. O. Box 77, Afton, VA 22920
804-361-9134
Citrus, medlars

Klehm Nursery
Route 5, P. O. Box 197, Penny
 Road, South Barrington, IL
 60010-9555
800-553-3715
Especially for peonies and hostas

McClure and Zimmerman
108 West Winnebago, P. O. Box
 368, Friesland, WI 53935
414-326-4220
*Species tulips and narcissi, unusual
 bulbs*

Merry Gardens
P. O. Box 595, Camden, ME
 04843
207-236-9064
Especially for geraniums and herbs

Miller Nurseries
5060 West Lake Road,
 Canandaigua, NY 14424
800-836-9630
Strawberries, fruit trees, quinces

Van Engelen, Inc.
Stillbrook Farm, 313 Maple
 Street, Litchfield, CT 06759
203-567-8734
Large bulb orders

Wayside Gardens
1 Garden Lane, Hodges, SC
 29695-0001
800-845-1124
Perennials and shrubs

Roses

Pickering Nurseries, Inc.
670 Kingston Road, Highway 2,
 Pickering, Ontario, Canada
 L1V1A6
905-839-2111

The Roseraie at Bayfields
P. O. Box R, Waldoboro, ME
 04572-0919
207-832-6330

Royall River Roses
70 New Gloucester Road, North
 Yarmouth, ME 04097
207-829-5830

Index to Recipes and Food Ideas

Index